Southern Literary Studies
LOUIS D. RUBIN, JR.
Editor

Parnassus
on the
Mississippi

PARNASSUS
ON THE
MISSISSIPPI

THOMAS W. CUTRER

The *Southern Review* and the

Baton Rouge Literary Community

1935–1942

Louisiana State University Press

Baton Rouge and London

Copyright © 1984 by Louisiana State University Press
All rights reserved
Manufactured in the United States of America
Designer: Barbara Werden
Typeface: Linotron Primer
Typesetter: G & S Typesetters, Inc.
Printer and Binder: Vail-Ballou Press

Publication of this book has been assisted by a grant from the
Andrew W. Mellon Foundation.

LIBRARY OF CONGRESS CATALOGING IN PUBLICATION DATA

Cutrer, Thomas W.
  Parnassus on the Mississippi.

  (Southern literary studies)
  Bibliography: p.
  Includes index.
  1. American literature—Louisiana—Baton Rouge—History and criticism.
2. American literature—Southern States—History and criticism.   3. Criticism—
Southern States—History—20th century.   4. Southern Review (Baton Rouge,
La.)   5. Baton Rouge (La.)—Intellectual life.   6. Brooks, Cleanth, 1906–
7. Warren, Robert Penn, 1905–   . 8. Authors, American—20th century—
Biography.   9. American literature—20th century—History and criticism.
I. Title.   II. Series.
PS267.B3C87   1984   810'.9'976318   83-24913
ISBN 0-8071-1143-0

For Lewis P. Simpson
in whose capable hands
the *Southern Review* lives again

Contents

Illustrations

Acknowledgments

MY THANKS are due primarily to Lewis P. Simpson, a scholar and gentleman without whose inspiration and material assistance I would scarcely have attempted this or any other study of southern literature. Cleanth Brooks is the first of many of the subjects of this book who shared with me not only their memories, their papers, and their valuable time, but vital guidance and encouragement as well. Robert Penn Warren, Eudora Welty, John T. Palmer, Andrew Lytle, Allen Tate, Leonard Unger, Peter Taylor, Jesse Cutrer, Fred Frey, Thomas Kirby, Thomas Thompson, Arthur Scouten, John T. Purser, and Robert D. Jacobs rank high among others, but by no means exhaust the list. I am indebted to Robert M. Crunden, William M. Stott, and Norman D. Brown for shepherding me through several drafts of manuscript, always giving sage counsel on focus, form, and diction. As well as teachers, they became firm friends. To other friends, George B. Ward III, William Donn Rogosin, William Richard Fossey, Joseph C. Porter, Charles Regan Wilson among them, I am grateful for the encouragement and good fellowship which kept the labor a pleasant one. My mother, whose faith in her son has been the principal inspiration of his life, is entitled to claim this work as her own; and to Emily, research assistant, typist, copyeditor, and wife, I owe a debt more special than any words of mine could ever repay. For daughter Katherine, who came into the world simultaneously with the epilogue, I wish the joy of such mentors, such friends, and such a family.

Parnassus
on the
Mississippi

Prologue

IN April, 1859, William T. Sherman received a letter from his old army comrade Don Carlos Buell informing him of a position which Buell was "disposed to think well of." Knowing that Sherman's Leavenworth law practice had failed and that he was in search of employment, Buell forwarded to the former brevet captain the prospectus of a new military college about to be inaugurated by the State of Louisiana. "If you could secure one of the professorships and the superintendency, as I think you could," wrote Buell, "it would give you the handsome salary of $3,500."[1]

With the aid of three prominent Louisiana friends, Braxton Bragg, P. G. T. Beauregard, and Richard Taylor, Sherman received the appointment and began the task of creating a college. A grant of federal land near Pineville, Louisiana, was designated as the site of the proposed seminary. The State Legislature, largely under the impetus of strong secessionist sentiment, appropriated funds for the maintenance of an institution of higher learning at which the youth of Louisiana would not be subjected to abolitionist doctrine and where they could be trained in military science against the pos-

1. Quoted in B. H. Liddell-Hart, *Sherman: The Genius of the Civil War* (London, 1930), 59.

sibility of war with the North. The school opened its doors on New Year's Day, 1860, with five professors and nineteen cadets. Despite severe disciplinary problems during the first semester, the second semester's enrollment grew to sixty-two cadets, and the seminary was endowed with a library and a state arsenal. The student body nearly doubled the following fall, but with Louisiana's secession on January 26, 1861, Sherman resigned his position as superintendent to return to the North. David Boyd, one of his faculty and later himself superintendent of the institution, long remembered Sherman's farewell to the corps of cadets. "The boys wept, the superintendent wept," he wrote. Sherman finally managed to say that he could not make the speech that he had intended, but he "put his hand to his heart saying, 'You are all here,' wheeled on his heel and was gone."[2]

Although gone from campus, William T. Sherman continued to make his presence felt in a far different way. The cadet corps, which had wept at its commandant's departure, took up arms to fight against his cause. Sherman was succeeded as superintendent of the all-but-deserted academy by a series of prominent Louisianans, all of whom left after brief tenures to enter Confederate service, and the seminary closed in the summer of 1863 with the approach of General N. P. Banks's Red River expedition. Its military equipment was donated to the Confederate cause and its library was burned by invading Federal troops. After its defeat at the hands of Sherman's former friend and benefactor, Richard Taylor, a division of Banks's army, on loan from Sherman, destroyed the remainder of the school's buildings on its retreat from Sabine Crossroads. General Taylor later bitterly observed that in view of Sherman's rampage in Georgia "It could hardly be expected that troops trained by this commander would respect *the humanities*."[3]

The seminary did not reopen until the war's end, when Colonel David Boyd returned from duty with the Army of Northern Virginia to become superintendent, a post he was to hold for twenty years. Almost as soon as the little college had struggled back to its feet, it was knocked down again by the burning of its remaining classroom

2. David French Boyd, *General History of the Louisiana State University and Agricultural and Mechanical College* (Baton Rouge, 1899), 2–7.
3. Richard Taylor, *Destruction and Reconstruction* (New York, 1879), 195.

building on the night of October 14, 1869. Colonel Boyd reported the fire as "the work of an incendiary" inspired by "the disturbed relations between the two races of our peoples."[4]

On the first day of November, the students, faculty, and such equipment as remained were removed to the campus of the State School for the Deaf at Baton Rouge. At this time, also, the institution changed its name to the Louisiana State University. Despite its promotion from "seminary" to "university" status, the struggling little school barely survived the period of Reconstruction. Colonel Boyd reported that in 1873, "owing to the distracted political status of Louisiana, the legislature failed to make the appropriations required by law for its support. Most students, and several professors, were compelled to leave; and the University hobbled along for four years, barely keeping alive."[5]

Although funds were cut every year, the university melded with the Louisiana Agricultural and Mechanical College in June, 1877, and could boast six professors "doing good and faithful work."[6] The military character of "The Ole War Skule" remained little changed. Although he never received official permission to do so, Colonel Boyd began to uniform the cadets in 1868 and to drill them with artillery. General Sherman, who never forgot the academy which he had organized and superintended, gave to the corps a battery of two James rifles and two ten-pound Parrott guns which he had captured at Charleston. These guns were used for drill until 1873 when the adjutant general of Louisiana sent two hundred Springfield rifles to the school.

The United States Congress greatly benefited the university in 1886 by transferring to it the military barracks and grounds at Baton Rouge. The new seat of the Louisiana State University had been the site of the westernmost battle of the American Revolution; also the "revolution" which wrested West Florida from Spanish control and turned it over to United States control in 1810; the plantation of President Zachary Taylor; and the 1862 battle of Baton Rouge. Although the buildings were in a state of near collapse,

4. Boyd, *General History of the Louisiana State University*, 3.
5. *Ibid.*
6. *Ibid.*, 5.

Colonel Boyd considered the bequest of 210 acres of fine land as "the Government's best gift to Louisiana," and felt that "this in the near future must be a grand Institution of Learning."[7]

Little by little the university grew as legislative funding increased. In 1920, during the tenure as president of David Boyd's younger brother, Colonel Thomas Duckett Boyd, John M. Parker campaigned for governor on a platform of securing funds from a severance tax on oil to acquire a new university site and build a "greater campus" just south of Baton Rouge. Parker believed that those who were profiting by the state's natural resources should be made to pay for the state's university. "The resources are gone forever," he said. "Then why shouldn't those who take them provide something to take their place, an education for the youth of the state?"[8]

Parker was elected and negotiated a 3 percent *ad valorem* tax with Standard Oil, whose attorneys drafted the bill. By 1921, the university had acquired 2,100 acres of an old plantation, and the following year made plans for buildings to accommodate 5,000 students. Professor W. H. Dalrymple noted that the general belief of educators was that "when completed, this greater institution will be one of the finest and best equipped in the South, if not in the entire country; one of the most valuable assets the state could possibly have; and a lasting credit to the commonwealth as a whole."[9]

However ambitious were Louisiana's plans for a great university, Louisiana State still had far to go to fulfill that dream. At the end of Governor Parker's tenure as governor LSU could boast only 1,800 students and 168 faculty members, placing it number 88 in size among American universities. In quality, it managed only to qualify for a class "C" ranking by the Association of State Universities.

After seeing his university moved to its new location, President Thomas Boyd retired in 1926 in favor of Colonel Campbell B. Hodges, son of a successful north Louisiana planter, a professional soldier, and commandant at West Point. The army, however, would

7. *Ibid.*, 12.
8. "New Home of Louisiana State University," *School and Society*, XXXI (October, 1925), 551.
9. William Haddock Dalrymple, *A Brief Sketch—Illustrated—of the Louisiana State University and Agricultural and Mechanical College* (Baton Rouge, 1922), 30.

not release Hodges from duty, so Thomas Atkinson, dean of the School of Engineering, was appointed as acting president.

Governor Parker was the last of the Bourbon class to fill Louisiana's state house. In 1928, at the end of his second term in office, he was supplanted by "an upstart red-neck" from the impoverished piney woods parish of Winn in north Louisiana, one of the last strongholds of southern populism. Huey P. Long was no more attractive to "the better class" of Louisianans than was William T. Sherman after the Civil War. But, like Sherman, he took the struggling little school to his heart; although by no means himself a scholar, he saw it through a time of rebirth and crisis as faithfully as its first superintendent had nurtured it at its beginning. Like Sherman, too, he left the college in the midst of controversy and on the eve of a war which stayed the progress that he had brought to it.

ONE

Huey Long's University

FREDERICK the Great? "He was the greatest son of a bitch who ever lived. 'You can't take Vienna, Your Majesty. The world won't stand for it,' his nit-wit ambassadors said. 'The hell I can't,' said old Fred, 'my soldiers will take Vienna and my professors at Heidelberg will explain the reason why!' Hell, I've got a University down in Louisiana that cost me $1,500,000 that can tell you why I do like I do."[1] So spoke the man whom some characterized as a "Frederick the Great from the piney woods" and others called a "tin pot Napoleon." But whatever his personal character and motivations might have been, Senator Huey Pierce Long did indeed have himself a university.

"As Governor and Senator, the 'Kingfish' has made [Louisiana State University] his biggest, most expensive plaything," reported *Time* magazine. "In small part his interest is due to pride in the educational and athletic advantages to his Kingdom. In large part it is due to his personal feud with Tulane University." Ironically, the senator's own formal education, such as it was, included nine months

---

1. "Give Him Honor or Give Him Death," *Time*, April 1, 1935, pp. 15–17.

6

at Tulane and but a single day at LSU. Long had won a scholarship to the state university in a declamation contest at LSU in 1909, but saw no chance to attend. His explanation was simple and sure to win the sympathy of his hard-bitten constituency. "The scholarship which I had won did not take into account books and living expenses. It would have been difficult to secure enough money." Nevertheless, the poor boy from Winn Parish did not forget LSU. He had fallen in love with the school at the 1909 contest, and the love affair was to bring great notoriety to the struggling little college on the banks of the Mississippi. The Kingfish's attentions would be the source of no small embarrassment to many on the Baton Rouge campus, but Long's devotion brought a building program to the physical plant and to the faculty of Louisiana State University that awakened the sleepy southern college and moved the center of literary criticism "from the left bank of the Seine to the left bank of the Mississippi."[2]

On May 21, 1928, Huey P. Long was inaugurated as governor of the State of Louisiana, and according to the new chief magistrate's memoirs, "The Old War Skule" became one of his first major concerns. "Efforts were renewed from the time I became Governor," he claimed, "to improve the standing of the institution. In November, 1928, it was given an 'A' rating by the Association of American Universities which established it on a parity with the best in the country."[3] While the AAU had indeed granted LSU an 'A' rating, the honor was a dubious one at best for the inadequate campus and its 1,600 students and was by no means a result of Long's efforts. As for the governor's claim of "parity with the best," it must have left college deans gasping from New Haven to Berkeley.

Governor Long did not so much as set foot on LSU's campus until 1930, and then his intrusion was not exactly in the best interest of the university. During the early fall of that year, Governor Long appeared in the president's office unannounced. President T. W. Atkinson had suffered a severe heart attack late in 1929, an occur-

---

2. "Huey Long's University," *Time*, December 10, 1934, pp. 42–45; Huey P. Long, *Every Man a King: The Autobiography of Huey P. Long* (New Orleans, 1933), 8; "Wessex and Louisiana," *Time*, June 20, 1940, p. 92.

3. Long, *Every Man a King*, 246–47.

rence which did not become public knowledge until early 1930. Governor Long told the secretary that he wished to see the president. She replied that he was at home ill. He then asked to see the business manager only to be informed that he too was off campus. Quite irritated by this time, Long demanded to know if there were "anybody on this campus that I can talk business to?"

Fred C. Frey, the dean of men, was next door, and the now-tearful secretary turned the governor over to him. Having made himself comfortable at the president's desk, Long got down to business. "Send for 'Pop' Gilbeau," he said. "I'm going to fire him." This was Frank Gilbeau, band master, grounds custodian, and jack-of-many-duties around campus. "I'm gonna get me a band leader. I'm also gonna fire quite a number more." Dean Frey recalls that Long took a list from his pocket and began to read off names. "Governor," Frey responded, "before we send for Mr. Gilbeau, I would like to discuss this matter with you at length." The dean of men then went on to point out that the firing of university personnel was a very serious matter and sure to get the university into trouble with accrediting agencies. Soon reinforced by the commandant of cadets, Major Troy Middleton, Frey began to make some headway against Long's hit list, especially when he pointed to the damage that Mississippi's former governor, Theodore Bilbo, had done to his state's university through political interference. When Frey at last mentioned that "Pop" Gilbeau was both popular and powerful among the voters of the "cajun" country of south Louisiana, Long pulled in his horns altogether.[4]

Or so it seemed to a relieved dean of men. In fact, Long was merely taking another tack. On November 17, 1930, he attended his first meeting of the LSU Board of Supervisors. At that meeting President Atkinson resigned "for reasons of ill health" and the governor had the responsibility of finding a new leader for the university. Campbell Hodges, released from his West Point duties, was still the first choice of most prominent Louisianans, but now Huey Long stood between the general and the president's chair. The Hodges family was deeply involved in anti-Long politics, and the general's

4. Fred C. Frey, "Reminiscences of Fred C. Frey" (n.p., 1975), n.p.

brother had been a prime mover in the impeachment proceedings brought against the governor the preceding year. Long was acquitted on May 16, 1929, but the opposition, again with Hodges in the van, formed the Constitutional League with the purpose of finding means to thwart the upstart governor. With Atkinson's resignation snugly in his pocket, one of Long's first acts was to inform Campbell Hodges that "he need not come to Louisiana to take charge of the State University. Instead," said Long, "a person of the highest collegiate standing was selected for that purpose."[5] That person was James Monroe Smith—next to the Kingfish himself perhaps the most controversial individual in all of Louisiana's Byzantine political history.

In 1930 Smith was forty-two years old. He was a native of Huey Long's own Winn Parish, but had attended LSU and had attained a Ph.D. from Columbia University in educational administration. The bulk of Smith's career had been spent as a country school teacher and principal, but after completion of the Columbia degree he had moved to Southwestern Louisiana Institute in Lafayette to become dean of the Department of Education. Dean Smith was popular with the students of SLI, who thought him quite "democratic." His colleagues found him to be an "excellent administrator, imaginative and bold in devising new educational policies."[6]

The meeting of the board at which Smith was elected has become a part of Louisiana folklore. According to local historians Smith arrived in Baton Rouge carrying an old-fashioned telescope hamper and wearing a decent but slightly worn suit. Long's first act was to peel off a couple of large bills and order Smith to a tailor. True or not, the story points to the fact that however imaginative and bold Smith might have been in Lafayette, in Baton Rouge "he took his orders running" from Huey Long.

His willingness to follow the Long line was not an indication that President Smith did not have the university's best interest at heart. Dean Frey remembers Smith as "the best all-around and most effective president" during his own forty years at LSU. Like many others who served under Smith's administration, Frey believes that "Dr.

5. Long, *Every Man a King*, 184–86.
6. T. Harry Williams, *Huey Long: A Biography* (New York, 1969), 529.

Smith was above all a genuine educator." In a system shot through with political machination, Smith more than any of his predecessors "knew how to work with the legislature and could sell them on the university programs." And President Smith seems to have shared the dream of seeing the state university become a great center of learning. "He was the first president under whom I served who showed any real interest in graduate work and research," says Frey. "He obtained the money and gave a great number of graduate fellowships, and in other ways as well he encouraged graduate work and offered special inducements to faculty members to do research."[7] But as *Time* magazine reported in 1934, "all Louisianians firmly believe that President Smith's resignation reposes in a drawer in the Kingfish's desk."

With the collapse of the stock market, colleges began to feel the pressure of the Great Depression. State universities were sorely affected as it became harder and harder to obtain operating funds, and in most states college enrollment fell off rapidly. Many state colleges and universities were forced to terminate some faculty members and to cut the salaries of others. Louisiana State University, however, had a powerful benefactor in the person of Huey Long. Manipulating the legislature by fair means and foul, Long was always able to provide the university with funds—not only to keep salaries stable, but in many cases to raise them. The governor's student aid fund, one of the largest in the country, provided tuition and living expenses for many who would otherwise have been unable to attend, so that from 1931 to 1937, the worst years of the Depression, LSU's enrollment shot up from 2,000 to 6,000, a 300 percent leap. "I served as a full time employee of Louisiana State University from 1922 to 1962," Dean Frey recalls, and "in all this time, it was during the years 1930 to 1939 . . . the university made more progress toward becoming a great modern university than in any other similar time span."[8]

During this period the institution's building program was explosive. Buildings to house the history, geology, mathematics, and English departments were going up almost simultaneously, as were

7. Frey, "Reminiscences of Fred C. Frey," 84; "Huey Long's University," *Time*, December 10, 1934, pp. 42–45.
8. Frey, "Reminiscences of Fred C. Frey," 76–77, 83.

women's dormitories, the law school dormitory, and the governor's beloved stadium. To finance such a tremendous program Huey Long had to campaign as boldly as his hero, Frederick the Great. "Go ahead with your buildings," he said to the university administrators. "Get your architect and start out on what you need." When the naturally skeptical board of supervisors asked where the money would be coming from, Long replied, "That will be part of my job."

As plans were drawn up and buildings began to rise, worried school officials and contractors were still asking how the bills were to be paid. "You have to dare a bit if you build this school," Long told them. "Start ahead. Let the people see what we propose, and we will find a way to do it." With administrators and builders near mutiny, the governor at last revealed his plan. Louisiana was at the same time building a new capitol, and the legislature had voted five million dollars to pay for its construction. With Long's prodding, the state's Department of Public Works paid $350,000 to the university for part of its old campus in north Baton Rouge to serve as the new capitol grounds. The state's Highway Commission, also booming with the administration's largesse, needed room to grow, so it too purchased a part of the old campus adjoining the capitol site and paid $1,800,000 to the university's building fund. The more fiscally conservative of the Louisiana legislators were outraged, but LSU had $2,150,000 to grow on, and when that ran out the governor once again called his contractors. "Go ahead with your work and within a short time, after you have completed everything we will find your money."[9] And, of course, largely at the expense of Standard Oil Company, he did.

For the state university, 1931 was a year of miracles. The College of Arts and Sciences inaugurated a department of speech and a school of library science, and the Louisiana State University Press came into being. Under the direction of former Metropolitan Opera baritone Pasquale Amato, the opera department carried on the tradition of the old French Opera of New Orleans, staging productions which were "the equal of many professional performances in quality of voice, costuming and direction"; and Louis B. Hasslemans made the university symphony orchestra the envy of maestros from Rome

9. Long, *Every Man a King*, 247–49.

to Los Angeles. Blithely ignoring the University of Texas, Vanderbilt, and Johns Hopkins, Huey Long's house journal, the *Louisiana Progress*, proudly announced on August 18 that LSU had joined the University of Virginia and the University of North Carolina as "one of the three colleges in the South whose educational facilities have developed to such a point that they are able to award" the Doctor of Philosophy, "the highest degree of learning." [10]

By the end of 1934, LSU's building fund reached the $3,000,000 mark, and the campus could boast a music building with eighty concert grand pianos, a football stadium enlarged to seat 35,000, a Huey P. Long Field House, and a Huey P. Long swimming pool, at the time the longest in the world. When the Kingfish learned that San Francisco had the world's greatest indoor swimming pool, he ordered that the one in Baton Rouge be built ten feet longer.

Despite its benefactor's penchant for grandeur and despite the inordinate haste with which the new campus came into being, the university received high praise for the beauty of its new facilities. When John Crowe Ransom visited the campus in 1933, he found the setting "more charming than others naturally, with its live oaks hung with moss, its subtropical flora, its soft air." To enhance the natural beauty of the university's new landscape, architect Theodore Link of Chicago designed Mediterranean style buildings whose light coloring made an attractive mass against the semitropical Louisiana scenery. Ransom's verdict was that "the builders conceived a harmonious plan for the campus in a modified Spanish, and it suits the regional landscape and is not altogether foreign to the regional history." [11]

At the same time that he was putting money into the construction program, Governor Long was seeing that the state allotted additional support to LSU for operating expenses. The appropriation to the university reached almost one million dollars in 1931 and was increased each year thereafter, totaling approximately $2,870,000 by 1935. "It is not necessary for the officers of the administration to beg and defend appropriations asked of the legislature," marveled

10. J. Harvey Cain, "Situation at Louisiana State University," *School and Society*, L (August 12, 1939), 215–17; *Louisiana Progress*, III, No. 2, (1931), 1.

11. John Crowe Ransom, "The Aesthetics of Regionalism," *American Review*, II (January, 1934), 309–310.

one national education leader. The state and university administrations have "exerted great influence in obtaining passage of this legislation, which adds so much to the stability of the institution's income."[12]

With its constantly expanding allocation, the administration was able to improve existing educational programs and start ambitious new ones. As the school widened the scope of its services, it enlarged the size of its teaching staff. The Baton Rouge campus employed 168 faculty members when Long became governor in 1928. By 1935 the number had increased to 245. This increase was not entirely quantitative. Many of the new professors were hired away from well-established northern and western universities and were already scholars of some national reputation. The LSU faculty for the first time attracted national attention, and Louisiana basked in the warmth of such unaccustomed admiration. Said one administrator, "We were no longer a little college stuck off down here but a first-class school or on our way to it."[13]

The school's administrators did not always welcome such precipitous expansion. "The students have come," President Smith lamented, and "we have found it most difficult at times to care for the unexpected increase." Each fall saw hundreds of LSU students sleeping in tents borrowed from the Army because of want of dormitory space. Realizing his administration's difficulties, Smith claimed to have made the best of the situation in his attempt "to extend the opportunities for which a state-supported institution is established, and in the meantime, as rapidly as we have been able, have increased our facilities to meet the student numbers."[14] This increase was even more phenomenal than the building program at LSU. Enrollment in 1936 passed the 6,000 mark, bringing LSU to thirteenth in size of all American colleges and ninth in size among state universities. Thus for the first time in its history, Louisiana State University came close to fulfilling its great commission to provide an education for all the young people of Louisiana.

With the larger number of students came a higher percentage of

12. Cain, "Situation at Louisiana State University," 216.
13. Frey, "Reminiscences of Fred C. Frey," 83ff.
14. James Monroe Smith, "The Old War Skule," *New Louisiana* (New Orleans, 1936), 26, 225.

good students. The average undergraduate at LSU in 1934 was by no means more remarkable than was his contemporary elsewhere, although *Time* was able to point out a few distinguishing local variants. "Since Sherman's time," the news magazine remarked, "Louisiana State has been proud of its military tradition," and cited military officers as the institution's most famed alumni. Besides the facts that many of the students were housed in barracks and wore uniforms, and that tuition was free and living expenses low, the *Time* correspondent found of interest the university's service *in loco parentis*. "Like most co-educational universities in the deep South where a large proportion of the female students are farmer's daughters, LSU keeps a firm hand on its students," he reported. "Forbidden are drinking, hazing, card-playing, visiting objectionable places of resort." Former students nevertheless recall the red light district blatantly open between campus and downtown Baton Rouge. "Several frame cottages with red-lighted transoms and huge illuminated numbers invited the students," one recounts, and he remembers as well the male students' joke of giving co-eds looking for work the telephone number of one of these establishments.[15]

Robert Penn Warren remembers the students as being "like students anywhere in the country in the big state universities, except for the extraordinary number of pretty girls and the preternatural blankness of the gladiators who were housed beneath the stadium to have their reflexes honed, their diet supervised, and—through the efforts of tutors—their heads crammed with just enough of whatever mash was required . . . to get them past their minimal examinations." But like Huey Long himself, "there sometimes appeared, too, that awkward boy from the depth of the 'cajun' country or from a scrabble-farm in north Louisiana, with burning ambition and frightening energy and a thirst for learning; and his presence there, you reminded yourself, with whatever complication of irony seemed necessary at the moment, was due to Huey, and to Huey alone. For the 'better element' had done next to nothing in fifty years to get the boy out of the grim despair of his ignorance."[16]

With a new campus, a supercharged building program, new aca-

15. "Huey Long's University," *Time*, December 10, 1934, pp. 42–45.
16. Robert Penn Warren, "*All the King's Men*: The Matrix of Experience," *Yale Review*, LIII (Winter, 1964), 161–67.

demic departments, and a steady influx of top-notch new faculty members, it is not surprising the Louisianans looked beyond the borders of their state for recognition of their accomplishment. Therefore, when Edwin P. Embree of Chicago, president of the Rosenwald Fund, visited the university in the spring of 1934, the state cheered his statement that "Louisiana has no finer chance for a 'place in the sun' than through its state university." Embree went on to say that in his theory of regional development each region must have at least one great university and that the lack of a university was the cause of the want of progress in some sections of the South. LSU's distinguished visitor cited the examples of the University of Chicago in the Great Lakes region and the University of North Carolina in its state as having remarkable influence in the development of their respective areas. The regions of the South, as Embree saw them, were those centered by North Carolina, by Atlanta, by Nashville, by Louisiana for the Deep South, and by Texas. According to his belief there must grow a great university in the deep Mississippi valley. "I have high hopes," said Embree, "that LSU will be that leader." He supported his hopes with the observation that the Louisiana State University "is the most promising in the section. It has grown very fast, and it has good leaders and professors." The latter, he added, were of particular importance in advancing the region's agricultural, educational, industrial, social, and economic standards. "I have been impressed with the amazing growth of LSU," he concluded. "From an unknown place twelve years ago, it has risen to be included in the nationally known universities. If the state will stand by, LSU has every right to come to be included in the first 12 or 15 universities in the United States, which means inclusion in the first 20 universities in the world."[17]

Justifiably proud of such approbation from so high a source, President Smith was quick to quote Embree as predicting the imminent inclusion of his institution among the first dozen American universities. Embree denied having predicted any such thing, and Senator Long charged that he "swallowed his words," and implied that Embree "lacked the code taught in Louisiana institutions: Truth, honor, gratitude, loyalty, and service to humanity are to be

17. Edwin R. Embree, quoted in Smith, *Biennial Report of the President 1935–1937.*

adhered to and double-crossing and selling your soul is to be deplored." In December, 1934, Embree rebutted the senator's charges with the blunt statement that no southern university could claim inclusion in the top twelve. "The great South," he claimed, had no school that could rank with Harvard, Yale, Columbia, Johns Hopkins, Wisconsin, California, or half a dozen other northern, midwestern, and western schools, and as for Louisiana State University, "it is not even among the best southern institutions: Virginia, Texas, North Carolina, Vanderbilt, Tulane, Duke, and Emory."[18]

Huey P. Long had created Louisiana State University, and he came to look upon it as his personal property. With his virtual ownership of the university went control—thorough, absolute, and unquestioned. Of the fifteen members of the board of supervisors who were political appointees, not more than two could have been counted as anti-Long by the end of 1934. As more than one observer concluded, "Huey showered material benefits on 'his' state university, but some students were placed on the state payroll or on political scholarships, and although apparently a high degree of academic freedom existed, its maintenance was conditional upon the whimsical good humor of the Kingfish." Even at the new university, with its mania for football and operas, "when the Kingfish moved abroad in the flesh of Huey P. Long, armed guards stirred too. The smell of violence—the drift of some sweet, lethal, intoxicating rottenness off the swamp—could be caught in the air."[19] The anti-Long commentators admitted, however, that under the Long tenure as governor, senator, and all but absolute sovereign of Louisiana, the state university followed its own academic destiny. "Huey is discussed frankly—and criticized frequently—on the campus and in the faculty rooms of Louisiana State University," reported one unofficial observer. His report concluded that "according to an imposing array of investigators, broad social and economic problems are discussed more freely than in most American universities." Yet one of Long's aides quoted the Kingfish as saying that he had appointed

18. "Two Heavy Brickbats Hit Huey Long's University," *News-week*, January 5, 1935, p. 34; "South's Shortage," *Time*, January 7, 1935, p. 34.
19. Allan P. Sindler, *Huey Long's Louisiana: State Politics, 1920–1952* (Baltimore, 1956), 104; Robert Penn Warren, "A Special Message to Subscribers from Robert Penn Warren" in *All the King's Men* (Franklin Center, Penn., 1977), n.p.

James Monroe Smith as president of the university because he had "a hide thick as an elephant"—a most unusual academic credential.[20]

John Earle Uhler, one of the English department's five professors, was a native of Pennsylvania who had acted in and directed various New York and New England stock companies and had worked as a reporter for the Baltimore *Sun* before earning his Ph.D. at Johns Hopkins in 1926. Two years later Uhler came to LSU as director of freshman English and teacher of Renaissance drama. Entranced by the customs and traditions of Louisiana's ethnic mix, he documented this unique blend of local colors in a 1931 novel called *Cane Juice*. Set on the sugarcane plantations of Bayou Lafourche and on the LSU campus, the novel exploited South Louisiana's peculiarities "too well for [Uhler's] own comfort," and he soon was under considerable fire for what "some readers considered too much realism in treatment of the local scene."[21]

Most vocal among the novel's and novelist's assailants was the Right Reverend Monsignor E. L. Gassler, pastor of St. Joseph's Catholic Church of Baton Rouge. Well-intentioned but with little understanding of science, the humanities, or human nature, Father Gassler, in a mimeographed broadside distributed around the Baton Rouge area, contended that "no professor at an up-to-date university has the right to dress up an unscientific theory," Gassler's opinion of evolution, "in the jewelled garb of romance. By such an attitude he lowers not only himself in the esteem of his hearers, but also damages the reputation of the institution which engaged him to teach correct English."

The principal target of Father Gassler's wrath was Uhler's "monstrous slander of the purest womanhood to be found in the United States," the young women of Acadiana and the co-eds of Louisiana State University. The author of *Cane Juice*, Gassler noted, "makes his characters seek dark corners of the sugar mill . . . there to satisfy their carnal passions." Such a thing, he contended, never could happen, for the "young ladies along Bayou Lafourche are brought

20. "Unofficial Observer" [John Carter Franklin], *American Messiahs* (New York, 1935), 15; Forrest Davis, *Huey Long: A Candid Biography* (New York, 1935), 227.
21. W. J. Olive, "John Earle Uhler," in Waldo F. McNeir (ed.), *Studies in English Renaissance Literature* (Baton Rouge, 1962), xi–xiv.

up differently. They do not meet in dark corners with members of the opposite sex."

Not only would "both the mothers and daughters of Bayou Lafourche" resent this "attack on the spotless purity" of the "Cajun" women, he predicted, but "the authorities at L.S.U. will hardly appreciate" the more intimate scenes in *Cane Juice* which, to Gassler's mind, "actually lower the co-eds to the level of bawdy women." Further, Gassler charged, Uhler "seems to delight in picturing L.S.U. as the champion breaker of the Eighteenth Amendment," with strong drink causing the male students of the university to become "unclean beasts too drunk to be responsible for their bestial behavior." Father Gassler's assessment of the novel ends with a personal attack on its author, characterizing Uhler as a "Turkey Buzzard," warning all of his potential readers to "dare not approach that ugly bird too close lest he vomit his stinking carrion all over you."[22]

In defense Uhler invoked the names of Ignatius de Loyola, Saint Thomas Aquinas, Saint Francis of Assisi, and Cardinal Newman, affirming that none of these great Catholic humanists would have "written in such an unchristian spirit as Father Gassler has shown toward me and my work." He protests that he has only "the greatest respect for the women students of our fine state university," and thus had made the "temptress" of the novel, "not only not a student, but not even a Southern girl."[23]

Father Gassler claimed ignorance of "what steps, if any," the university administration would take against Uhler, but predicted that the students would not "stand for such an imputation" and that parents would no longer "entrust their daughters to an institution where their daughters' chastity has to be safe-guarded by locked doors." These dire predictions were enough to stampede the university administration, and President Smith soon announced the termination of Professor Uhler's contract.

Cane Juice was, in fact, an unlikely cause for scandal. Although hardly great literature, it did not impunge the reputation of the 'Cajun' people nor, even by the standards of its day, were its sexual

22. Right Reverend Monsignor F. L. Glasser, quoted in Baton Rouge *State Times*, October 6, 1931.

23. John Earle Uhler, quoted in Baton Rouge *State Times*, October 6, 1931.

scenes very torrid or explicit. Almost as surely as Father Gassler misread the novel, Huey Long never read it at all. Yet LSU was his university; its professors, he felt, should be his loyal minions, and any staff publication which damaged the reputation of the university, intentionally or otherwise, was a direct attack upon the Kingfish. Further, Huey was ever sensitive to any undermining of his already shaky support from the Church and the bayou parishes of Louisiana. Thus, when Professor Uhler found himself jobless, it was almost universally assumed that Governor Long had ordered his puppet president to do the firing.

Uhler, having found Saints Francis, Aquinas, and Loyola too weak a defense, turned to the American Civil Liberties Union and the American Association of University Professors to help him regain his lost job, and their combined strength overcame LSU's scruples and reinstated the disgraced professor in the spring of 1932. The rumor that Huey P. Long had ordered Uhler's firing lingered beyond the lives of both men, however, and more than thirty years after the incident the former governor's son, Senator Russell B. Long, was still defending his father against the charge. Russell, who had been a high school student at the time, remembered "considerable protest from the moralists" over the publication of *Cane Juice*, but thought that President Smith had merely given Uhler a leave of absence rather than firing him. At any rate, Russell declared, "as far as Huey Long was concerned, he had nothing to do with the matter."[24] Few observers of the Louisiana scene in the early 1930s agree that there was much of any consequence at LSU that Huey had nothing to do with, but his link to the firing of John Earle Uhler cannot at this late date be verified. Two years after Uhler's reinstatement, however, occurred an incident that demonstrates beyond question Long's tampering with the university administration and his slight regard for the principle of academic freedom.

In September, 1934, a young man from San Francisco named Wes Gallagher moved to Baton Rouge to study journalism. Huey Long, he said, "was making a big uproar at the time and it seemed a good place to go if you were going to be a good newspaperman." Gal-

24. Russell B. Long, quoted in Baton Rouge *State Times*, undated clipping in "John Uhler" file, Louisiana Collection, Middleton Library, LSU.

lagher was a good newspaperman, becoming during World War II chairman of the Associated Press, the largest news-gathering organization in the world. But the journalism school at LSU became the scene that fall of Senator Long's most flagrant tampering with academic freedom and freedom of the press in an incident which nearly cost the new university its hard-won accreditation. As Senator Long explained, "I like students, but this state is puttin' up the money for that college and I ain't payin' nobody to criticize me."[25]

The *Reveille*, a biweekly student newspaper, was, according to a statement issued by President Smith in the spring of 1934, "an absolutely uncensored publication."[26] But in November of that year an event occurred which not only decisively disproved Smith's statement, but also called into question the existence of academic freedom at Louisiana State University. Despite his duties in Washington, the LSU football team was the senator's first love, and on the eve of the Tigers' game with George Washington University on Saturday, November 10, Long rushed back to Baton Rouge to conduct the student pep rally himself. Perhaps somewhat carried away by the spirit of the occasion, Long proclaimed that the rally constituted a parish meeting and solemnly had halfback Abe Mickal elected state senator. It was the Roman emperor touch, the next thing to Caligula's appointing his horse a consul.

The point was raised that Mickal was a Syrian, under twenty-one, and a resident of Mississippi, hence unable to qualify for the job. Senator Long retorted that his legislature would seat senator-elect Mickal and that was all there was to it. With breathtaking irrelevance Long declared that "Mississippi has annexed itself to Louisiana," and "anyhow, Napoleon came from Corsica, didn't he?"[27]

Mickal failed to show up for his induction on Monday morning, but that afternoon an LSU undergraduate named D. R. Norman asked in a letter to the editor of the *Reveille* if "there is one serious-minded student in this University that is in sympathy with the proposed attempt to seat a popular member of the LSU football squad in the Louisiana Senate?" Calling the previous week's events "a mockery of Constitutional government and democracy," Norman

25. Wes Gallagher, *Broadcasting*, July 9, 1973, p. 57; Davis, *Huey Long*, 227.
26. "Huey Long's University," *Time*, December 10, 1934, pp. 42–45.
27. "Headlong Week," *Time*, November 19, 1934, p. 17.

praised Mickal for not being a party to the "burlesque" and attacked Senator Long by implication for his "serious mockery of our legislative body." The letter was to appear in the November 16 issue of the student newspaper, but that day's *Reveille* never made it to the news stands.[28]

The letter was set and laid out on the editorial page, but when the first proof copy rolled from the press, a journalism student named Frank Cayce took fright and carried the page to Helen Gilkinsen, a Baton Rouge journalist and close friend of Huey Long. Miss Gilkinsen was in the press box of the senate when the paper arrived, and she promptly handed it over to the senator. Within minutes two state troopers burst into the Ortlieb Press, where the *Reveille* was printed, and ordered the presses shut down. They took the 4,000 papers that had been printed and shredded them. Only two copies escaped destruction. Editor Jesse H. Cutrer got away with them stuck in his pants.

While the raid on the *Reveille* press was in progress, Long was raving on the senate floor. The next morning's papers quoted him as shouting: "If that little —— prints that, we gonna have a new editor. And as for the little —— who wrote this, why he's not gonna be in school. That's my university and I'll fire any student that dares to say a word against Huey Long. I'll fire a thousand, we've got 10,000 to take their place."

On the following day, Cutrer was summoned to the president's office and given a severe dressing down. "These are abnormal times," said Smith. He further informed the *Reveille* editor that "Senator Long was a virtual dictator of the University," and stated that he would not do anything that would offend the senator or jeopardize "the good of the University." Cutrer reports that Smith threatened that he "would fire me, my staff, destroy the School of Journalism, and fire 4,000 students before he would offend the Senator."[29]

President Smith imposed a program of censorship upon the paper, in response to which Cutrer and his editorial staff resigned from the *Reveille*, and forty journalism students, nearly the entire department, went out on strike. Of the strikers, twenty-six were

28. Interview with Jesse H. Cutrer, August 17, 1977.
29. Baton Rouge *State Times*, November 16, 1934, p. 9; Interview with Jesse H. Cutrer, August 17, 1977.

summarily suspended from the university. "I was out of touch with the whole thing," Long claimed. "However, I have been working and trying to get enough money to provide facilities for 1,000 additional students. Maybe Dr. Smith got impatient. You know, this is one way to solve the problem of overcrowding."[30]

Further student agitation in opposition to Long's and Smith's blatant disregard for academic freedom and freedom of the press resulted, on December 5, in the expulsion from the university of Jesse Cutrer and four of his former staff members. As commandant of cadets, Lieutenant Colonel Troy Middleton was ordered to serve the five with dishonorable discharges from the corps of cadets. An admirer of honesty and courage, Colonel Middleton prefaced his sentence with the remark, "Jesse, I sure don't want to do this. But I don't have any choice."[31]

The National Student Federation of America had five days earlier condemned the action of James Smith for the suspension of the twenty-six journalism students, and now a resolution adopted by the executive committee of the Southern Association of Colleges and Secondary Schools asked the Commission on Higher Education to investigate charges that Senator Long "is running Louisiana State University." The association's president, Frank L. McVey of the University of Kentucky, reported that a subcommittee of his organization would investigate the situation thoroughly, "probably for several months." The association, McVey said, "is gravely concerned regarding any harmful influences in the proper conduct of an educational institution in this area." If Senator Long were found guilty of exerting undue influence on the administration of the state university, action could result in the removal of LSU from the list of accredited colleges. To add insult to this injury, a straw-stuffed effigy was found swinging from the greased flagpole in front of the Huey P. Long Field House on the morning of December 8. It bore a placard reading, "Jimmie the Stooge." The next day a similar effigy labeled "James Moron Smith" was discovered suspended from a tree near the field house. Both hangings made the New York *Times*.[32]

30. New York *Times*, November 29, 1934, p. 27.
31. Interview with Jesse H. Cutrer, August 17, 1977.
32. New York *Times*, December 6, 1934, p. 2; Baton Rouge *State Times*, December 5, 1934, p. 1.

At the same time that the *Reveille* incident at LSU was gaining negative notoriety for the university throughout the nation, a similar occurrence on the Baton Rouge campus was threatening to add greater ignominy to the institute's bruised reputation. On December 27, the Association of American Law Schools adopted a report of its executive committee which found political influence undermining the educational facilities of Louisiana State University. This investigation stemmed from an incident concerning the belated bestowal of an LL.B. degree on one of the senator's circle. Kemble K. Kennedy, a Long protégé, had sought to follow his hero into the legal profession, but despite honor grades in his courses, he was expelled from the LSU School of Law following the publication of a scurrilous magazine called the *Whangdoodle* by a secret society called *Theta Nu Epsilon*, of which he was leader. "Always illustrating the rough side of humor," one issue of the magazine so outraged LSU Business Manager R. L. Himes that he sued Kennedy for criminal libel. Kennedy was convicted and imprisoned, but was pardoned by Long just before the Kingfish resigned from the governorship to take his seat in the Senate. Long then insisted that the faculty of the law school grant Kennedy a degree. The faculty refused, but overriding the obstacle, Long had the university's supervisors bestow a "special" LL.B. on Kennedy. Governor Allen and President Smith signed the diploma, but Dean Ira Flory of the law school refused. Out of consideration for the law faculty, which, the AALS report stated "has acted with propriety so far as it has power to do so," the committee did not expel the school from the association. Without dropping the Kennedy incident, the group recommended further investigation of it and the entire situation at the university.[33]

However ruthless he may have been in using the university to stamp out personal opposition or to grant favors to friends, Long retained an astonishingly high degree of regard among LSU officials who appreciated the good that he had done there. Dean emeritus Fred Frey, fondly known in Baton Rouge as "Mr. LSU," is one such administrator. "I would like to point out," he says, "that many of the news releases of the day . . . accused Governor Long of completely politicizing LSU. I want to go on record here as saying that most

33. New York *Times*, December 28, 1934, p. 23.

23

of these statements are untrue." Frey further says that "in all of the appointments that I was making at the time, I had not one single suggestion from the governor . . . as to whom I should appoint. I certainly cannot say this about some of our other governors who have indeed tried to engineer appointments."[34]

This, then, is the paradox of Huey P. Long. Unlike many of his contemporaries, Long never held higher education in contempt. Like many a man deprived of an academic education, Long had an almost reverent faith in it, and certainly cheaper and better public schooling was one of his central objectives. However impetuously he stamped out criticism of himself in the student newspaper at LSU, he also saw to it that the state employed good professors and that they enjoyed academic freedom. Raymond Swing, who drew an explicit analogy between Long and Adolph Hitler, admitted that "the incident of the *Reveille* is not to be explained by a philosophic hostility to free speech," but because the editor was a kinsman of Long's bitter political enemy and because he thought his enemies "were using 'his' university against him and were getting away with it."[35]

Long's greatest pride was what he did for education, from the free textbooks and school buses in the elementary schools to the new university at Baton Rouge. As Arthur M. Schlesinger, Jr., says, "He led the brass band at State, meddled with the football team, and invented the Sugar Bowl, but at the same time he was building a first-class university."[36] On a campus where able people pursued their studies without hindrance, and professional schools flourished, faculty members were fired and students were expelled for printing what the Kingfish found objectionable and felons were granted special degrees in law because they were the senator's friends.

34. Frey, "Reminiscences of Fred C. Frey," 77.
35. Raymond G. Swing, "The Menace of Huey Long," *Nation*, January 9, 1935, pp. 36–39, 138.
36. Arthur M. Schlesinger, Jr., *The Politics of Upheaval* (Boston, 1960), 42–68.

TWO

"My Boys at LSU"

It was great Canaan's grander
   counterfeit.
Bold Louisiana.
It was the landfall of my soul.
Or then it seemed—

ROBERT PENN WARREN
Brother to Dragons

AMONG the bright young men that Louisiana State University was hiring under Huey Long's munificent, if unpredictable, hand was Robert B. Heilman, a specialist in Renaissance drama and the possessor of a recently acquired Harvard Ph.D. When he arrived in Baton Rouge in the fall of 1935, Heilman found the academic and political climate very different from that which he had experienced in Cambridge. "The university," he recalls, "shared the mixed atmosphere of the state. Officially, at least, it maintained a certain abstention from high seriousness." If the young zealots of the English department deplored this situation, "as is the wont of young men ever alert to the imperfections of campuses to which they bring their new Ph.D.'s," Heilman and his new colleagues shared a sense of the excitement which now pervaded LSU—an excitement which he characterized as springing from "a great feeling of freedom, particularly of expression. We sensed vigor, imaginativeness, gusto, and along with the ever present political sense in some quarters, a great feeling for quality," especially in the College of Arts and Sciences. The Long spirit transformed a provincial military school into an exciting and zestful, if uneven, university. "If

25

there was money to buy a football team and a band, there was also money for a music school."[1]

Baton Rouge in the 1930s was "one of the most socially congenial places that ever has been on this earth," recalls John E. Palmer, who knew LSU as an undergraduate, a graduate student, and a faculty member during this period; and after leaving LSU to edit the *Sewanee Review* and the *Yale Review*, he still "cannot think of any academic community that has been pleasanter to be in." Palmer's LSU mentor, Cleanth Brooks, remembers that "by the middle of the 1930's there were at least 35 or 40 young family people on the campus whose talk I still remember as the most stimulating I have ever heard."[2] The range of the scholars and artists was broad, including writers and critics, painters and sculptors, geologists, political scientists, historians, and linguists, and their relationship was cordial, extending beyond the campus to dinner and cocktail parties perhaps twice a week.

As important as the influx of northern and midwestern Ph.D.'s, was the tide of distinguished refugees from Europe which began arriving in the late thirties. There were, for instance, George Jaffe, a physicist from Leipzig, and Rudolph Heberle, a sociologist from Kiel, and Eric Voegelin, whose monumental *Order and History* is recognized as one of the key works of the twentieth-century restorationist movement. Voegelin wrote much of his magnum opus at LSU after being driven from his native Austria by the Ausschluss; but "without the impact of Long on the university," Heilman believes, "no one there would have heard of Voegelin, and more conventional 'respectable' places were afraid of him."

But if such names as Pasquale Amato and Louis Hasselmans loomed large on the LSU scene, the names Brooks and Warren were rising into view as well. Cleanth Brooks was born on October 16, 1906, in the town of Murray, Kentucky. "The south Kentucky country of his nativity is distinctive among landscapes, and the

1. Robert Heilman, "Williams on Long: The Story Itself," *Southern Review*, n.s., VI (Autumn, 1970), 935.

2. Interview with John E. Palmer, May 16, 1979; Cleanth Brooks, "Brooks on Warren," *Four Quarters*, XXI (May, 1972), 21.

sense of it is intimate and constitutive in the consciousness of its inhabitants," John Crowe Ransom has remarked. "His breed, the population of that country, acknowledges more firmly than another the two bonds of blood and native scene, which individuate it." Like Ransom, Brooks was the son of a Methodist minister, a fact which Ransom feels was responsible for the form of Brooks's critical method. In his boyhood he "heard many a sermon preached where the preacher unpacked the whole burden of his theology from a single phrase of Scripture taken out of context," the same type of exposition which Ransom feels would characterize Brooks's approach to imaginative literature as a critic. The similarities between Brooks's and Ransom's biographies do not end with their region or their fathers' professions. In fact, said Ransom, "Brooks and I were about as alike as two peas from the same pod in respect to our stock . . . the kind of homes we lived in, the kind of small towns; and perhaps we were most alike in the unusual parallel of our formal education."[3]

Young Brooks attended preparatory school at the McTyeire School, a small classical academy at McKenzie, Tennessee, and from there moved on to Vanderbilt in 1925 where, in his freshman year, he developed a keen and abiding interest in English literature. Brooks arrived on the Nashville campus in the year before the last issue of the *Fugitive* was issued, and "by a lucky series of accidents" met Robert Penn Warren and through him Andrew Lytle. As Brooks recalls, "the campfires [of the *Fugitive*] were still glowing" when he was a freshman, and he was able to direct his path by their light. Those chance meetings produced a dramatic change in his notion of the glamorous life—"which was originally that of being a really shifty halfback"—to the writing of books. For the first time he was in the company of people "who actually wrote poems and stories and got them printed."[4] This redirection of interest solidified by the end of his sophomore year in the classroom of John Crowe Ransom,

3. John Crowe Ransom, "The Inklings of 'Original Sin,'" *Saturday Review of Literature*, May 20, 1944, pp. 10–11; John Crowe Ransom, "Why Critics Don't Go Mad," *Kenyon Review*, XIV (Spring, 1952), 331–39.
4. Rob Roy Purdy (ed.), *Fugitives' Reunion* (Nashville, 1959), 220.

and although he came too late to contribute to the *Fugitive*, Brooks did place some poems in *Facets*, a small volume of verse produced by a group of Vanderbilt undergraduates.

In 1928 Brooks took his Bachelor of Arts degree in English with Phi Beta Kappa honors, and in 1929 moved to New Orleans to pursue graduate study at Tulane University. At Tulane, where he shared an apartment with Hodding Carter, Brooks encountered an English department far different from the one he had known at Vanderbilt. His interest in literature carried him through the year it took him to receive the Master of Arts degree, but the young scholar found himself "appalled at the fact that so much of the conventional graduate study seemed to have nothing to do with the interior life of the poem." The curriculum was solid enough and he certainly profited from it, but, as Brooks says, "the question of whether a given poem was good or bad was either waived or never asked." The biographical and cultural facets were given fullest consideration, but one "consulted a book to find out whether somebody had said it was a good poem. If you couldn't find anybody who had passed judgment on it, you were at sea."[5] The graduate schools provided no equipment with which to make aesthetic judgment.

If Brooks received little in the way of aesthetic training at Tulane, he certainly did not waste the year. Not only did he receive his degree but he won a Rhodes Scholarship to Oxford as well. Believing that "at Oxford I should attempt the traditional Oxford degree," Brooks began an honors B.A. in 1931 and took the B. Litt. in 1932 under David Nichol Smith, Merton Professor of English. In the summer of 1932, Brooks came home and began to look for a job. As he later recalled, "the depression had set in and university posts were hard to come by. At the very last minute I had the luck to get a post at the Louisiana State University at Baton Rouge."[6] Times were hard, indeed, but it was not blind luck that brought Cleanth Brooks to LSU.

In December, 1929, Brooks first met Allen Tate. The place was

5. Robert Penn Warren, "A Conversation with Cleanth Brooks," in Lewis P. Simpson (ed.), *The Possibilities of Order: Cleanth Brooks and His Work* (Baton Rouge, 1976), 4–5.
6. *Ibid.*, 19, 21.

the Café des Deux Magots in Paris, and Tate recalls that "even then
. . . he was wearing his thick spectacles, and one had the fleeting
thought that like Eliot's Donne he was looking into one's skull beneath the skin. The amusing, if somewhat disconcerting, thing
about this was that it seemed to be a one-way scrutiny; his lenses
were so thick that I couldn't see through to his eyes to surmise what
he was thinking." Dramatic though this description is, it is much
too macabre to be quite the accurate portrait of the man. Despite the
thickness of the lenses, others felt Brooks's eyes fairly danced with
intelligence, good humor, and even a scarcely suppressed hint of
mischief. Tate was more correct in observing that this small, mild-
mannered man was "so perfect a gentleman that one cannot understand that he has faced Eliot's 'horror and boredom.'"[7]

The third party at the Deux Magots with Brooks and Tate was
Charles Wooten Pipkin, a former Rhodes Scholar. Pipkin was born
in Little Rock, Arkansas, in 1899, and, like Ransom and Brooks,
was the son of a Methodist minister. He had received a B.A. from
Henderson-Brown College, an M.A. from Vanderbilt, had been a
Hopkins fellow in economics and social sciences for three years at
Harvard, and, in 1925, had received his Ph.D. from Oxford. When
James M. Smith became president of LSU, he wrote to some of the
scholars that he had met at Columbia, asking for the names of qualified people to fill some key posts at his new university. From the
names sent him, he chose Pipkin, then only twenty-six years old
and a full professor of government at the University of Illinois, to
serve as dean of the graduate school.

Perhaps the first of the dynamic new generation of scholars to
come to LSU during this period of greatest growth, Pipkin "blew
like a bracing current of arctic air into a campus which for decades
had gone its languid way amid the faint smell of magnolia blossoms."
One former colleague remembers Pipkin as full of vigor, candor, and
daring. He "deferred to no one, acknowledged no sacred cows, and
spoke his mind with a startling lack of regard for what was considered discreet academic policy. He was fluent, witty, affable; but he

7. Allen Tate, "What I Owe to Cleanth Brooks," in Simpson (ed.), *The Possibilities
of Order*, 125, 126.

had a keen eye for frauds and a caustic tongue merciless in their exposure."[8]

Despite the surface raillery, Pipkin was an idealist and a crusader. Exemplifying "the recrudesence of Jeffersonian cosmopolitanism in the post-World War I age," Pipkin was a twentieth-century philosophe. His two main causes were world peace and the redemption of the South through education, and the latter goal was his constant theme during the years that he was dean of the graduate school. In 1930 the South had not yet thrown off the affliction of the Civil War, and Louisiana's condition was typical of the region. The South was "the nation's number one economic problem" and it contained a major part of that third of the nation which President Roosevelt described as "ill-fed, ill-clothed, ill-housed." Pipkin deplored the inadequacy of the efforts by southern universities to cope with these problems. He criticized university programs which "had grown from catechisms of denominational colleges to the vast catholicity of curricula which mean nothing," and referred to the South's system of higher education as "this animated circus of mediocrity and miscellany." He derided the righteous contentment of many college professors who "are embalmed with the shroud of a Ph.D.," and surveying the result of much that passed for academic research, observed that if Dr. Johnson were still alive "he would not overlook the word 'research' as the last refuge of the scoundrel." The minimum objective he set for the graduate school was "a greater immediate realization of the inherent capacities of the southern regions and a more vital reintegration of the regional culture in the national scene."[9]

In addition to his duties in the government department, Pipkin served from 1928 to 1930 as a member of the advisory council of the League of Nations, was editor of the *American Political Science Review* and associate editor of *Candid Opinion*. As summers permitted he took postdoctoral courses in Berlin, Freiburg, and Paris, and from 1929 to 1930 he was a Carnegie fellow in international law at

---

8. Alex Daspit, *LSU Graduate Report*, XXI (Spring, 1976), 5.

9. Lewis P. Simpson, "*The Southern Review* and Post-Southern American Letters," *Triquarterly 43: The Little Magazine in America: A Modern Documentary History*, XLIII (1978), 87–88.

the Sorbonne. On a subsequent trip to Paris he once again encountered Cleanth Brooks, a young man whom he had recommended for a Rhodes scholarship in 1928. Although neither Brooks nor Tate knew it at the time, "Pip" was even then planning to bring the young Kentuckian to Louisiana after he took his Oxford degree.

When in April, 1931, Pipkin had become dean of the newly created graduate school, President Smith's mandate was that money was to be no object and Pipkin was to bring in scholars to every department of the university and to pay higher salaries than any other institution. He was required, however, to work properly through current department chairmen and to persuade them to initiate these new appointments. Although the job brought Pipkin serious stomach ulcers within two years of his appointment, he was astonishingly skilled at the type of departmental diplomacy required to work around and through some old and unimaginative department heads and was able to bring to LSU some extraordinary scholars. As one of Brooks's colleagues heard the story, for example, Pipkin told English Department chairman William A. Read that "Cleanth Brooks was the son of a Methodist minister in Shreveport and that LSU should hire some local people." Whether this story is accurate or not, Pipkin did engineer a speaking engagement for Brooks on the LSU campus, at the end of which he was sought out by Read and offered a teaching position on the English faculty.[10]

Limited but significant sections of the university to which Brooks came were bursting with intellectual energy and with funds to put ideas into action. With characteristic understatement Brooks remembers it as a "highly interesting time." LSU was one of the very few American universities actively recruiting faculty at the time and, Brooks recalls, "it threw its net wide, and it swept in all sorts of people: those who could only be regarded as so-so; those who were undistinguished but solid and useful . . . and those—they were in considerable number—who were intelligent, imaginative, and intelligently vigorous."[11]

Shortly after Cleanth Brooks arrived on the Baton Rouge campus to take his post as lecturer in the English department, Pipkin set

10. Scouten to author, September 23, 1979.
11. Brooks, "Brooks on Warren," 21.

afoot a project which employed the talents of the two former Oxonians beyond their normal roles of teaching government and composition. Early in 1933 Pipkin, who was interested in starting a scholarly publication at LSU, approached Southern Methodist University political science professor S. D. Myres with a hint that LSU was interested in sharing the expense and the prestige of publishing the *Southwest Review*. This periodical, established as the *Texas Review* at the University of Texas at Austin in 1915 under Stark Young, moved in the autumn of 1924 to the campus of SMU in Dallas. There it came under the editorial direction of Jay B. Hubbell, whose policy it was "to follow Carl Sandburg's advice and get into the pages of the *Southwest Review* the five-gallon hat of the cowboy as well as the skyscrapers of Dallas and Denver."[12]

In April, 1927, a new regime took over the editorial duties of the Dallas quarterly, but John H. McGinnis, a classic New England liberal, and his young protégé, Henry Nash Smith, did little to alter the quarterly's distinctive character as an expression of the cultural interests peculiar to the Southwest. To Smith's mind, the Southwest was a region "bounded on the east by the western edge of the Mississippi and Red River bottoms," a definition which left Baton Rouge and most of the rest of Louisiana out of the area of interest of the magazine. The editors in Dallas had serious reservations as to whether Baton Rouge based editors might not be more concerned with the problems of the Deep South and were worried that there was not a sufficient common tradition within the two regions to warrant the joint publication of a magazine devoted to the interpretation of both. In Pipkin's estimation "this regional business was quite a racket," and the LSU dean did little to allay Smith's fears with his stated belief that rather than Louisiana being part of the Southwest, Texas was part of the South.[13]

SMU was not supporting its publication adequately, however, and LSU, thanks again to Huey Long, had funds to underwrite a journal. James M. Smith, especially, was desirous of acquiring the prestige of a national publication for LSU, and so, on hearing of the

12. Jay B. Hubbell, "Southern Magazines," in W. T. Couch (ed.), *Culture in the South: A Symposium of Thirty-one Authors* (Chapel Hill, 1934), 163.

13. Henry Nash Smith, "A Note on the Southwest," *Southwest Review*, XIV (Spring, 1929), 269; Charles Pipkin to Henry Nash Smith, April 1, 1935, in *Southwest Review* Papers, Southern Methodist University, Dallas, Texas.

Dallas quarterly's financial difficulties, approached Myres with an offer which he hoped would benefit both LSU and SMU. Myres, who knew Pipkin well, brought Pipkin and McGinnis together, and for some months there was considerable discussion, both in Dallas and in Baton Rouge, of the proposed merger. On a trip to Dallas in April, 1933, Pipkin confirmed that Louisiana State would appropriate as much money for the support of the magazine as Southern Methodist would provide, specifically $800 per annum. In return Louisiana was to share equal editorial control with the staff in Dallas. Pipkin proposed an editorial board of five members, consisting of three editors from the current staff and two from Baton Rouge, further suggesting that it would be best if the editorial and business offices remained in Dallas.

Although Smith thought that the arrangement offered the attractive prospect of an "intellectual adventure through association with the remarkable group who were in the process of remaking the university at Baton Rouge," McGinnis was initially against the merger of the boards, fearing that such an action would cause a retrogression into provincialism. McGinnis especially feared the self-effacing but brilliant young Brooks, who although technically neither a Fugitive nor an Agrarian, was by his association with Donald Davidson and John Crowe Ransom at Vanderbilt branded a neo-Confederate conservative. Working in favor of the merger, however, was the belief that the magazine would be greatly improved by "more material from the eastern part of our region," and the board regarded the connection with Louisiana as one which could "broaden and improve the *Review* in every way." The Dallas editors further believed that "the prestige of the University would not be diminished by sharing the publication with so excellent a school as Louisiana State," but rather would be increased because of the expansion of the magazine which the new arrangement would produce. The clinching argument was financial. The situation in Dallas was rapidly becoming one of accept the merger or discontinue publication; the SMU board saw LSU's offer as "an excellent solution to our problem." [14]

14. Henry Nash Smith, "McGinnis and the *Southwest Review: A Reminiscence*," *Southwest Review*, XL (Fall, 1945), 306–308; S. D. Myers [unsigned] to Charles Selecman, April 19, 1933, quoted in Trippet, "A History of the *Southwest Review*," 157–58.

The fall, 1933, number announced the association under the terms that Dean Pipkin had suggested. The new editorial board consisted of McGinnis, Smith, and Myres from SMU and Pipkin and English Department chairman William A. Read from Baton Rouge as editors. B. A. Botkin, Jay B. Hubbell, Howard Mumford Jones, William Alexander Percy, and a half dozen others from Southern Methodist would serve as associate editors, and Cleanth Brooks, Roark Bradford, Lyle Saxon, and John Gould Fletcher would represent Louisiana State. Mary Austin, J. Frank Dobie, and Stanley Vestal of SMU were later named as "contributing editors" from Dallas, as was Taylor Cole from Baton Rouge. McGinnis, however, remained suspicious of the Louisianans and wrote to Smith that the SMU editors "were going to have to make it clear to the LSU people that final editorial decisions were going to have to be made in Dallas." In the hands of so large and heterogenous an editorial board a certain amount of drift and confusion was perhaps inevitable. This conflict of interest was not enough to impair the basic quality or change the basic direction of the magazine, but, Brooks believes, "it took no prophet to see that if the situation prevailed very long, the magazine would lose its old virtues without acquiring new ones." Though personally friendly, the editors were uneasy, with both editorial camps fearing that the collaboration would eventually "reduce the magazine to an academic hodgepodge." [15]

Adding yet another anomaly to an editorial board already as incongruous as the appearance of the cowboy and the pelican in the *Southwest Review* logo was the addition to the editorial board of Robert Penn Warren. Warren was born on April 24, 1905, in Guthrie, Kentucky, less than sixty miles to the east of Cleanth Brooks's birthplace. Warren remembers the area around that part of the state as a "mixed country" with "fine rolling farmland breaking here and there into barrens, but with nice woodlands and plenty of water, a country well adapted to the proper pursuits of boyhood." [16] Warren

15. John McGinnis to Henry Nash Smith, quoted in Mary Maude Trippet, "A History of the *Southwest Review*: Toward an Understanding of Regionalism" (Ph.D. dissertation, University of Illinois, 1966), 160; Cleanth Brooks and Robert Penn Warren (eds.), *Stories from the Southern Review* (Baton Rouge, 1953), xii.

16. Robert Penn Warren, "Some Important Fall Authors Speak for Themselves," *New York Herald Book Review*, XXX (October 11, 1953), 10.

attended school in Guthrie and in Clarksville, Tennessee, and in 1921 entered Vanderbilt University.

Allen Tate, one of Warren's classmates, recalled meeting the young Robert Penn Warren no less vividly than he remembered his first sight of Cleanth Brooks. Tate was in the office of Vanderbilt professor and fellow Fugitive Walter Clyde Curry one day in 1923 when, becoming aware of a presence at his back, he turned around to see "the most remarkable looking boy I had ever laid eyes on. He was tall and thin, and when he walked across the room he made a sliding shuffle, as if his bones didn't belong to one another. He had a long quivering nose, large brown eyes, and a long chin—all topped by curly red hair. He spoke in a soft whisper. . . . This remarkable young man was Robert Penn Warren, the most gifted person I have ever known." Having abandoned an early ambition to become a chemist, Warren, in his second college year, had begun to spend a good deal of time writing poetry and keeping company with the "group of poets and arguers" called the Fugitives. On a campus where the writing of poetry "was almost epidemic"—"Even an all-Southern center on the football team did some very creditable lyrics of a Housmanesque wistfulness," Warren recalls—the red-headed sophomore gained the greatest part of his education at the Fugitive meetings. Before he had graduated summa cum laude in 1925, he had published twenty-four poems in the group's magazine.[17]

After Vanderbilt Warren did graduate work at the University of California, where he shared rooms with Howard Baker and Lincoln Fitzell. Receiving his Master's degree from Berkeley in June, 1927, he began a Ph.D. at Yale in September but quickly won a Rhodes Scholarship to Oxford. While in England he added to his growing canon his first piece of published fiction, a short story in *American Caravan* called "Prime Leaf." Also at Oxford he made his first contributions to the Agrarian cause with his 1929 biography of John Brown and "Briar Patch," one of the twelve essays which comprised *I'll Take My Stand*, a joint venture with his Vanderbilt mentors and companions. Warren returned from Oxford with his B. Litt. in Eliza-

17. Allen Tate, "*The Fugitive, 1922–1925*: A Personal Recollection Twenty Years After," *Princeton University Library Chronicle*, III (April, 1942), 81–82; Warren, "Some Important Fall Authors," 10.

bethan literature in June of 1930 and was hired as an assistant professor of English at Southwestern University in Memphis. At the end of his one-year appointment there he returned to Vanderbilt for three years as a visiting professor.

Pipkin visited Warren at Nashville in the summer of 1934 with the ostensible purpose of soliciting from him some poems for the *Southwest Review* and of inviting Warren to Baton Rouge to give an informal lecture. Warren, at loose ends, was happy to accept the invitation, tendered at the end of the lecture, to join the LSU faculty as a member of the English department. "Having been found expendable by my university," Warren left Nashville and headed south to Baton Rouge where, when most universities were laying off members of their staff, "thanks to Huey's complex respect for learning, LSU was hiring faculty, football team and live tigers." So the young poet from Guthrie entered a phase of his career in a city "where a strangely beautiful landscape, human charm, corruption, cynicism, and social warmth and ready wit created a peculiar amalgam for the untutored to get acquainted with."[18]

Warren, of course, was already well acquainted with one of his new colleagues, Cleanth Brooks. They had met at Vanderbilt in 1924, where from the first, Brooks remembers Warren as "warm and kind to me," even taking an interest in the entering freshman's "attempts to write English prose." The two had then renewed their friendship at Oxford in 1929, where Warren introduced Brooks to I. A. Richards' *Principles of Literary Criticism* and *Practical Criticism*, epoch-making books which would be the keynote of their work together for more than forty years. Brooks's admiration for his fellow Kentuckian, Vanderbilt alumnus, and Oxonian increased as they became co-editors of the *Southwest Review*. Besides his "great gifts as an editor, a practical critic, a teacher and an executive," says Brooks, "the one thing that impressed me from the beginning, perhaps more than his keen intelligence or original ideas, was the enormous energy that he possessed."[19]

Another trait in Warren which Brooks soon came to recognize and admire was his "carefulness and zeal for accuracy. At this pe-

18. Warren, "A Special Message to Subscribers," n.p.
19. Brooks, "Brooks on Warren," 21–22.

riod of my life," Brooks confesses, "I still retained some lingering traces of the romantic notion of a poet. A poet worked by inspiration, flashes, insights. He was therefore privileged to be a little cavalier with facts and figures. . . . In Warren the flashes of insight were clearly visible and one was conscious of his creative surge. But for him facts were important too. If one was to edit a magazine or write a textbook or engage in any other enterprise, there were mundane obligations that had to be honored." As Warren has remarked, there was between himself and Brooks a "vast difference in temperament, character and sense of the world. So every agreement has, in the end, to be regarded in the dramatic context of a hard-won agreement." Yet in the offices and classrooms of Allen Hall, the new home of LSU's English department, and on the editorial board of the *Southwest Review* the two young professors were able to reach such accord and forge an alliance which sparked a revolution in the teaching and criticism of literature. "Like Blake or Boswell," a former student recalls, "both Brooks and Warren had a sense of destiny which was observed by a number of people at the time and is not a reconstruction by hindsight."[20]

In September Warren settled into his new home on Park Drive, not far from the Brookses' home on Convention Street, and took up his new duties at the university. Each semester he taught creative writing and "Modern English Prose and Poetry," an introduction to the study and appreciation of literature, and on alternating semesters, the non-dramatic literature of the Elizabethan period and the dramatic and poetic works of Shakespeare. With Warren was his wife, the former Emma Brescia, the daughter of a professor of music at Mills College in Oakland. Cinna, as she was called by her friends, was a graduate of the University of California, where she and Warren had first met. Born in Ecuador of Italian parents, she spoke Italian, Spanish, English, German, and Polish fluently and became a welcome addition to the LSU department of Romance langauges.

His new life in Baton Rouge fascinated Warren, for he saw in it facets of the human condition undreamed of in his previous experi-

20. *Ibid.*; Warren, "A Conversation with Cleanth Brooks," in Simpson (ed.), *The Possibilities of Order*, 1; Scouten to author, September 23, 1979.

ence. "Having spent a number of years in Tennessee, I was not entirely innocent of politics, from the blood-spattered days of General Jackson to the corrupt shenanigans that ushered in the Depression," a subject which Warren later treated in *At Heaven's Gate*. Nowhere, however, had he encountered corruption and the use of raw power on the scale evident in Huey Long's Louisiana. "Melodrama was the breath of life" in Warren's new environment. "There had been melodrama in the life I had known in Tennessee," he testifies, but somehow it was not the same thing. For "in Tennessee the melodrama seemed different from the stuff of life, something superimposed upon life, but in Louisiana people lived melodrama, seemed to live, in fact, for it, for this strange combination of philosophy, humor and violence. Life was a tale that you happened to be living—and what 'Huey' happened to be living before your eyes."

Of course this new assistant professor at the state university did not view all of Louisiana in mythic proportion. He remembers as well "the world of ordinary life." Plenty of common people were just trying to get by as common people everywhere must. But besides the insurance and used car salesmen, the farmers and storekeepers, were the swampers—"visible even from the new concrete speedway that Huey had slashed through the cypress swamps toward New Orleans"—fishermen, trappers, and moss pickers whose palmetto-leaf and sheet-iron hovels rose "like some fungoid growth" from the marshlands above Lake Maurepas and Lake Pontchartrain. In contrast to the clean, cool waters of "the land between the rivers" of his native Kentucky, Warren found a face of evil in the "scum-green water that never felt sunlight." Only minutes from his front door was "the Freudianly contorted cypress gloom," whose sights and sounds were "cottonmouth moccasins big as the biceps of a prizefighter, and owl calls, and the murderous metallic grind of insect life." In this primordial ooze the poet also found a fitting metaphor for some of his new colleagues, only a few miles up the road at LSU, "some as torpid as a gorged alligator in the cold mud of January and some avid to lick the spit of an indifferent or corrupt administration." But in Cleanth Brooks and many others of the faculty he found able and gifted friends, "fired by a will to create, out of the seething stew and heavy magma, a distinguished university." Withal, he was able to write to John Gould Fletcher at the end of the fall semester of 1934, "I am delighted with my job here, and with my associates. It is a good place in many respects . . . certainly good as places go; and it promises to be better."[21]

No sooner had Warren arrived on campus than he found his name on the editorial board of the *Southwest Review*. As mentioned, the Dallas members of the board had been somewhat apprehensive about their editorial alliance with LSU, but until the addition of Warren they had had little to complain of in their relationship with the editors from LSU. McGinnis, Smith, and Myres had much in common with the liberal Pipkin, whom they found to be "a very agreeable person." In a letter to the SMU president Charles C. Selecman, Myres had stated that the old board members "anticipate no difficulty whatever in working with him. His conception of the aims of the *Review* is entirely in harmony with our own." John McGinnis remembers with pleasure Pipkin's tough-minded but generous approach in editorial discussions and especially his ability to reconcile the differences of the several editors; and Mary Maude Trippett, the principal historian of the *Southwest Review*, has written that "to a considerable degree, Brooks fulfilled the role of junior editor, in charge of the mass of routine details" while Pipkin led the Louisiana group—"our Ulysses," Brooks called him—making editorial decisions, issuing directives, and working out schemes. If the Dallas group had been suspicious of Brooks's close association with the Nashville Fugitive-Agrarian group, Warren, as a charter member of the conservative fellowship, was absolute anathema. On hearing of Warren's appointment to the board of editors, the vacationing McGinnis wrote to Smith, "We shall have to look to the foundations of the *Review*: I suspect an invasion of termites—Agrarian termites. We'll wake up some day and find we're just the shell of what we thought we were."[22]

Smith had already made public his view of the southern conser-

21. Warren, "*All the King's Men*: The Matrix of Experience," 161; Robert Penn Warren to John Gould Fletcher, December 13, 1934, in *Southern Review* Collection, Beinecke Rare Book and Manuscript Library, Yale University. Unless otherwise indicated, all letters cited in this volume are to be found in this collection.

22. Myres [unsigned] to Selecman, April 19, 1933, in Trippet, "A History of the *Southwest Review*"; Trippet, "A History of the *Southwest Review*," 160–61; Brooks to Henry Nash Smith, June 8, 1933; McGinnis to Smith, September 6, 1934, in *Southwest Review* Papers.

vatives in a *Southwest Review* article published five months before Warren joined the magazine's staff. In an essay-review entitled "The Agrarian Dilemma," Smith attacked *I'll Take My Stand* on a number of counts. Claiming that the Agrarians had taken advantage of the early stages of the Depression to publish their manifesto, Smith found virtue in the Twelve Southerners' "delicate but vigorous prose" and their "defiance of Mammon." He further admitted that the Agrarian program "exhibits certain complexities" which he found admirable. Where Smith began to take exception was in the practical applicability of the program. Smith saw that "in addition to defying the wounded dragon of Big Business the Agrarians profess to advocate a number of reforms." The Agrarian philosophy, said Smith, is the identification of the drive toward industrialization with the uncritical cult of Progress and the rejection of the whole movement. Thus it is hoped that, by discouraging the introduction of mechanized industries into the South, the region will avoid "the brutality, and the general starvation of life which are associated with the modern factory wherever it has reached the scale of large-scale production." The remedy for this situation—what Smith saw as the positive side of Agrarianism—was to be found in a faith in agriculture as a way of life able to foster the values destroyed by the factory. "To put the matter simply," said Smith, "the Agrarians advocate an exodus from the cities and a return to the land." But Smith echoed W. T. Couch's question to the Nashville group: "In what way is tenant farming superior to work in a factory?" Pointing out the pitiable plight of the sharecroppers barely eking out a living on depleted cotton lands in the South, Smith concluded with heavy sarcasm that the Agrarians "must be thinking of something besides the kind of farming which is now usual in the South: an ideal, not an actual Agrarianism."[23]

Assessing the state of affairs in the cotton states, Smith saw only two "theoretically possible" ways of making the South more ideally agrarian. Either the Negroes must be reenslaved and the plantation system reestablished or tenantry and one-crop farming must be abolished and factory and office workers returned to subsistence

23. Henry Nash Smith, "The Dilemma of Agrarianism," *Southwest Review*, XIX (April, 1934), 216, 222.

farming of the land. Both of these "solutions" were, of course, unthinkable, and so the program advocated by the writers of *I'll Take My Stand* was reduced, in Smith's estimation, to a simple nostalgia for a real or imagined past. In his words, Agrarianism "is simply the name for a discontent with the contemporary situation in the South." When it seeks concrete reforms to advocate, it can find only impossible anachronisms or measures that have been proposed by the very liberals whom it scorns. Thus "when the Agrarians are intent upon their myth, they can form no program; when they begin to consider practical measures, they have to turn their backs upon their myth. This is their dilemma."[24]

The battle lines were clearly drawn between the liberalism of the Dallas editors and the conservatism of the energetic young Agrarians from Baton Rouge. But for all of McGinnis' and Smith's fears of a neo-Confederate takeover by the "damned mummies," for eight months the partnership went smoothly. Although the influx of Louisiana money enabled the *Southwest Review* to print twelve issues in an eight-month period, thus clearing the backlog created by SMU's financial troubles, the cooperation did little to change the character of the magazine, and, in fact, actually strengthened one area of McGinnis's interest, the magazine's treatment of social and economic problems of the region. "Pipkin was interested in the problems of the South," Smith has commented, "but he was not an Agrarian." Furthermore, the New-Deal-oriented Smith was gratified that "neither Brooks nor Warren showed any serious intention of carrying forward the discussion of Agrarian economics in the pages of the magazine."[25] Pipkin promoted essays and articles by University of North Carolina liberal Howard W. Odum and his followers in the school of "sociological regionalism," including Rupert Vance, Benjamin Kendrick, W. T. Couch, Clarence Carson, and George Fort Milton, and the Baton Rouge editor himself contributed an essay on his favorite subject, "Legislation and Social and Economic Planning." The appearance of these writers served to make

24. *Ibid.*
25. Henry Nash Smith, "The *Southwest Review*, 1924–1943," quoted in Thomas F. Gossett, "A History of the *Southwest Review*: 1915–1942" (M.A. thesis, Southern Methodist University, 1948), 145.

clear the editorial policy of the magazine to be based on an intention to concentrate upon the region and its needs and yet to be intelligently national, not narrowly provincial.

Through the months of cooperation, the editors from Baton Rouge made their voices heard not in political theory but in literature. First Brooks and later Warren were responsible for introducing good poetry to the magazine, including Warren's own "Problem of Knowledge," an intimation of his later greatness. The pages dedicated to poetry were few, however, and the fiction section was scantier still. None of the short stories published in 1933 and 1934 were distinguished, and most were contributed by Southern Methodist University supporters and written from a distinctly southwestern bias.

In the issues which LSU supported, however, new life was sparked in the book review section of the magazine. In that area the *Southwest Review* had been almost wholly devoted to the review of nonfiction writers, many of them bad. In his extensive review section, which finally became a tradition under the title "Son-of-a-Gun-Stew," J. Frank Dobie reported at some length on his patient and laborious reading of vast quantities of southwestern and western writings. In a letter expressing disappointment in general over the fall, 1934, number, Pipkin wrote to Smith that "the most disappointing part to us all is the Book Review Section. There was not a single contemporary book treated. I wish you would read again the first paragraph of Dobie's review." That review read as follows:

"This is the best western story about a horse that I have ever read," wrote Owen Wister in a foreword to *The Pinto Horse*, by Charles Perking, which appeared six years ago. I myself thought the story true to cowhorse nature and beautifully written. It appeared in distinguished format under the imprint of Wallace Habberd, of Santa Barbara, California. Now in format equally handsome but from another publisher, as a kind of companion to pinto, *The Phantom Bull*.

The conscientiously literary Brooks found this reviewing situation unfortunate at best, especially in an era of fierce and exciting literary activity. Brooks wished to bring the book review section into line with the example set by T. S. Eliot at the *Criterion* and to provide a sounding board for the nascent and as yet unnamed New Critics. After a lengthy correspondence between the Baton Rouge and Dallas offices, LSU personnel took over the book reviews and the review section was moved to a more prominent space in the magazine. By early December, 1934, the two factions were in agreement, with McGinnis writing to Pipkin, "We are heartily in accord with your wishes to make the *Review* more contemporary, and rejoice that you mean to intervene at last in regard to the book section."[26]

The next issue, January, 1935, was a special Louisiana number, devised in hopes of bolstering the Louisiana subscriptions and opening the pathway for more congenial recognition in the state. The contents were a satisfying reversal of much of the mediocrity that had previously appeared in the magazine, with Brooks writing a scholarly appraisal of "Edna Millay's Maturity," and Warren contributing an evaluation of the "Fiction of Caroline Gordon." In the books section, Brooks reviewed T. S. Eliot's *The Use of Poetry* and other reviewers looked at works by contemporary writers like Archibald MacLeish, Roark Bradford, and Paul Horgan. "Son-of-a-Gun Stew" went to the back of the magazine. Dallas responded with a sincere letter of congratulations to Pipkin, and Warren rejoiced in a letter to Smith, "The winter issue is a handsome object! It is probably the best looking magazine on the stands for the season."[27] The honeymoon, alas, was short-lived.

In 1934 Charles Scribner's Sons published *So Red the Rose*, the fourth novel of the *Southwest Review*'s founding editor, Stark Young. *So Red the Rose* is a story of antebellum and Civil War era Mississippi. The book's heroes are the McGehees and their kin, an aristocratic planter clan who represent the best traditions of the Old South. Its principal villain is General William T. Sherman, the archetype of modern man as soulless pragmatist, who, in the course of the novel, resigns as superintendent of the Louisiana Seminary of Learning and Military Academy to turn upon his former friends, stu-

26. Pipkin to Smith, December 4, 1934, in *Southwest Review* Papers; J. Frank Dobie, "Son-of-a-Gun Stew," *Southwest Review* (Fall, 1933), 13; McGinnis to Pipkin, December 12, 1934, in *Southwest Review* Papers.

27. Warren to Smith, March 1, 1935, in *Southwest Review* Papers.

dents, and benefactors in the name of practicality and expediency.

Young, like Warren a charter member of the Agrarian movement, used Sherman to represent all that is hostile, in principle and in deed, to the Old South tradition. Sherman is the enemy in rational intent as well in military fact. In trying out his policy of "total war" in the Natchez-Vicksburg area—long before he applied it to Georgia and elsewhere—Sherman, in Donald Davidson's estimation, represented "the logical and realistic side of humanitarianism to which Lincoln at this time was giving a very persuasive but misleading rhetorical expression." Young's Sherman typifies the opposite of the type of unified personality which the Agrarians believed that the Old South had produced. To Davidson "Sherman is a grand apotheosis and cataclysmic realization of the cult of the divided personality." Between Sherman the man and Sherman in his efficient function as a general there is no connection. The man is kind, generous, and courteous; but the general, the political thinker, is the polar opposite. He worships the god of expediency, and everything and everyone is expendable in the service of that deity.[28]

Robert Penn Warren secured Albert Erskine, an LSU graduate student who had studied at Vanderbilt under John Crowe Ransom, to review *So Red the Rose*. Erskine's review was unqualifiedly favorable, stating that although Young "has limited his view to include only a special class, the highest," such a limitation is in no way dishonest. "A deeper and more inclusive treatment would be valuable, too, but that would be another book." Erskine further conceded that Young's novel is "propaganda," but, he maintained, it is propaganda that "argues not for some contemporary cause but for a historical interpretation." More important, the cause which the novel is defending is not dead, Erskine maintained, but merely out of fashion. The standard of values which is held by the Mississippi planter class and defended by the author "is not compatible with the general modern temper, and probably could not be understood by a society to which money has become the *summum bonum* of existence." The reviewer admitted that the Natchez planters did have money,

28. Donald Davidson, Introduction to Stark Young, *So Red the Rose* (New York, 1953), v–xxxvi.

but averred that their wealth did not "relieve them of the responsibility of being ladies and gentlemen."[29]

If Young's attack on modern man and his defense of a traditional and conservative view of society and an orthodox conception of religion were likely to upset the liberal sensibilities of the Dallas editors, Erskine's interpretation of the Old South system of labor was certain to drive them into violent reaction. The plantation aristocrats owned their own labor "which, however, sinful," Erskine contended, "put them in a more humane and responsible relationship with their slaves than is usually enjoyed by hirelings: nominal freedom is of doubtful value to wage slaves." Receiving Erskine's manuscript, Smith fired back a reply to Warren stating flatly that he and the other SMU editors were very displeased with the review. To them the tone of the piece implied an attitude of "I know this isn't a great novel, but I dare any (liberal) white trash to say so." Although Smith claimed that he, McGinnis, and Myres had tried "to put aside for the moment [their] feelings about Agrarianism and to discount mere difference of opinion," the Dallas editors still could not agree that slavery "even in enlightened Natchez," was necessarily superior to absolutely any relationship of employer to employee. "I for instance," says Smith, "once worked for the Dallas *News*, and received a paycheck every Tuesday afternoon. I do not feel the relationship to me of Mr. G. B. Dealy, owner of the paper, was less humane than that of the McGees [sic] to their slaves."[30]

Responding to Erskine's claim that *So Red the Rose* "is largely non-fiction," Smith retorted that "it never occurred to me to regard it as history . . . I do not believe Mr. Young himself would defend his book as history. . . . On the other hand much could be said in defense of it as art." To Smith's mind, the review blew "both hot and cold." He found inconsistent Erskine's reading of the novel as both history and propaganda, and dubious the reviewer's claim that *So Red the Rose* was firmly grounded in fact. "It remains an open question with us," Smith told Warren, "what are the reviewer's historical

29. Albert Erskine, "The Sempiternal Rose," *Southwest Review*, XX (April, 1935), 21–27.

30. Smith to Warren, January 10, 1935, in *Southwest Review* Papers.

sources and evidences for declaring that Stark Young's portrayal of life in Natchez are [sic] accurate." Smith also was disturbed by his feeling that Erskine's review seemed "to surrender all claims of the book to artistic merit." Instead, Smith charged, the reviewer read the novel only as a sort of historical reconstruction and special pleading for a cause, thus basing his entire judgment upon the question of historical accuracy.[31]

Upon this question of accuracy, Smith was highly dubious. Erskine, having declared the book to be history, went on to remark that Natchez in 1860 "demonstrated one of the highest points ever attained by collective human nature." Smith deplored such a claim, and admitted to "a malicious suspicion" that Erskine had forgotten how immensely general such a statement can be. "Does he then really know so certainly?" Smith asked Warren. Such a statement Smith regarded as one which might be expected from a Daughter of the Confederacy, perhaps, but not one which was suitable for the *Southwest Review.*[32]

The controversy was clearly based upon conflicting views of the antebellum South. Smith had already gone on record in his essay on Agrarianism as believing that "the gracious civilization, the ordered society with every man in his place, and the aristocratic subtlety which the Agrarians attribute to the Old South are evidently in the best sense mythical." Brooks and Warren, however, sided with Erskine in his belief that the portrait of a society which fellow Agrarian Stark Young had painted was not only mythically satisfying but literally true. They agreed with the view of Katherine Anne Porter, who wrote that the planters of the lower Mississippi valley

> had on their side the strong arm of slave labor, and definite views on caste, morals and manners. They pushed back [the virgin wilderness] mile by mile, uncovering rich lands, and raised splendid crops. They built charming houses and filled them with furniture from France and England. Their silver and porcelain and linen were such as befitted their pride, which was high, and their tastes, which were delicate and

31. *Ibid.*
32. *Ibid.*

expensive. Their daughters sang, danced, and played the harpsichord; their sons played the flute and fought duels; they collected libraries, they hunted and traveled and played chess, and spent the winter season in New Orleans. They traveled much in Europe, and brought back always more and more Old World plunder. Everywhere, with ceaseless, intensely personal concern, they thought, talked, and played politics.

Even Pipkin, usually the bridge between the Dallas liberals and the Baton Rouge Agrarians, added his voice, however softly and qualifiedly, to the defense. In a later essay on social legislation in the modern South, Pipkin came down on the side of the southern tradition of paternalism and *noblesse oblige* in the treatment of the Negro. The "tradition of proprietary responsibility for dependents has survived in an environment of free labor," he claimed. "The existence of a large servile and inferior class, first as slaves and later as freedmen, made such a philosophy not only humane but also expedient."[33]

Warren's reply to Smith, six days later, was conciliatory but firm. "I see now that it looks pretty dogmatic," the Baton Rouge editor conceded, "but we have drafted it in this way as a matter of convenience." Erskine had done some rewriting, which Brooks and Warren believed to have improved the tone of the review, and asked for Smith's opinion. Warren defended the review against Smith's charges of categorical statements about the nature of slavery and the accuracy of the description of the life of the planter aristocracy at Natchez and on points which Smith had raised challenging the internal consistency of the review. Denying that Erskine presented a moral defense of slavery, Warren contended that "it seems rather that he is pointing to the obvious fact that the relationship was more concrete and personal, and therefore responsible, than the relationship ordinarily existing between employer and employee." In reply to Smith's objection that the review blew "hot and cold," the Baton Rouge editors suggested, "Surely you do not mean to imply that a

33. Katherine Anne Porter, "Happy Land," in Frank Crowinshield (ed.), *Vogue's First Reader* (New York, 1942), 75; Charles W. Pipkin, "Social Legislation," in Couch (ed.), *Culture in the South*, 646.

review should not make certain qualifications, that it should be absolute in praise or blame." What Erskine was attempting, Warren wrote, was "to define the sense of values held by the limited society" portrayed by Young. He and Brooks could not agree with the Dallas editors that it violated the findings of the best historians, and they did not find Erskine inconsistent in the review but believed the review quite suitable for a quarterly journal.[34]

The Dallas camp was not fully satisfied by Erskine's rewriting or by Warren's explanation. "The whole business begins to give me an acute malaise," Smith wrote. "We are bound by our lack of money; but I believe I'd rather see the *Review* go under with dignity than become an Agrarian sheet." Nevertheless, they backed away from further controversy over the matter. "I have reread the revised review and protocol which accompanied it," Smith wrote to Warren the following month, "and hasten to say that we do not want to make an issue out of the matter." Indeed, Smith conceded that "on reflection it seems that while we do not see eye to eye with you on every point, there is not enough difference between our points of view to justify prolonging the argument," and he promised to run the review in the magazine's spring number.[35] Even though Smith, McGinnis, and other Dallas editors of the *Southwest Review* were willing to accept Erskine's revised version of the *So Red the Rose* review, the rupture between the two editorial camps was far from healed, and years later Smith recalled that he and his SMU colleagues decided to accept the piece only because LSU had already announced its decision to pull out of the joint publishing venture.

Brooks and Warren had of course been busy collecting manuscripts and promises of manuscripts for the *Southwest Review* from their Agrarian friends and allies, and when the end of the collective editorial board was announced, they had on hand essays by Frank Owsley, John Crowe Ransom, and Cleanth Brooks and stories by Caroline Gordon and John Peale Bishop. The Baton Rouge editors had also acquired reviews by John Gould Fletcher, Caroline Gordon, and Brooks as well as promissory notes from Herbert Agar, John

34. Warren to Smith, January 25, 1935, in *Southwest Review* Papers.
35. Smith to Chapman, n.d. [1935], in *Southwest Review* Papers; Smith to Warren, February 27, 1935, *ibid.*

Gould Fletcher, Randall Jarrell, and Donald Davidson among others. Although it is quite likely that the Dallas contingent of the *Southwest Review* editorial board would never have allowed so much material from the Deep South and from conservative writers to appear in the magazine, this collection of material represented a compendium of some of the finest writing being done in America at that time, and provided Brooks, Warren, and Pipkin with a tremendous advantage in their next publishing venture.

On March 20, 1935, Pipkin wrote to his Dallas associates signaling the end of the Louisiana–Southern Methodist partnership and the beginning of a new era in the American little magazine. "There is no need to tell you that we have enjoyed the association and look forward to its continuance in all the things that we together are interested in," Pipkin wrote to the SMU editors, but, he announced, Louisiana State University had just granted Pipkin, Brooks, and Warren a $10,000 annual stipend with which to publish their own journal under the LSU imprint.[36] Its name was to be the *Southern Review*, and it became one of the finest literary magazines in the English language.

36. Pipkin to McGinnis, Smith, and Myres, March 30, 1935, *ibid.*

THREE

"The Athens of
the Nation"

THE beginning of *The Southern Review* was casual,
sudden, and in so far as the future editors were concerned, quite
unexpected," Brooks and Warren recall. On a bright Sunday afternoon in late February, James Monroe Smith drove up to the door of
Robert Penn Warren's home and invited Warren, his wife, and their
guest, Albert Erskine, to go for a drive. Erskine and the Warrens
settled back into the soft upholstery of the official black Cadillac and
listened as President Smith unfolded his plan. "Was it possible," he
wanted to know, "to have a good literary quarterly at the university."
Warren's reply was "yes" with certain qualifications. If the journal paid a fair rate for contributions, and if it gave writers "decent
company between the covers," and if editorial authority were suffi-
ciently concentrated to allow the magazine its own distinctive character and quality, then LSU could have as good a quarterly as any in
the land. Almost as an afterthought, Warren added one more stipu-
lation to his list. Remembering, perhaps, the high-handed fashion
in which the university administration had sought to censor the
Reveille, Warren insisted that interference by academic committees

and officials must not dilute the quality of the magazine. President Smith gave the matter only a few minutes meditation and then suggested that Warren and Erskine confer with Brooks and Pipkin. They were to prepare a statement of feasibility concerning the proposed magazine, and if the statement was in by the next day, he would sign an authorization for the project.[1]

Brooks, Warren, Erskine, and Pipkin lost no time in getting to their task. That evening a plan for the quarterly was drawn up, and the next day Smith signed the authorization. They were no less hastened in setting afoot the review's first number. The new editors—and President Smith—had hoped that the first issue would come from the presses in June, and to that end they began a furious campaign of letter writing in search of contributors.

Agrarian sympathizer Herbert Agar was among the first from whom the new quarterly solicited a contribution. "I want to ask your service in a project which, I hope, is a good deal more important than the *Southwest Review*," wrote Warren. "A week ago we obtained funds for the founding of a large quarterly, which will combine fiction, poetry, criticism, and essays on social matters. Our rates will be better than those proposed for the *Southwest Review*, but we have not yet reduced them to a final statement. Our budget, however, will certainly permit us to pay a good deal better than a cent a word for prose and something above thirty-five cents a line for verse." Warren further stated that the new review was "aiming at a national distribution," and remarked that "since we have a rather large promotion fund that ambition does not seem too remote." Two days later Warren wrote to John Gould Fletcher, also an Agrarian destined to be a Pulitzer Prize winner. "As you may observe from the letterhead," he wrote, "the University has embarked on a new project. . . . This has all happened within the last week, and so we are extremely busy trying to put together the first issue by June 1. I believe that this is a fine step, for it gives us a great deal more scope for our activities."[2]

Cleanth Brooks assumed the responsibility for contacting many

1. Brooks and Warren, *Stories from the Southern Review*, xi.
2. Robert Penn Warren to Herbert Agar, March 23, 1935; Robert Penn Warren to John Gould Fletcher, March 25, 1935.

of the non-Agrarian authors whom the review wished to publish. Typical of the dozens of letters that he wrote to potential contributors is his March 25 communication to E. E. Cummings:

> On June 1 the first issue of *The Southern Review* will appear. Despite its title, this quarterly does not aim, especially in its literary aspect, at a sectional program, nor will it have an academic bias. We hope to provide a large quarterly which will be a ready index to the most vital contemporary activities in fiction, poetry, criticism, and social-political thought, with an adequate representation in each of the departments. In each issue there will be a large display of poetry. We are especially anxious to have some of your work for the opening exhibit, preferably several pieces. It is our hope to provide a market for longer poems than are ordinarily in other magazines.[3]

By the first of April such letters had gone out to Conrad Aiken, Sherwood Anderson, James Agee, Kay Boyle, Kenneth Burke, Erskine Caldwell, Donald Davidson, Bonamy Dobrée, T. S. Eliot, Dudley Fitts, F. Scott Fitzgerald, William Faulkner, F. R. Leavis, Archibald MacLeish, Marianne Moore, Katherine Anne Porter, Herbert Read, Thomas Wolfe, and a host of others. Not all of the requests for material were honored with manuscripts in the return mail. Stark Young, for example, wrote that although he "was much interested to have your letter and to hear your plans for the magazine," he regretted that he would "not be able to write anything for you, at least not for some time to come." He explained that he had contracted for "a great deal more than I could hope to get done within several months, perhaps a year or so." He did, however, congratulate the editors for their distinguished and promising list of contributors and hoped that they would do a great deal of writing for the magazine themselves. F. Scott Fitzgerald replied, "Thanks for your letter. I wish to God I had something for you, especially as I understand that Louisiana State University is to be the Athens of the Nation."[4]

3. Cleanth Brooks to E. E. Cummings, March 25, 1935.
4. Stark Young to Robert Penn Warren, March 5, 1935, in John Pilkington (ed.), *Stark Young: A Life in the Arts: Letters, 1900–1962* (Baton Rouge, 1975), I, 583; F. Scott Fitzgerald to Robert Penn Warren, April 5, 1935.

Other requests bore fruit, and by the end of March the *Southern Review* had manuscripts or promises from John Peale Bishop, Herbert Agar, John Crowe Ransom, Katherine Anne Porter, Caroline Gordon, Ford Madox Ford, Andrew Lytle, and Allen Tate.

One factor that helped to influence President Smith's decision in favor of founding the new publication was the fact that 1935 was Louisiana State University's seventy-fifth year, and the "Old War Skule," reinvigorated by a new campus, new faculty, and a new prestige, celebrated the event in a grand style. As part of the birthday celebration and as an announcement party for the university's new magazine, the editors conceived and planned a Southern Writers' Conference to convene in Baton Rouge in April. Although the guest list was dominated by Brooks's and Warren's Agrarian friends, it was by no means the "genuine, dyed-in-the-wool, True Rebel Southerners' Convention" that Donald Davidson had hoped for.[5] Liberal southern, northern, and even British writers were invited. The sole criterion seemed to be that those were welcome who might have something to contribute to the success of the new quarterly.

Not all who were invited attended, and some who did attend were not perfectly pleased with the prospect of fresh competition. Stark Young, for example, wrote a charming letter to the Warrens begging off the trip to Baton Rouge, citing a pile of proof which had gotten the better of him. To Allen Tate, however, he wrote, "I was invited to the Louisiana affair, but my foot has been troubling me so badly, so that made as easy an excuse as any." In fact, he admitted, "I detest all meetings and groups." Even when Mrs. Warren telephoned the reclusive Young with a personal invitation, he refused to reconsider. "I get reported often as being or going to be in places," he told Tate. "It's always a safe bet I'm not."[6]

An even bigger disappointment to the planners of the conference was William Faulkner's decision to decline the invitation. Although he telegraphed the university on the morning of April 10 that he

5. Donald Davidson to Allen Tate, October 29, 1932, in John Tyree Fain and Thomas Daniel Young (eds.), *The Literary Correspondence of Donald Davidson and Allen Tate* (Athens, 1974), 274.
6. Stark Young to Allen Tate, April 9, 1935, in Pilkington (ed.), *Stark Young*, I, 599.

might be able to fly down for a day from Oxford in his private plane, he did not do so. Explaining his reason for not attending a similar conference at the University of Virginia four years earlier, he had told its planner, James S. Wilson, "You may have seen a country wagon come into town, with a hound dog under the wagon. It stops on the square and the folks get out, but the hound never gets very far from the wagon. He might be cajoled or scared out for a short distance, but first thing you know he has scuttled back under the wagon; maybe he growls at you a little. Well, that's me." The most vicious growls, however, came from the planners' one-time partner, Henry Nash Smith. Still angry, perhaps, over Albert Erskine's review of *So Red the Rose*, Smith outdid his usual sarcasm in a letter to John Chapman. "We are supposed to have the [*Southwest*] *Review* out by April 10 for Pipkin's big triple brass band super-heated air cooled oil filter knee action SOUTHERN WRITERS' CONFERENCE at Baton Rouge. The magazine would look nice as a program for the second banquet."[7]

Despite these unpleasant notes, as well as regrets from John Crowe Ransom, Donald Davidson, and Elizabeth Madox Roberts, the Baton Rouge conference was well attended. On March 27 Warren acknowledged Ford Madox Ford's intention of driving down to Baton Rouge with Allen Tate and Caroline Gordon, and thanked him "for being able to give us some material immediately for *The Southern Review*."[8] In all, forty men and women of letters took part in the conference plus a mix of spectators. Robert Penn Warren served as chairman, and besides Allen Tate and Caroline Gordon, Agrarians and their allies John Gould Fletcher, John Peale Bishop, John Donald Wade, Frank Lawrence Owsley, and Randall Jarrell attended. Among the southerners of a more liberal persuasion at the conference were Lambert Davis, managing editor of the *Virginia Quarterly Review*, William T. Couch, director of the University of North Carolina Press and editor of the influential anthology *Culture*

7. William Faulkner to James S. Wilson, September 24, 1931, in Joseph Blotner (ed.), *Selected Letters of William Faulkner* (New York, 1977), 51; Henry Nash Smith to John Chapman, undated letter, in *Southwest Review* Papers.
8. Robert Penn Warren to Ford Madox Ford, March 27, 1935.

in the South, and B. A. Botkin, Oklahoma folklorist and editor of two short-lived journals in Norman, as well as John McGinnis of the *Southwest Review.* Also adding their prestige to the occasion were the two reigning lions of the Louisiana literary scene, Roark Bradford and Lyle Saxon of New Orleans. Whether because of a hostile review that Warren had recently given to Bradford's *John Henry,* or because they felt their preeminence threatened by the talented and energetic young men from Baton Rouge, or perhaps from a genuine philosophical commitment, Bradford and Saxon sided with the New South liberals from the start, in a conference which was the stage for the continuation of the controversy that had shaped the dissension in the editorial board of the *Southwest Review.*

Ford Madox Ford remembered the morning as "insupportably hot" when Robert Penn Warren called to order the first session of the Conference on Literature and Reading in the South and Southwest on Wednesday, April 10, on the roof of the Heidelberg Hotel. This was the very location from which Senator Long managed the affairs of the State of Louisiana when away from his Washington office, and Ford was struck by the view of the levee of the Mississippi River behind which "the continent of North America [was] hurrying overhead to throw itself into the sea."[9] Warren introduced Dean Pipkin to the conference, and Pipkin in turn welcomed the participants and guests in the name of Louisiana State University. The theme of Pipkin's opening remarks was the fellowship of the community of letters. "You and I believe in ideas," he declared, and "we are here to discuss the permanence of ideas through writing." Referring to the economic crisis which was then disrupting all of Western society and the military crisis then brewing in central Europe, Pipkin noted that "there are so many things which happen whose passing seems momentous. But the ideas and ideals are important. You who manage to put this into words are thinking of the past and looking ahead to the future. The chief purpose of this group is fellowship—a community of ideas. Genial tolerance and congeniality must characterize it." Pipkin called upon his listeners to

9. Ford Madox Ford, *The Great Trade Route* (New York, 1937), 351–52.

forgo their provincial world view and to "think of the South today as a way of life toward the future. And it is to that future," he concluded, "that we have given ourselves." [10]

Pipkin's plea for "genial tolerance and congeniality" went unheeded from the first, however, as did his suggestion that the discussions of the conference be international in scope. In his opening comments, Warren brought the subject into a much tighter focus with the injunction that "the aims of this conference particularly are to discuss reading and literature in the South." The writers, editors, and publishers present spent most of their time debating the special meaning of the South's cultural heritage, the literary status of the region as a province of the Northeast, and the role of "progress" in its future. Given the geographical and philosophical mix of participants, controversy was all but inevitable and overt hostility was avoided only with the forbearance of gentlemen.

The program's first speaker was John Peale Bishop, who delivered a prepared statement on the nature of provincial literature and the audience for such a literature in the South. Bishop, seconded by Allen Tate and John Gould Fletcher, declared that great art had traditionally been the result of an interaction of an artist and his public when the two have "the same reactions and those reactions are serious ones." The southern writer's relationship "to the soil, to neighbors, friends, and history," the Agrarians agreed, was the most outstanding feature of its art, but such a relationship was fast breaking down beneath the onslaught of modern industrialism. Although unquestioned in the West in the seventeenth century, such a rapport between the artist and his public was exceptional in the twentieth century as a result of modern society's insistence that art and culture be made to serve economic ends.

With the nation's wealth concentrated in the Northeast, the southern artist had no significant audience in the South. He thus wrote for an audience outside of his native region. Such southern writers as T. S. Stribling and Erskine Caldwell, therefore, created "a criticism of Southern life from standards not Southern" but of New

10. "Transcript of the Conference on Literature and Reading in the South and Southwest," Baton Rouge, Louisiana, April 10–11, 1935, p. 1, in possession of the author.

York. "From 1850 on," said Allen Tate, "we see the rise of the national point of view in politics. We in the South know that this is not
national but Eastern sectionalism disguised as nationalism. We
have been asked to accept nationalism which is Eastern." John
Gould Fletcher extended this point with the observation that since
the metropolitan critic seeks to define all of American experience
through his own limited vision, the provincial critic should relate
the southern experience to its own history and the creative writer
should "define the point of view that emerges from his environment
without doing violence to it." [11]

A bit awed and defensive in the face of the Agrarians' self-
consciously intellectual stance, the New Orleans writers rose to the
defense of the metropolis, with Saxon declaring that "New York has
treated us perhaps better than we deserve" and Bradford agreeing
that the tyranny of the New York publishers was no greater than the
tyranny of self-conscious regionalism. "I don't think I know what
Southern culture is," Bradford told the conference. It is perfectly all
right to talk about southern arts and southern press and a southern
audience "if you are going to stay in the South all the time," he
maintained, but further insisted that the real dichotomy in the arts
was not between North and South but between good and bad. [12]

The most spirited defense of the New York establishment, however, came from the conference's distinguished English guest, Ford
Madox Ford. Like T. S. Eliot, Ford was deeply responsive to the se-
ductive myth of the Tory past. Although London born, he had for
years subsisted as a small farmer in Sussex and harbored a personal
reverence for the land and an admiration for those who worked it. In
his memoir *The Great Trade Route*, Ford revealed one of his three
lifelong obsessions to be "the conviction that green growing objects
are necessary to the saving of the world as we know it," and he
claimed "Stonewall" Jackson as his childhood's hero. Indeed, Ford
believed that the repulse of Pickett's charge sealed the fate of humanity. "Destiny cried with a loud voice: *All aboard for the industrial system*, and heaven knows when we shall disembark." Yet Ford
took the floor at the Baton Rouge writers' conference "for the in-

11. *Ibid.*, 1–5, 10–12.
12. *Ibid.*, 14, 31.

trepid purpose of saying nice things about New York to Mr. Long's subjects" and to the "violent secessionists of the hot South." [13]

Since there was not a publishing center in the South, and since he could see no harm done to the South by the metropolitan literary establishment inasmuch as "Southern books fill the reviewing pages of all the Literary Supplements" and are "enthusiastically heralded to an enthusiastically waiting public," then the name of the metropolis should not be anathema to the southern literati. Ford had been gassed during World War I, and few in the audience could hear him distinctly. Nevertheless, at this point in his speech Ford looked up to see John Gould Fletcher "prowling the back of the audience asking them why they did not lynch me." In the discussion that followed— "a literary chit-chat" as Botkin later called it—Ford insisted that provincial writers needed a distributing center and New York was as good a place as any. "You must have a social center where you can meet your fellows in your craft. New York," he claimed, "is such a place." "Oh, not at all!" Caroline Gordon and John Gould Fletcher shouted in unison. "New York is just a market place," Fletcher expounded, and Miss Gordon vowed that "the Southern writer has no chance in New York for such contact with fellows in his craft." [14]

Ford's impromptu closing remarks, however, did much to settle the ruffled Agrarian feathers and to end the meeting on a note of optimism. "You in the South have the world at your feet," he declared. "The North and East are exhausted, and the industrialism of the Middle West is even worse than Eastern industrialism." The Southern Writers' Conference was only possible because the South was once again becoming prosperous, and, if the South desires it, he claimed, the most glorious revenge was its for the taking. "You were conquered in a war; now, at peace, you are conquering the conqueror of your conquerors. That is *revanche noble!*"

By Ford's analysis the power of the other regions of North America was quickly eroding, as was the case with their equivalents all over the world. "Seventy years ago you stood for the fruits of the earth and the treasures of the craftsman, means of wealth that

13. Ford, *The Great Trade Route*, 3, 151, 271.
14. "Transcript of the Conference on Literature and Reading in the South and Southwest," 47.

alone can be coterminous with life on this earth." Ford saw in the years since 1865 the rise of the industrial system and the consequent eclipse of the values of the Old South. The industrial system was, by 1935, "crumbing into its final decay" while the South continued to keep faith with its traditional role as an agricultural region. "Measured by human lives, the pursuits and earnings of the husband-man constitute the only wealth that is and must be as durable as humanity itself." The survival of the South, therefore, Ford felt to be "inevitable." Not only did Ford predict the survival of the region, but he also prophesied that, endowed with wealth and an undisturbed tradition, "your dominance of the hemisphere is as inevitable as your survival." [15]

The true high point of the Conference, though, at least so far as its planners were concerned, was the announcement of the *Southern Review* at the banquet at the end of the first day's proceedings. Significantly, Brooks and Warren took almost no part in the heated debate between their Agrarian and progressive guests, but absorbed as much information as might be valuable to their new magazine while remaining above the sectional rivalry. Unfortunately, almost all of the reports on publishing in the South were of a negative nature, and the prospects for the success of the new magazine were gloomy indeed, to judge from the remarks of the conference's participants. Lambert Davis, for example, commented that the economic poverty and physical isolation of the region had been massive deterrents to the success of his *Virginia Quarterly Review*, and W. T. Couch added that "the general lack of interest in books and the feeling that the intellectual life is of no importance" made the South a poor risk for the publisher. Ford pointed out that any magazine must be either commercial or noncommercial and neither is completely satisfactory. With the former, the editor must cater to the tastes of the least common denominator among his readers, and with the latter "some capitalist gives money and it runs out." Thus, Ford told his listeners, "the imaginative magazine is precluded from commercial success." McGinnis commented on the financial instability of his *Southwest Review*, and Botkin, editor of Oklahoma's

15. *Ibid.*, 48.

defunct *Space* and *Folk-Say*, had some even more dreary comments to add based on his ill-fated tenure as patron of the arts in the Southwest.[16]

The conference itself was only a qualified success. Botkin, viewing the proceedings through western eyes, saw the group solidarity of the Agrarians as "an object lesson in what can be accomplished through joint action in fostering regional literature," and concluded that such a movement was needed in other regions of America as well. Donald Davidson, who had been unable to attend the Baton Rouge conference, mailed his congratulations and total approval to its planners, branding Ford and the New Orleans, Dallas, and Chapel Hill progressives as "the villains, and the Agrarians among the heroes quite clearly." The equally partisan New Orleans *Item* took the opposite stance, citing Roark Bradford and Lyle Saxon as the only clear heads in the group and labeling the conference as "amusing" but "completely ineffectual." For the conference hosts, however, the outcome was not so clear cut. "The sporadic 'Conferences' and 'Congresses' of writers in different sections of this country have been non-political and have tended to define differences of opinion rather than concord," Warren observed in an early *Southern Review* editorial. "Certainly no program or dogma has emerged."[17]

The significance of Ford Madox Ford's participation in the Baton Rouge conference, as Max Webb correctly points out, was that "it shows the *Southern Review* editors' determination to take their stand for a responsible literary internationalism." The *Southern Review* served two states—the state of letters and the state of the South—and Ford was symbolic of the *Review*'s commitment to the supranational spirit of literary modernism within a regional framework. This twofold commitment—"doubleness of vision" Allen Tate might have called it—saved the *Review* from the dead end of sentimental patriotism of earlier generations of southern writers which Lambert Davis had warned against, while keeping it firmly an-

16. *Ibid.*, 34–37.

17. B. A. Botkin, "*Folk-Say* and *Space*: Their Genesis and Exodus," *Southwest Review*, XX (July, 1935), 321; Donald Davidson to Robert Penn Warren, May 14, 1935; K. T. Knoblock, New Orleans *Item*, April 14, 1935, Metropolitan Section, 1; Robert Penn Warren, "Some Recent Novels," *Southern Review*, I (Winter, 1936), 632.

chored in a concrete and meaningful tradition which even Ford could not quite understand.[18]

With the end of the conference Brooks, Warren, and Pipkin went back to their campus duties. They spent much of the remainder of the month putting the transcript of the conference in shape and mailing it out to the participants. But along with these more or less mundane occupations, Brooks, Warren, and Pipkin had the responsibility of preparing the first issue of their new magazine. Letters of encouragement came almost daily. John Gould Fletcher, back in Arkansas after the Baton Rouge conference, wrote to Pipkin, "It is very good news to know that the deep South is to have its own magazine, after all," and B. A. Botkin wrote from Oklahoma, "congratulations on the announcement of the first *Southern Review.* From the typographical dress, prospectus, and table of contents it looks as if the *Hound and Horn* had moved south of the Mason Dixon line."[19]

Despite the general congratulations, however, 1935 was not an auspicious year for the launching of a literary magazine, whether in New York or in the provinces. The decade of the 1930s had seen a marked decline in the circulation of little magazines, and many of the best had gone into receivership or oblivion. The Depression, the radio, the moving pictures, and the metropolitan Sunday newspaper with its numerous magazine features left the literary magazine hard pressed to command a large enough circulation to secure the advertising necessary to make a profitable venture. Especially in the South, literary magazines lacked adequate support and all but a handful had been forgotten. Morton Dawen Zabel, editor of *Poetry,* found "among the Depression's harshest dealings in the world of civilized intelligence" the blow which it struck against critical journalism. "Whatever had been left undone by commercial decay among the older monthlies," he wrote, "was completed by the crippling effects of economic disaster on the younger quarterlies. . . . The

18. Max Webb, "Ford Madox Ford and the Baton Rouge Writer's Conference," *Southern Review,* n.s., XX (Fall, 1974), 892.

19. John Gould Fletcher to Charles W. Pipkin, July 22, 1935; B. A. Botkin to Cleanth Brooks, July 21, 1935.

end of *The Dial* forecast the early doom of its successors, *The Symposium* and *Hound and Horn*."[20]

The death of *The Dial* in 1929 and of *Hound and Horn* in 1934 had left America no journal with the critical standards they had advocated, and the *Southern Review* editors hoped to pick up their banner. Yet, as dedicated as they were to the international republic of letters, they also saw themselves following in the tradition of the little magazines of the South. Among the oldest of these were the *Southern Review*, founded in Charleston, South Carolina, in 1828 by Hugh Swinton Legaré. The new Baton Rouge journal's namesake had modeled itself on *The Edinburgh* and Britain's *Quarterly Review* and had followed in those worthy footsteps for four years before lack of public interest stopped its presses. The nineteenth century's *Southern Review* had, moreover, a twofold purpose; the motives behind its founding were "first, the desire to take away the northern and British reproach of cultural inferiority, and second, the ambition to develop and give expression to an independent southern culture."[21] The new *Southern Review* saw itself carrying this banner into the twentieth century.

The history of the little magazines and critical quarterlies had clearly demonstrated the necessity of solid and stable financial backing, and the example of the *Sewanee Review*, the oldest living quarterly in the United States, showed that connection with a university was perhaps the most reliable means of insuring such backing. Nevertheless, the difficulties of publishing successfully a serious quarterly review identified with a college or university are considerable, as one such editor has pointed out. "Such a review must," he said, "content itself with a few subscribers and exact a heavy subsidy." Such a magazine can always be printed, of course, "if its backers are able and willing to support it," and although its subscription list may be small, if well edited it may yet serve a useful function. "Although it is hardly possible to imagine encouraging commercial prospects for a newcomer in the field," the editor of the *Harvard Alumni Bulletin*, who had witnessed the demise of the Harvard *Graduates Magazine* and the *Harvard Quarterly* in 1933,

---

20. Morton D. Zabel, "Recent Magazines," *Poetry*, XLVIII (April, 1936), 51.
21. Hubbell, "Southern Magazines," in Couch (ed.), *Culture in the South*, 161.

extended his "greetings and good wishes to *The Southern Review*."[22]

Despite such grim prospects, the editors took over three contiguous rooms in the LSU administration building, David Boyd Hall, and on March 23, 1935, Albert Erskine requested a copyright patent on the name "The Southern Review." At the same time the editors announced the first issue for June 15. The *Southern Review* listed Charles W. Pipkin as editor, Cleanth Brooks and Robert Penn Warren as managing editors, and Albert Erskine as business manager. Erskine, who "looked like a blondish younger brother of Gary Cooper,"[23] had been born in Memphis, Tennessee, April 18, 1911, and had taken his bachelor's degree at Southwestern College there in 1932, one year after Warren left to accept a position at Vanderbilt. Erskine soon followed Warren to Nashville, where he enrolled in a Master's program under John Crowe Ransom. Erskine finished his course work at Vanderbilt and returned to Memphis to run a bookshop, "The Three Musketeers," and to work on his thesis; but with undergraduate enrollment at LSU skyrocketing, Warren secured for him an instructor's position in the English department after the beginning of the fall semester in 1934.

Despite the fact that Pipkin, a member of the government faculty, took as his chief concern the discussion of public affairs, and Brooks and Warren of the English department worked primarily in the field of literature, there was never any real division of function among the members of the staff. "Every member of the staff read every item that could seriously be considered for publication, and by and large, all decisions were joint decisions," Brooks and Warren have revealed. Erskine's role, if not his official title, was that of managing editor. "There were, of course, disagreements on matters of taste and policy, but the disagreements worked, on the whole, to keep the atmosphere of the office brisk and healthy." In an era and profession in which a former editor of the *Partisan Review* claims that the friendship of Damon and Pythias "would have been severely taxed" if they had tried to co-edit a little magazine, John E. Palmer, who served as the magazine's managing editor in 1941 and 1942, never

22. *Harvard Alumni Bulletin*, n.d., n.p., in clipping file, *Southern Review* Collection, Yale.

23. Thomas Thompson to author, October 2, 1979.

knew of a serious disagreement between Brooks and Warren and considered his tenure with the *Review* to have been as genial as it possibly could have been.[24]

With the mortality rate among little magazines so alarmingly high, the subsidy which Louisiana State University granted the *Southern Review*—apparently beyond the hazard of popular response or personal caprice—must have seemed like manna from heaven to its editors. In the minds of some people it did carry a taint, however, and that was the reputation of the *Review*'s benefactor, Senator Huey P. Long. To some critics no enterprise could be pure whose source of funding was a political demagogue. "*The Southern Review* was completely free to print whatever its editors, men of integrity, thought best," stated Robert Gorham Davis, for example. "And yet by that very fact, and by the presence of such men at the University of Louisiana, Long's ambitions were being served." Davis concluded that in order to forestall blacklisting by national education organizations and to placate intellectuals, Long was shrewd enough to have able writers and teachers brought to the university and given freedom of expression and teaching as long as they let him have his way in politics. Brooks and Warren have granted that when they began the magazine they did so "with some fear of political interference. In the atmosphere of Louisiana at that time, the apprehension was real." Pipkin, Brooks, and Warren agreed, however, that if the senator or any of his minions should attempt to influence the *Review* in any way, they would resign. Their resolution was never put to the test: Brooks and Warren testify that there was never any interference with the magazine, academic or political. As Warren recalls from the summer that he joined the LSU faculty, "It was Huey's University, but he, I was assured, would never mess with my classroom. That was to prove true; he was far too adept in the art of power to care what an assistant professor might have to say." In fact, the only time that the senator's presence made itself felt in Warren's classroom was during the two weeks of each year that he taught *Julius Caesar*. During that time, says Warren, "backs

24. Brooks and Warren, *Stories from the Southern Review*, xiii; William Barrett, *The Truants: Adventurers Among the Intellectuals* (New York, 1982); Interview with John E. Palmer, May 15, 1979.

grew straighter, eyes grew brighter, notes were taken, and the girls stopped knitting in class or repairing their faces."[25]

The first issue of the *Review* appeared July 22, 1935, and for the remainder of the summer a shocked American press commented on the paradox that "one of the best and purest literary quarterlies in the United States" was being "paid for by a brilliant and unscrupulous vulgarian who had imposed a naked dictatorship of fraud and force on the State of Louisiana."[26] The maiden issue contained articles by Kenneth Burke, whose political leanings were far to the left, Donald Davidson, the most conservative of the Agrarians, Aldous Huxley, a nihilistic pessimist, and Herbert Agar, defender of democracy and denouncer of dictatorship. From the Deep South came such reactions as that of the Montgomery *Advertiser*: "If the first issue of *The Southern Review* . . . is an example of what future numbers will be like, those Southerners who appreciate good literature will soon forget that it emanates from a college which bears the stained fingerprints of Huey P. Long." The Norfolk *Virginia-Pilot* thought

> the most curious thing about *The Southern Review* . . . is that it should come out of what is popularly believed to be Huey Long's university. Louisiana State University is obviously Huey's so far as the football team is concerned, and the band, and the student newspaper; and it seems, after a recent episode, to be Huey's administration. It appears to be his in its new financial development. But there is a catch in this theory. The new *Journal of Southern History*, which was born on its campus, has no greater affinity with Huey than Thomas Jefferson with Thomas Heflin. And now *The Southern Review* confirms the suggestion that Louisiana State University has scholars of energy, initiative and independence.

The New York press echoed, "no matter how much Huey Long may cut up, his antics can't cast disrepute on a state that, through its

---

25. Robert G. Davis, "Dr. Adam Stanton's Dilemma," *New York Times Book Review*, August 18, 1946, pp. 3, 24; Brooks and Warren, *Stories from the Southern Review*, xiii; Warren, *"All the King's Men*: The Matrix of Experience," 162.

26. Davis, "Dr. Adam Stanton's Dilemma," 3.

leading university, issues a magazine of high literary quality as *The Southern Review*." And John Chamberlain of the New York *Times* was "moved to an ironic smile" by the appearance of the first issue of the *Southern Review*. He averred that Long was a demagogue and pointed out that "when Huey didn't like the way that the football team was being run, he made things hot for the head coach, Howard Jones." To the *Times* columnist, it was all the more amazing, therefore, that "Huey's own pet college" should be publishing "an extremely liberal magazine." Chamberlain concluded that although "Huey may dictate to the Louisiana Legislature . . . he evidently permits free controversy in the new quarterly published by 'his' university."[27]

As a United States senator, Long did indeed control the State of Louisiana through a caretaker governor named O. K. Allen, after whom, ironically enough, the new English department building at LSU was named. Like James Monroe Smith's new suit, Allen's lack of spine became a part of Louisiana folklore. Huey's younger brother, Earl, once remarked sarcastically that so accustomed to following the senator's orders was the puppet governor that when a leaf blew through his office window and onto his desk he promptly signed it. But as Earl Long's biographer, A. J. Liebling observed, "whenever there was a bit of political hocus-pocus to be brought off that Huey thought was beyond Allen's limited competence, he would come home to put the legislators through the hoops himself."[28] So it was that the Kingfish was in Baton Rouge in the summer of 1935.

While the reviews greeting the debut of LSU's new magazine were coming to Baton Rouge—applause for the quarterly counterpointed by hisses for its benefactor—the Brooks household was host to a young kinsman who had the misfortune of swallowing a class pin. Professor Brooks called on Carl A. Weiss, a well-respected Baton Rouge physician, to minister to the child. The old doctor was not in, but his son, Dr. Carl Austin Weiss, Jr., responded. Mr. and Mrs.

27. Montgomery *Advertiser*, July 26, 1935; Norfolk *Virginia-Pilot*, August 2, 1935; Yonkers *Home News*, August 1, 1935; John Chamberlain, "Books of the Times: Huey Long's Quarterly," New York *Times*, August 6, 1935, p. 15.
28. A. J. Liebling, *The Earl of Louisiana* (Baton Rouge, 1970), 11.

Brooks found him to be competent, courtly, well educated, soft spoken, and perfectly professional in manner. Three weeks later this unlikely Brutus assassinated Huey Long in a corridor of the Louisiana state capitol and was himself shot ninety-one times by the senator's bodyguards.

Robert Heilman, the newest addition to LSU's English department, had arrived in Baton Rouge on Labor Day, 1935. He and his wife "happened on a two-room apartment just off the capitol grounds," and one week later walked the block or two to the capitol to observe a meeting of the legislature which, they understood, the senator was to attend. After sitting in the visitor's gallery for the better part of an hour waiting for him to appear, Huey strode out, passing near to where the Heilmans were seated. "My memory is of many henchmen running around or following," says Heilman, "and of a chamber still officially at business by now semi-empty, all but dead. A few seconds later there was a strange outburst of sounds in a rapid but irregular sequence. Firecrackers, I thought. . . . Then men came running back into the chamber below and ducking behind desks. It had to be gunfire, though to a new Ph.D., fresh out of Harvard, this was unbelievable." Gunfire it was indeed, and to Robert Penn Warren, Long myth and Long fact "merged only at the moment when in September, 1935, in the corridor of the capitol, the little .32 slug bit meanly into the senatorial vitals." Long was removed to Our Lady of the Lake Hospital, within a pistol shot of the capitol, and there died on September 10.[29]

With the passing of the Kingfish, activities at Louisiana State came to a halt. The chairman of the English department, William A. Read, called his faculty members and said, "I don't know whether the university will open." He did not mean that there would be a temporary and ceremonial delay of the beginning of the fall semester as a period of formal mourning; rather he indicated that it was quite possible that a state of general collapse was possible in the administration of the campus and of the state. "It was my only expe-

29. Heilman, "Williams on Long," 938; Warren, "*All the King's Men*: The Matrix of Experience," 162.

rience," Heilman recalls, "of a situation in which, to an apparently competent observer, the whole life of a state, from its political fabric to its educational system, seemed tied to the life of one man."[30]

On the day that the senator's death was announced, Warren's friend Howard Baker wrote from Berkeley, "The news of Senator Long's death is a terrible shock. I hope that your university will not suffer too severely from it."[31] On the same day Agrarian historian Frank Owsley offered the most perceptive and the most prophetic analysis of the probable result of Long's assassination. In a letter to Cleanth Brooks, his former Vanderbilt student, Owsley delivered a eulogy and a prediction: "It is bad for you fellows that Huey is gone. What else may be said, of a bad nature, of the dead dictator, at least he was a sincere patron of the University of Louisiana. . . . The last thing that Huey said was 'what will become of my LSU boys now?'"

Perhaps, thought Owsley, Long's last words would have a good effect on his successors and enable them to carry on the best of his plans. Yet, as a shrewd observer of southern history and politics, Owsley was worried. He hated the thought that "the Standard Oil Company and petty minded politicians bent upon revenge" might gain control of the state, but he was also afraid that Long's supporters, "all 'yes' men," were too weak to control the opposition. "Any way you put it," Owsley concluded, "I am concerned over the position of my friends at L.S.U. and, of course, over the future of *The Southern Review*."[32]

Despite Long's general reputation as a despot, the *Southern Review* offices received a remarkable amount of mail in the next two weeks which spoke in glowing terms of the martyred senator. S. S. Field, whose first published short story had appeared the month before in *American Mercury* and was later included in the 1936 edition of *O'Brien's Best Short Stories*, enclosed the following letter with the manuscript of "Goodbye to Cap'm John," a story which appeared in the winter number of the *Southern Review*:

30. Heilman, "Williams on Long," 939.
31. Howard Baker to Warren, September 10, 1935.
32. Frank L. Owsley to Cleanth Brooks, September 10, 1935.

I should always consider it a privilege to submit work of mine to a magazine whose inception seems to have been at least indirectly responsible to Senator Long; he was capable of such versatility as to have even managed the insignificant matter of personal friendship to me. This story—since its protagonist, too, is the symbol of great human understanding—belongs, if anywhere, in *The Southern Review*. For the story seems to have been an almost prophetic Goodbye to that symbol and, after a fashion, to the only real prototype of that symbol I have ever known. God knows many of us here are heartbroken over his death.[33]

The "here" to which Field refers is the office of the *American Progress*, a weekly newspaper sponsored by Huey Long, of which Field was the editor. Field's talent was as genuine as his regret. He went on to publish two stories in the *Review*, both of which received favorable critical attention. But his enthusiasm for Senator Long could perhaps be explained as hero worship and by the fact that the senator had gotten him a good job within his organization. Harder to explain is the letter that Warren received from his friend Lincoln Fitzell at the University of California: "I was shocked to hear of the death of Huey Long. It is hard for me to understand why the good guys are so often assassinated, or failing that, persecuted. I hope this does not darken the prospects of the university, or work you any harm." From Paris Katherine Anne Porter sent her congratulations and her concern. "Do send me a subscription to *The Southern Review*," she wrote to Warren. "It is the best magazine I know, judging from the first number. I can't do without it. I hope that nothing has occurred that will change or destroy your plan." And John Gould Fletcher enclosed a stamped, addressed envelope for the return of his manuscript of "Three Poems About Trees" in case "you have to give the review up (I do not know how Long's death will affect the University.)"[34]

33. S. S. Field to Charles W. Pipkin, September 17, 1935.
34. Lincoln Fitzell to Robert Penn Warren, September 19, 1935; Katherine Anne Porter to Robert Penn Warren, November 22, 1935; Fletcher to Warren, September 25, 1935.

This close association of Huey Long with the *Southern Review*, assumed by the quarterly's friends and foes alike, amused and amazed its editors. Brooks and Warren never met the Kingfish, and both believe that Long did not know that the *Southern Review* existed. In fact, untimely as the senator's assassination might have seemed for many of the *Review*'s readers, it is just possible that his demise came at a fortunate time for the new magazine. Charles Pipkin had contracted for a review-essay on former Fugitive William Y. Elliott's anti–New Deal book, *The Need for Constitutional Reform*. The article was written for the second number by Norman Thomas, who, after the magazine had gone to press, fell into a violent political feud with Long. Perhaps remembering the fate of the *Reveille* editor who had dared to publish even a letter by an anti-Long undergraduate, Pipkin may have become fearful of what the senator might do to him. Perhaps fortunately for the editor and his magazine, Long did not live to see issue number two.

Indeed, he may never have heard of the *Southern Review*. Cleanth Brooks thinks it unlikely that Long ever knew of the magazine, and William Faulkner in "Knight's Gambit" has Gavin Stevens tell his nephew, Charles Mallison, that "Huey Long in Louisiana had made himself founder, owner, and supporter of one of the best literary magazines anywhere, without ever once looking inside it and probably not even caring what the people who wrote and edited it thought of him." At any rate, the university and the magazine survived Long's passing, and, as Warren wrote to Katherine Anne Porter three months after the senator's funeral, "It looks as stable now as ever, barring a communistic revolution or a new prohibition law."[35]

35. William Faulkner, "Knight's Gambit," *Knight's Gambit and Other Stories* (New York, 1949), 229–30; Robert Penn Warren to Katherine Anne Porter, December 6, 1935.

FOUR

The *Southern Review*

With the establishment of *The Southern Review* in 1935 the center of the avant garde of American literary criticism shifted temporarily to the banks of the Mississippi at Baton Rouge. Gradually the pundits and critical moguls on the Hudson began to alter their tone about the "Sahara of the Bozart."

C. VANN WOODWARD
The Burden of Southern History

I N the years that followed the passing of *The Symposium* and *Hound and Horn*, many critics doubted if America would again see a regular critical journal of anything approaching the importance of *The Criterion* in England. Thus it became "a matter for general congratulation that this gloom has been relieved," wrote Morton D. Zabel of *Poetry* magazine at the end of the Baton Rouge quarterly's first year, "and a cause for special rejoicing that relief has come, not in the form of such feeble compromises with popularity as are usually put up in luring public support, but through a quarterly of unquestionable integrity in its literary and editorial aims."[1]

Although somewhat disappointed that the *Southern Review* had not become the house journal for the Agrarian cause which they had hoped for, Brooks's and Warren's Nashville friends and colleagues were first and warmest in their praise of the new review. From his farm, "Cornsilk," at Guntersville, Alabama, Andrew Lytle declared that "the *Review* is a swell piece of getup. . . . You gentle-

---

1. Zabel, "Recent Magazines," 51.

men must place the right hand across the belly and bow to one another." John Crowe Ransom agreed that "the *Review* is swell," liking especially the poetry format and the fiction. To Frank L. Owsley the magazine "made a beautiful show in its first issue," although he maintained his stance that a truly southern review was yet to be established. And John Gould Fletcher wrote that he thought it was "all on the extremely high level of intention and performance. So high, in fact, as to be definitely superior to the *Yale Review* in which the ideas are neither so new or so stimulating." Donald Davidson called the *Review* "a notable, a most notable magazine" which "shows distinction and balance that we look for in a good quarterly. I was glad to see the Southern, the political-and-topical, the creative, the critical all given their place." Herman C. Nixon sent "congratulations on the form and content and the physical make-up," and second-generation Agrarian George Marion O'Donnell wrote that "at last the South has a literary quarterly of which to be thoroughly proud." William Y. Elliott thought that the editors were "doing a good job on the *Review*," and Allen Tate saw the magazine as the standard of excellence in the field. "Between academic futility and journalistic ignorance," he wrote on the fifth anniversary of the *Review*, "critical standards without you would have lapsed in this period of America. May you continue as the finest literary magazine in English."[2]

Other southerners responded in kind. Thomas Wolfe sent his congratulations and passed along those of William Faulkner. Professor Richmond C. Beatty thought that "the first number was grand," and Katherine Anne Porter wrote to Warren that she was "so glad there is to be a really substantial review published in the South, and even more glad that you have some authority in it. It seems to be a beautiful opportunity to make something you want and believe in."[3]

2. Andrew Lytle to Cleanth Brooks, August 5, 1935; John Crowe Ransom to Albert Erskine, September 8, 1935; Ransom to Robert Penn Warren, November 12, 1935; Frank L. Owsley to Brooks and Warren, n.d.; John Gould Fletcher to Charles W. Pipkin, December 13, 1935; Donald Davidson to Erskine, March 10, 1938; Herbert C. Nixon to Charles Pipkin, July 26, 1935; George Marion O'Donnell to Albert Erskine, July 31, 1935; William Y. Elliott to Charles Pipkin, February 3, 1937; Allen Tate, quoted in Baton Rouge *State-Times*, May 20, 1940, p. 5.

3. Thomas Wolfe to Robert Penn Warren, October 14, 1935; Richmond C. Beatty to Warren, August 8, 1935; Katherine Anne Porter to Warren, April 1, 1935.

From Columbia University, Kenneth Burke wrote to Brooks that the magazine was "a literary man's paradise. Hence, I read it greedily." F. O. Matthiessen wrote from Harvard: "I have considered the founding of your quarterly a very enheartening event for American letters. With the passing of the (none too perfect) *Hound and Horn* there has been none except a few little magazines seriously devoted to the arts." And Howard Baker, then at Berkeley, told Brooks, "I think *The Southern Review* is a really grand publication, and I'd do anything short of breaking my neck for it."[4]

In England, *The Criterion* first noticed the new journal with cautious optimism. "The first number of *The Southern Review*," commented the reviewer with a curious mixture of metaphors, "is interesting. While not, perhaps, filling the gap left in American periodicalism by the suspension of *Hound and Horn*, it none the less throws open a new platform to those whom it may concern. And one is bound to admit that the platform is thus far well held." After the second number, he admitted further that "*The Southern Review* continues to maintain its comparatively high standard which it set with its first number." Randall Jarrell, unimpressed with the cool tone and scanty regard of the British reviews, wrote to Warren that "the dope that writes them is a little too pleased with himself and England to get very moved with anything"; but with a few more issues of the *Review* and a change of *The Criterion's* staff, T. S. Eliot's journal began to take a decidedly kinder view of the new magazine. By 1939 *The Criterion* was ready to admit that the *Southern Review* was "the best literary periodical of all the American publications."[5]

By the second issue, the new magazine had a paying circulation of over nine hundred, and by November, 1935, almost all the major colleges and universities in the East and South and some in the Midwest had subscribed. The editors were a bit concerned, as Warren indicated in a letter to Howard Baker, that the response from northern California had been very slight. No college or university in

4. Kenneth Burke to Cleanth Brooks, January 6, 1936; F. O. Matthiessen to Cleanth Brooks, April 1, 1936; Howard Baker to Brooks, July 22, 1936.
5. D. G. Bridson, "American Periodicals," *Criterion*, XV (January, 1936), 368, and XV (July, 1936), 777; Randall Jarrell to Robert Penn Warren, April, 1937; A. Desmond Hawkins, "Periodicals: American," *Criterion*, XVII (July, 1938), 796, and XVIII (January, 1939), 405–406.

the West had subscribed, and only one public library, that of Los Angeles, took the journal. In August of the next year, Erskine confided to John T. Flynn of the *New Republic* that he was having "a much tougher time with the problems of circulation than I feel is justified on the merits of what we are offering"; but one month later Pipkin wrote to Flynn that "*The Southern Review* is reaching a wider group with each issue, and we are hopeful that our editorial policy will make a contribution that is useful to clearer thinking on the American scene."[6]

Within two years the subscription figure had jumped from 900 to 1,500, where it remained more or less constant for the career of the magazine. The subscription list, however, did not come close to indicating the impact of the magazine, for many of those 1,500 subscribers were libraries, with presumably a fairly high ratio of readers per copy. In terms of geographical distribution, the magazine sold most heavily in the middle South, New York, and the East; the West Coast and Great Britain also had a relatively high percentage of readers. Brooks and Warren have also pointed out that both Tokyo and Calcutta had more subscribers than Atlanta, Georgia. "The editors never quite decided what this meant about their self-appointed mission."[7]

Assessing the importance of the various critical reviews that had been published during the 1930s, critic, editor, and publisher Alan Swallow singled out *Hound and Horn* and the *Southern Review* as unquestionably the best, "and surely it is no stretch of the imagination to consider them the two most important literary journals ever to appear in the United States," he declared. In seeking the formula which made them so excellent, Swallow determined that the first standard of judgment was appearance. "The best of the reviews had been printed with a consciousness of their literary worth."[8] The paper and printing of the *Southern Review* were undeniably superior to those of rival publications. The designing and typographical specifications for the new magazine were done by Paul Johnson, a

6. Albert Erskine to John T. Flynn, August 21, 1936; Charles Pipkin to Flynn, September 29, 1936.

7. Brooks and Warren, *Stories from the Southern Review*, xv.

8. Alan Swallow, quoted in Elliott Anderson and Mary Kinzie (eds.), *The Little Magazine and Contemporary Literature* (New York, 1966), 23, 24.

native of Augusta, Georgia, who had studied painting at the Yale School of Fine Arts, the National Academy of Design, and the Art Students' League. He also had studied type and typography under Egmont Arens and had taught himself the craft of printing. By 1935 Johnson had written two books on printing and publication and had contributed articles on the art and history of typography to magazines in the United States, France, Great Britain, and Germany, and he had become the chief designer for a major New York press.

Another major factor on the side of the *Review* was the fact that it was able to pay its contributors much more handsomely than was almost any other contemporary magazine. "That the funds subsidizing the *Review* were supplied by the late Huey Long's Louisiana legislature is of incidental interest," wrote Zabel. Although the source of the money which the editors were able to offer the magazine's contributors "will doubtless worry all upright defenders of humane and enlightened progress," this fear "may be greatly reduced and even eliminated, if one keeps the eye on the object, for the *Review* has announced and maintained a distinction that immediately makes it superior to political affiliations."[9]

Despite the generous remuneration which the editors were able to offer to their writers, bureaucratic red tape often tied up payment for contributions, much to the exasperation of authors and editors alike. "A continual scandal" was created by the fact that the university paid only for work completed. Thus the *Review* could offer no advances against forthcoming work. Caroline Gordon, among others, complained bitterly of this policy to her friend Warren: "Paying on publication is taking advantage of the writer," she contended, and when the magazine fails to render payment immediately on publication, as the university's financial office often did, "the wrath that's been accumulating all those months boils over pretty quickly when the cheque doesn't come." Miss Gordon was not the only contributor to resent the university's tardy bursar or to visit her frustration on the *Review*. In November, 1935, after vainly waiting through weeks of the Great Depression for payment for an article, John Crowe Ransom sent a scolding letter to Baton Rouge: "I'm

9. Zabel, "Recent Magazines," 51.

waiting for the paycheck. The more quickly you can send that, the happier I. . . . I don't want to get in the habit of regarding *The Southern Review* financially as a version of the *American Review*; don't let me." [10]

One year later Warren was able to report to Ransom that "at last we have managed to get a fund, at least so I'm told, set aside for payment in advance on request. This greatly relieves our situation, and I hope will encourage some of our contributors. I say in advance, but this really means that the requisition will go in a week after acceptance of the manuscript, because we cannot issue a requisition until proof is received in our office. This means that payment will come approximately ten days after acceptance. That is a good deal better, however, than three months." By October, 1937, however, the situation was apparently unimproved. Ransom wrote to Allen Tate that he expected to send his newest essay, "Shakespeare at Sonnets," to the *Virginia Quarterly Review*. He would have sent it to the *Southern*, he said, but for the fact that he felt "a little resentful of the paying end of their arrangement down there." They paid a little better than the Charlottesville magazine, he explained, but "infinitely later." With the financial scandals which toppled Louisiana's political administration in 1939, a new accounting system came to LSU which was designed to place university funds beyond the reach of grafters in the statehouse. For Brooks and Warren, however, it brought the additional difficulty of upsetting the already shaky working relation with the bursar's office. In fact, in November, 1939, Brooks admitted to R. P. Blackmur that the new university administration "has so many financial checks and balances that I can't absolutely guarantee an early payment." [11]

The editors continued throughout the run of the magazine to attempt to bring the administration to the understanding that tardy payments were injuring their journal's reputation, but never with much success. "The problem hinges," Brooks explained to the uni-

10. Caroline Gordon to Robert Penn Warren, 1936; John Crowe Ransom to Warren, November 12, 1935.

11. Robert Penn Warren to John Crowe Ransom, October 7, 1936; Thomas Daniel Young, *Gentleman in a Dustcoat: A Biography of John Crowe Ransom* (Baton Rouge, 1976), 293; Cain, "Situation at Louisiana State University," 217; Cleanth Brooks to R. P. Blackmur, November 10, 1939.

versity's comptroller, "on the technical consideration of whether payment for an article which has been formally accepted by our office, and which has been set up in type, but which has not yet been actually published, constitutes payment in advance of receipt of goods or services. So far as we can see such payment does not constitute an *advance* payment in the language of university regulations, since to all intents and purposes we have, on the formal acceptance of the article, committed ourselves to its purchase; and since it actually is in our hand and subject to our disposition, the manuscript, considered as either goods or services, has obviously been delivered." One rather important case in point was that of the *Review*'s acquisition of Katherine Anne Porter's short novel *The Leaning Tower*. Brooks and Warren were among the first to know that Miss Porter was at work on a new piece and had urged her for more than a year to give them the opportunity to publish it when it was finished. As Brooks explained to Daniel Borth, the LSU comptroller, "Miss Porter is one of the few writers of the time who can deliberately choose her publisher. And it is only because she has a personal interest in the *Review* that we are able to secure any of her work for publication." Because of her affection for the editors of the *Southern Review*, Porter turned her manuscript over to them in August, 1941, but before the story appeared in the winter number she wrote to Brooks that she was building a house and needed her check. "It seems to us bad business, if nothing else," Brooks told the comptroller, "to prejudice our future relationships with this distinguished contributor to refuse her payment at this time." The editor's request was not granted, and Katherine Anne Porter was not surprised. "I know a great deal about procedure in *Southern Review* business at LSU, none of it to LSU's credit," she wrote to the editors from Yaddo, "and I wouldn't expect any sudden change for the better." [12]

Far more important than format or financing to the success of a little magazine, wrote Swallow, was its editors' program—"not merely eclecticism, or definition of program by negatives, but a powerful sense that some new ideas were being developed into liter-

12. Cleanth Brooks to Daniel Borth, n.d.; Katherine Anne Porter to John E. Palmer, October 6, 1941.

ary form and significance." To develop such a program had been the aim of the editors of the *Southern Review* from its very inception. In the prospectus which they presented to President Smith, they promised "to define large issues and to attempt interpretation of the contemporary scene" as the chief aim of the quarterly. "Through the *Southern Review* the University hopes to make a major contribution to the life and thought of the nation." In general, the magazine followed a fairly consistent format. Most often three or four essays, "extended discussions of issues of contemporary importance, and matters of purely technical or academic interest," led off the issue. These were followed by the fiction section, then the longer critical articles, then poetry, and finally, the book reviews and shorter pieces of criticism. [13]

The magazine's essays were most often political or economic in nature and were the special province of Dean Pipkin. Pipkin's circle of friends was large and highly regarded, and although of a generation more given to retrospective speculation than to avant garde experimentation which marked the journal's fiction, poetry, and criticism, could be counted on to supply the *Review* with consistently high-quality articles on fascism, Marxism, the New Deal, Agrarianism, and New South progressivism, and ran the political spectrum from Herbert Agar and Donald Davidson on the right to Sidney Hook and Kenneth Burke on the left. Unlike such magazines as the *Partisan Review*, the *Southern Review* was never merely the house organ for a single strand of the American political fabric. "Let's hear the best voices on all sides," was the editorial credo, and Brooks, Warren, and Pipkin were seldom content with a simple juxtaposition of opposing views. Instead they engineered debates among the best minds representing all sides of an argument, thus revealing the strengths and weaknesses of contending political and literary dogmas. The editors, from the first, attempted "to build up a pretty consistent staff of reviewers and critics, whose reputations will be to a degree associated with the *Southern Review* and whose reputation will support the reputation of the magazine itself," Warren wrote to

13. Swallow, quoted in Anderson and Kinzie (eds.), *The Little Magazine and Contemporary Literature*, 24; "Prospectus" of the *Southern Review*, quoted in the *Reveille*, April 16, 1935, p. 1.

Howard Baker. "Taken together," Zabel said, "these essays show a competence almost wholly unrivaled . . . in American magazines."[14]

The duty of the critical quarterly, Allen Tate had written in the *Review*'s third issue, was to "supply its readers with coherent standards of taste. . . . A sound critical program . . . allows to the reader no choice in the standards of judgment." The *Southern Review* was by no means so rigidly programmatic as Tate would have had it, but its book reviews in particular applied such rigorous standards as to incur considerable protest among offended authors, some of whom were friends or allies of the editors. Although the editors depended on what the mails would bring for poetry and fiction, they always commissioned their reviews and essays. "We hope to be one quarterly in this country that really gives attention to the critical review," Pipkin informed Crane Brinton in 1936. "We intend to select our reviewers with the greatest possible care," Warren told John Gould Fletcher, "but we also intend not to indicate what special line of treatment they shall adopt toward an individual book." Although they called upon reviewers and essayists of such divergent political and aesthetic beliefs as John Dewey, Hilaire Belloc, Crane Brinton, Kenneth Burke, F. O. Matthiessen, and Arthur Mizener and not infrequently upon their own more promising graduate students such as Leonard Unger, the editors depended to the greatest degree on their Agrarian colleagues and the nascent school of "New Critics" of which Brooks and Warren comprised so large a part and the golden age of which coincides almost exactly with the period of the *Southern Review*.[15]

Brooks and Warren had no intention, however, of making the *Southern Review* an exclusively southern or even an exclusively American journal. In August, 1938, Brooks wrote to William Empson, then teaching with the Associated Universities at Mengtzu, China, to explain that he and Warren were "trying, in so far as we can, to make *The Southern Review* a clearing house for literary criti-

14. Robert Penn Warren to Howard Baker, November 9, 1935; Zabel, "Recent Magazines," 52.

15. Allen Tate, "The Present Function of the Critical Quarterly," *Southern Review*, I (Winter, 1935–1936), 552; Charles Pipkin to Crane Brinton, February 24, 1936; Robert Penn Warren to John Gould Fletcher, April 29, 1935.

cism." He told Empson, who had not yet seen a copy of the magazine, that they had published "rather frequently" the American critics whom they thought best, but that they had not yet been able to get in contact with as many British critics as they would have liked. Bonamy Dobrée, Brooks admitted, sent the *Review* an occasional piece, and he and Warren soon published an essay by T. S. Eliot, but, despite overtures to what he called "the *Scrutiny* crowd," neither F. R. Leavis nor L. C. Knights had yet submitted an article.[16] Nor was the *Southern Review* any more successful in getting a manuscript from I. A. Richards. Brooks's letter-writing campaign soon paid off, however, with Leavis placing one essay with the *Review*, Empson placing two, and Knights placing three. Although Richards never published in the *Southern Review*, Brooks did manage to coax him to Baton Rouge in January, 1941, to lecture at the University Artists Series at LSU.

Citing the work of these critics published in the *Southern Review*, Randall Jarrell found their criticism to be "extremely catholic and extremely acute: there has been no analysis too complicated, delicate, or surprising for these critics to undertake. Modern criticism has accomplished a change in taste, a critical revolution, even greater than the change in poetic performance which modernist poets have effected."[17]

The *Southern Review* hoped to offer its readers a consistent format in the book review section but was forced by circumstances to change its policy at the end of the second volume. Devoting their reviewing section "largely to extended studies of a carefully selected list of current books, with emphasis on analysis and criticism rather than mere description," the editors' original intention was that novels would be reviewed not as individuals but together with others of the same season in an omnibus review by a single reviewer. Warren explained to R. P. Blackmur in March, 1936, "We feel that in general it is a better policy than that of scattering the novels among a number of reviewers. By the present arrangement the reader at least can gain an impression that is consistent in its premises. We

16. Cleanth Brooks to William Empson, August 2, 1938.
17. Randall Jarrell, "Contemporary Poetry Criticism," *New Republic*, July 21, 1941, p. 88.

have in the past given one separate treatment of a book that had been treated in a group review and shall do this more frequently in the future." Warren conceded the point that some novels deserved longer treatment than others, but maintained that "it would be difficult to make such a policy general."[18]

Within a year and a half, however, the editors were forced to re-evaluate their position. To James T. Farrell of Vanguard Press, Warren confided that the *Review* was "experimenting with a change of policy in the reviewing of fiction." In the future, he and Brooks had decided, "we shall run a very long annual fiction chronicle in the fall and in other issues run shorter reviews of individual novels." As Brooks explained the change of policy to Howard Baker, "Red and I have felt for a long time that there was no point in reviewing run of the mill books, but we have felt that there would be some value in having a competent and sensitive critic look over the whole batch and make some general comments about the season as a whole and point out any real discoveries that ought to be pointed out, and, if necessary, puncture reputations that have been inflated by enterprising blurb writers."[19]

Kenneth Burke was but one of the many readers of the *Southern Review* for whom the poetry section was the magazine's greatest contribution. To Brooks Burke wrote of his satisfaction at "the great amount of attention you give to poetry. For it is in the 'poetry exchange,'" he believed, "that the problems of 'cultural distribution' come to a head. One cannot properly 'discount the news' until one sees how events are reflected in the trends of poetic valuation." Both of the associate editors would have liked to have been able to devote even more of the magazine's pages to poets and poetry, but as Brooks informed Richmond Beatty, "we are obliged, despite our major interest in that department, to maintain a proper balance."[20]

From the first issue it was the policy of the *Southern Review* to publish long groups of poems by single authors, with an accom-

18. "Prospectus" of the *Southern Review*, quoted in the *Reveille*, April 16, 1935, p. 1; Robert Penn Warren to R. P. Blackmur, March 26, 1936.
19. Robert Penn Warren to James Farrell, October 6, 1937; Warren to B. A. Botkin, October 18, 1937; Cleanth Brooks to Howard Baker, July 26, 1938.
20. Kenneth Burke to Cleanth Brooks, n.d.; Robert Penn Warren to Richmond C. Beatty, September 20, 1935.

panying critical note. In returning a short poem submitted by James Agee, Warren outlined the magazine's poetry program: "We do not publish miscellaneous pieces," he wrote. "We try to publish long groups of poems by a single author, so that the reader may be able to get a sample of the poet's work . . . say up to 20 or 25 pages."[21] Accompanying these poems would be a critical note on the poet's work and discussion of the specific poems published in the *Review*. Much to the editors' credit, they did not go to their friends among the outstanding living poets and ask for poems to help them out once the magazine became established. Instead they printed the best poems that came across the desk through the mails, and by doing so gave a much-needed boost to many promising but unpublished poets.

As to the nature of the review printed with the poems—as with the criticism of novels in the magazine—the editors chose their reviewers with care and then allowed them a great deal of freedom in stating their opinions. They did not, however, give the reviewers of verse the absolute freedom which they allowed to their fiction reviewers. "We do not demand a laudatory review," Warren explained to Howard Baker, but "we do not wish to accept a man's work for publication merely in order to make a butchery of it. Our objective in these critical notes is primarily expository. And that means a definition of the limitations, and perhaps the defects of the poem, as well as the definition of his virtues."[22]

On one occasion the editors invited R. P. Blackmur, a poet as well as an influential critic, to prepare the critical commentary on his own work for the *Review*. The editors did not insist, understanding "why you might choose to decline to do so," but, they believed, such a note "might serve the purpose of helping some of our readers who are sincerely interested in the poetry we publish, but who do not have an experienced approach to it. We have hoped, perhaps vainly, that the *Review* might extend the audience, at least a little, for poetry, and I am sure that many other readers will also be very much interested in whatever you might have to say about your intention and method."[23] Although Blackmur demurred from commenting on

21. Robert Penn Warren to James Agee, November 8, 1935.
22. Robert Penn Warren to Howard Baker, November 9, 1936.
23. Robert Penn Warren to R. P. Blackmur, December 11, 1936.

his own compositions, Brooks and Warren did not abandon the idea of combining text and criticism by the same author, and in their third textbook, *Understanding Fiction*, prevailed upon Eudora Welty, Katherine Anne Porter, and John Cheever to supply commentary on their stories anthologized in the text. Warren himself provided commentary on "Blackberry Winter" for the book.

Impressive as were the reviews, essays, and poems printed in the *Southern Review*, no section of the magazine received higher praise than the short fiction. Although the editors occasionally commissioned a story, such as Andrew Lytle's "Jericho, Jericho, Jericho," their general principle for the publication of short stories was always to hunt for new writers and to use the work of established writers only when the editors had a genuine enthusiasm for it. Brooks recalls that during the run of the magazine both he and Warren were teaching three courses per semester in addition to the basic problems of their editorial work: soliciting articles, reading manuscripts, scribbling notes on rejection slips, and making plans for future numbers. The two associate editors once calculated that they were reading ninety fiction manuscripts for every one that they printed. Thus, for a while, they considered the idea that the *Review* stop publishing any short fiction except from writers whose work was known to be good. The selection of articles and reviews consumed far less time, and short stories could be commissioned at need. With such a policy made general, unsolicited material would constitute a far smaller drain on the editor's time. Brooks and Warren worked hard on every submission, often typing out a multi-page rejection letter to a contributor whom they did not even encourage to resubmit. They at last came down on the side of the young short story writer, however. They decided that "a great part of our job as editors of a literary quarterly was precisely that of providing a publication channel for the young fiction writer, who most of all, needed to see his work in print. We simply couldn't take the short cut, hard-pressed for time though we were." [24]

The *Review* was run by three quarter-time editors, a quarter-time business manager, and a full-time secretary, making the maga-

24. Brooks, "Brooks on Warren," 22.

zine severely understaffed. The result, according to Albert Erskine's successor, John E. Palmer, was "except for a few intervals," a "state near chaos." In August, 1939, John Berryman spoke for a number of *Southern Review* contributors when he loosed a barrage at the hapless editors for neither accepting nor returning promptly a group of poems he had submitted months earlier. When the staff replied to his attack, they could only concede that they entirely understood and sympathized with his feelings, and asked that he bear with them. Their tardiness, the editors explained, was not due to want of interest or respect but to a case of over-extension. Berryman's wrath was turned by the gentle answer, and he replied that he was grateful to hear that his poems had "not been lost or burnt." "I sometimes think," he confided, "of resigning my precarious status'as *Southern Review* contributor and taking up normal life again," but the admiration that he held for the magazine and its editors overcame his exasperation with delays, and he admitted that his "principal aim in life at present is a large group in *The Southern Review*." To that end, he told Brooks, he was holding back his normal contributions elsewhere.[25]

The arrangement of three editors, all of whom were harassed by a good many other things besides editing, made agreement among the *Southern Review* staff difficult and slow. "For one thing," said Warren, "we cannot have conferences often enough." Each of the editors read independently each manuscript that showed any promise whatsoever, and then "compared notes and found that our conclusions were [usually] in thorough agreement." Often, however, one or more of the staff would be out of town, and then new manuscripts would have to be discussed by mail, "a method dictated by necessity," Brooks observed, "and not making for promptness."[26] A random sampling of the kinds of comments that Warren returned to the Baton Rouge office with proffered typescripts indicates the tone which the editors used among themselves when dealing with all but the best contributions to the *Review*:

25. John E. Palmer to John Berryman, October 21, 1941; Berryman to Cleanth Brooks, August 23, 1939.
26. Robert Penn Warren to Howard Baker, February 4, 1937; Cleanth Brooks to John Berryman, July 27, 1937.

Promising, but nothing we can use, I imagine. I have taken the liberty of attaching a note, which you can jerk off if you don't approve.

Better, by a lot than the last story . . . but even this is rather thin. Probably publishable in a pinch.

Horrible.

I have written a note to him, to be sent back with the MSS. The stuff is hopeless.

No opinion. But it leaves me colder than a dead herring. It's a damned phony piece of work. It seems that I do have an opinion after all.

On the whole superficial, I feel. We can get better criticism than this.

No sale; I've attached a letter which can be sent on to the author with the rejected stuff if you think it's all right.

A full bust.

An almost for me; I've attached a note. But if you all happen to like this I'll string along with pleasure.

What do you think of this? I'm inclined to think that there's some good stuff in it, but I think that the thing is pretty unusable in its present form.

Very nice writing, taken page by page, but I don't get a real kick out of the pieces . . .

Nothing usable, but the boy seems to have the stuff.

Very well done, but essentially trivial, I think.

This has something, even if it does come from the Coast Guard Academy. I wouldn't mind seeing it published.[27]

To Caroline Gordon, Brooks's and Warren's editorial style was a

27. Warren to Brooks, n.d. [1941].

little baffling. So "accommodating" and encouraging were they that she once confessed that she did not know exactly what changes they intended her to make in a typescript. "I suppose," she wrote to Warren, that this is "because I am used to editors saying, 'Cut out five pages and I'll take it.' Anyhow, I judge that no matter how soft-spoken an editor is, he always wants things cut."[28] Cleanth Brooks, especially, often suffered the tension between his natural kindliness and his natural love of literature, but however "soft-spoken" and polite he may have been, the quality of the magazine and his commitment to first-class writing always came first. In justifying the *Southern Review* budget to the university, the editors explained fully their views on solicitation of materials, judgment of materials received, and payment for manuscripts published:

> Consider for a moment the kind of "merchandise" which the editors buy. There are no "objective" standards; it is impossible for one to ask authors to submit bids on ten pages of poetry or a 5500 word short story. From first to last the editors have of necessity to rely on their own judgment—to deal in subjective reactions, to weigh intangibles. Their only check is their standard of what a "good" magazine is, itself a matter resting on subjective judgments of all kinds. Indeed, with whatever rules they are hedged around, great confidence has been placed in their judgment. How is one to know that they are choosing wisely from the vast amount of MSS. that goes through their office? Or for that matter, how is one to know that they are not misusing their power for patronage, taking a short story from this unknown writer for reasons other than literary or taking a worthless potboiler from that famous author for reason of literary politics?[29]

"Literary magazines devoted to experimental writing are usually filled with works by middle-aged or old people," Warren observed in an interview with Richard Wright. Such was seldom the case

28. Caroline Gordon to Robert Penn Warren, 1936.
29. Cleanth Brooks and Robert Penn Warren, "Note on Section 2" to LSU Budget Committee, n.d., in *Southern Review* Collection, Yale.

with the *Southern Review*. Not only was the "new criticism" new, and largely practiced by young men—Kenneth Burke, Theodore Spenser, R. P. Blackmur, Delmore Schwartz, and L. C. Knights all achieved their reputations largely through exposure that their ideas were given on the pages of the *Review*, and Leonard Unger was still a graduate student at LSU when his first critical work appeared there—but Brooks's and Warren's writers of fiction also were mostly in their twenties, thirties, and even late teens. The editors tried not to inspect the reputation of the author who submitted any manuscript, but only the manuscript itself. "Despite awe and human frailty," Brooks and Warren did their best "not to let the greatness of a name sway their judgment. Work by Nobel Prize winners was on occasion rejected, and work by college sophomores was published." T. S. Eliot, Wallace Stevens, Aldous Huxley, and a host of other such names were represented in the *Review*, but there was also the very early work of writers whose names have become almost as familiar: Mary McCarthy, Nelson Algren, and Peter Taylor, then a student in Warren's creative writing class, placed stories in the magazine that were among their very first, and W. H. Auden and John Berryman, who were barely beyond their apprenticeship, and Randall Jarrell, still a graduate student at Vanderbilt, appeared early and often in the *Southern Review*.[30]

"This policy evokes the risk of giving space to one-story and one-essay people," the editors were aware, and the magazine printed some of these, but they were willing to take the risk rather than merely to play it safe with writers of established reputations. Brooks and Warren have conceded that "since many contributors were very young, some of the names that appeared in the magazine are of people who have long since found vocation elsewhere than writing."[31] If the names of S. S. Field, Allen McGinnis, Michael Seid, and Mary King are less than household names today, it is neither because the editors of the *Southern Review* failed to publish their promising

30. Robert Penn Warren, quoted in Malcolm Cowley (ed.), *Writers at Work: The Paris Review Interviews*, 1st series (New York, 1959), 198–99; Brooks and Warren, *Stories from the Southern Review*, xiv; Warren, "Conversations with Cleanth Brooks," in Simpson (ed.), *The Possibilities of Order*, 95–96.

31. Robert B. Heilman, "Cleanth Brooks, Some Snapshots, Mostly from an Old Album," in Simpson (ed.), *The Possibilities of Order*, 139.

work nor because their talent went unrecognized by other critics once Brooks and Warren had brought it to light. Each of the young fiction writers listed above had at least one story chosen from the *Review* for publication in Edward J. O'Brien's collection of *Best Short Stories*, an annual anthology of impeccably high standards.

In addition to reprinting in his annual volume a selection of the best short stories of the year, O'Brien graded the stories printed in American magazines, assigning one star to stories of merit, two stars to stories of superior merit, and three stars to stories of highest merit. The *Southern Review* in the years from 1936 through 1940, the year in which O'Brien died, was rated highest in the percentage of its stories which were given two stars or three stars—that is, the stories of very highest merit among all literary magazines. By way of comparison, in 1936 approximately seventy-five magazines were publishing short stories in the United States. Only ten of these received even O'Brien's passing notice. He gave even a one-star rating to fewer than 10 percent of the stories printed in *Cosmopolitan*, *Redbook*, *Pictorial Review*, and *American Magazine*, to only 15 percent of those in the *Saturday Evening Post*, while *Story* magazine got that coveted asterisk for nine-tenths of its stories; and every one of the sixteen or seventeen short stories printed in the *Southern Review* and the *Atlantic* won at least one star in 1937.

Not only did the editors not inspect a writer's reputation, they did not inspect his birth certificate either. True to its prospectus, the *Southern Review* aimed at "presenting and interpreting Southern problems to a national audience and relating national issues to the Southern scene." But however staunchly southern in their regional loyalties, Brooks and Warren felt that the best way they could serve their region was by "insisting upon the highest possible standards of excellence" for the magazine. As the editors pointed out, however, "it is only natural that when an affinity is discovered between a magazine and a writer the work of that writer will appear there rather often." By unofficial count, approximately 51 percent of the items appearing in the *Southern Review* were by southern authors, with the names of Ransom, Tate, Lytle, and Davidson—original Agrarians—among the most frequent contributors.[32]

32. "Prospectus" of the *Southern Review*, quoted in *Reveille*, April 16, 1935, p. 1; Brooks and Warren, *Stories from the Southern Review*, xiv, xv.

Despite the editors' conscientious attempt at doctrinal balance and overall excellence, Donald Davidson expressed his belief that the *Southern Review* had not done all that it could for young writers in the South. "I would have imagined," he wrote to Brooks in August, 1939, "that you might conceive of the *Southern Review* as owing a certain consideration to young writers of the South, especially to those who . . . may find it difficult to get a start because of the character of their production which may be quite out of line with what goes as approved in the usual magazine story." Although he readily conceded that the editors had been "more than generous" in soliciting and publishing his own work, Davidson took the *Review* to task for its recent rejection of a story by Mildred Haun, a Davidson protégé.

> I do not know that this will happen again, but there may be other young writers turning up here, and looking for an outlet. What am I to tell them? The *Virginia Quarterly Review* (as long as L. Lee is editor) will probably boycott their productions. The *Southwest Review* hates us, of course. That ends the Southern list just about. And can they try the *Kenyon Review*? Too esoteric by far, I think—and besides John Crowe Ransom [who founded the *Kenyon* in 1938] has broken (if I understand him) with some of his old [Agrarian] tenets. Where do I go to seek editors and sponsors for my young hopefuls (of whom there will be, after all, a rare few worth recommending to an editor)? I find myself reflecting on a curious situation, in which Wilbur Sahram of Iowa, or John Frederick, or even the chilly and distant Edward Weeks of *The Atlantic* are more interested in the young writers whom I have to recommend than are my own dear friends of *The Southern Review*.[33]

Brooks's reply was a long and detailed letter defending the policy of his magazine and refuting Davidson's charges against it. Marshaling names and statistics, he completely overwhelmed Davidson's objections. "Red and I turned down for the first number a story by a Nobel Prize winner, because we felt that to accept an unworthy story—it was poor—merely to have a name, would be the

---

33. Donald Davidson to Cleanth Brooks, August 5, 1939.

worst way to start out," Brooks wrote. "We have made mistakes, it is true, though some of our worst mistakes were in taking stories from young writers—stories which we later decided were inferior." Citing the *Southern Review*'s first volume, Brooks pointed out they had published at least seven stories by new writers and only two by writers with established reputations such as Caroline Gordon and Katherine Anne Porter. The same had been true in volumes two, three, four, and five. "Actually," Brooks concluded, "we have run very few established writers and of the young writers which we have run I imagine that a good 75% have been from the South and Southwest."[34]

Davidson still was not entirely satisfied, and said so to Allen Tate. "I had it in mind to reproach Cleanth but have never got up courage to write in stronger terms than I have already used," he told his old *Fugitive* colleague. "Besides," he added, "Cleanth is always so extremely nice to me, and always so completely explanatory." Following the career of a single contributor to the *Southern Review*, however, from almost absolute obscurity to national fame, will perhaps demonstrate that Davidson, in his zeal to promote southern writers, and especially his favorite students, was unfair to the editors of the *Southern Review*. And while it is perfectly true that Eudora Welty is not exactly typical of the run of young writers whose stories found their way to the desks of Brooks and Warren, the distance between her obscurity in 1937 and her fame in 1941 was spanned to no small degree with the aid of the Baton Rouge magazine. To the "quiet, tranquil-looking, modest" Mississippi girl, the *Review* was the perfect blending of rigorous critical standards and international recognition with the gentle and courteous manner of its associate editors. Miss Welty's admiration for the *Review* soon became a mutual one, and the enduring partisanship of Brooks, Warren, and Erskine helped to place the name of Eudora Welty among the great.[35]

Miss Welty says that she has always written, but that she was "a late starter." She never took a creative writing course—"Mississippi State College for Women did not offer one"—so she studied litera-

34. Cleanth Brooks to Donald Davidson, October 3, 1939.
35. Donald Davidson to Allen Tate, February 23, 1940, in Fain and Young (eds.), *Literary Correspondence of Donald Davidson and Allen Tate*, 321; Interview with Eudora Welty, June 17, 1978.

ture and wrote short stories in the time that she was not attending to more "normal pursuits." After finishing her B.A. degree at the University of Wisconsin and attending for one year the Columbia University School of Business, Miss Welty returned to her hometown of Jackson, Mississippi, in 1931, to work for a local radio station and to act as society correspondent for the Memphis *Commercial Appeal*. In 1933 she took a job with the Writers' Project of the W.P.A., "trying to earn a living taking pictures." Miss Welty's job ended with the reelection of Franklin Roosevelt in 1936, but she submitted her portfolio, which she called "Black Saturday," to a publisher, hoping to "break through into publishing by using captioned photographs." The collection was rejected, but all of the time that she had worked for the W.P.A. she had been writing in her spare time.

Although Miss Welty claims to have been "quite timid about showing anything I'd written back then," she did finally send out a short story to John Hood at *Manuscript*, a little magazine which printed the work of new authors without pay. "She could not believe that anyone would buy a story from her," says Katherine Anne Porter. The story was "Death of a Traveling Salesman," and *Manuscript* published it in June, 1936.[36]

Somewhat emboldened by her initial success, she sent her first manuscript to the *Southern Review* three months later. "The *Southern Review* was very prestigious," she recalls, and to appear there was a great step toward recognition; "publishers in New York might see your stories, because it was a respected quarterly." Remarkably, Miss Welty's first contribution to the Baton Rouge journal was not one of her short stories but a collection of poems. "We find much to interest us in your verse," Warren wrote, "but have decided against immediate publication." Keeping the door open to later contributions, however, the editor did ask to see more of her work.[37]

Miss Welty took Warren at his word, and before the end of 1936

36. *Ibid.*; Katherine Anne Porter, Introduction to Eudora Welty, *A Curtain of Green and Other Short Stories* (New York, 1941), xi, xviii.

37. Interview with Eudora Welty, June 17, 1978; Robert Penn Warren to Eudora Welty, September 23, 1936, Mississippi Department of Archives and History, Jackson, Mississippi.

submitted a group of short stories. Of them, the editors liked best "The Petrified Man" and "Flowers for Marjorie," finding them both to be "extremely interesting," and being for quite a while "on the verge of publishing them." The comic effects in "The Petrified Man" especially "struck us as first rate," Warren reported, and so the editors were very sorry to have to return them. They were "absolutely confident," however, "that, if you are good enough to submit other work to us, we can publish your things in *The Southern Review*." [38]

With such encouragement Welty persisted and continued to send her stories to Baton Rouge, and on May 17, 1937, Warren informed her that the *Southern Review* would publish "A Piece of News" in the summer issue. "A Piece of News" was followed in the *Review* by "A Memory" in the fall of the same year and by "Old Mr. Grenada," which Warren characterized as a "very brilliantly done" story, in the following spring. Paul Brooks, then an editor with Houghton Mifflin, saw Welty's work and wrote to Warren in March, 1938, requesting that he ask her to compete for the Houghton Mifflin award that year. "If you are interested," Warren told her, "the *Southern Review* will certainly do everything it can to push your case." For sponsors, he added, "you might name Cleanth Brooks and myself and Katherine Anne Porter, who, I happen to know, likes your work." Within the week Welty had returned to the *Southern Review* editors a plan for a novel and a sample of its style. Warren wrote back commending both as excellent and expressing every confidence that Houghton Mifflin's judges would agree. When the Houghton Mifflin Literary Fellowship Committee failed to appoint Welty, Warren reacted with surprise and disappointment. He did assure her, however, that "if it isn't that it will be something else soon." [39]

In the meantime, however, Welty continued to place stories in the *Southern Review*. "A Curtain of Green" appeared in the *Review*'s fall number, and in the same letter that informed her of its acceptance, Warren asked for the third time if they might again see "The Petrified Man," as he was now sure that they had erred in returning

38. Robert Penn Warren to Eudora Welty, January 13, 1937, Mississippi Department of Archives.
39. Warren to Welty, February 22, 1938, March 23, 1938, and September 28, 1938, all in Mississippi Department of Archives.

it. Miss Welty had not been coy or petulant in not returning the story to Baton Rouge at Warren's first request. It simply no longer existed. "When 'The Petrified Man' was finally sent back, I tore it up," she says, "burned it up in the kitchen stove." At Warren's third request for another look at it, she rewrote it and sent it on, but "my conscience burned me for some years," she later recounted, "because I thought I might have done something wrong—this couldn't be exactly the story they thought they'd bought." Since "The Petrified Man" is a "told" story, however, Miss Welty maintains that it was easier to remember. "You know, it's sort of like playing back a record in my ear. I couldn't have written an internal story over again, but I wrote that." Later, after she and Warren had met and become friends, she told him of her "deception," and asked if it had been "an unethical thing to do." "You wrote both of them, didn't you?" was his reply.[40]

"The Petrified Man" became the first of Welty's stories to be selected by Edward O'Brien for his annual Roll of Honor and it also appeared in Herschel Brickell's 1940 volume of *O. Henry Prize Stories*. Brickell, an LSU graduate, was living at that time in Yazoo City, Mississippi, and he first took Miss Welty to Baton Rouge. On that first trip she met Albert Erskine, who always regarded Eudora Welty as his personal discovery, but Brooks and Warren were both out of town. On subsequent trips, however, the three became lasting friends. "If Cleanth Brooks isn't the sweetest man in the world, then Red Warren is," she has since said.[41]

Returning one of her earliest contributions to the *Southern Review*, Cleanth Brooks commented to Miss Welty that "one cannot ask a very competent author to rewrite stories," but suggested that if she changed the ending a bit he and his co-editors would like to see it again. Miss Welty demurred and later placed the story elsewhere. When she forwarded "The Hitch-Hikers" to Baton Rouge in January of 1939, however, Brooks quickly accepted but mentioned "by the way" that Albert Erskine had suggested that the story's last sentence be dropped and that he was in agreement. The editors did not

40. Interview with Eudora Welty, June 17, 1978.
41. *Ibid.*

persist, but only asked what the author thought. "It was for the better," she agreed, and remembers it as the only time an editor ever changed any of her stories.[42]

In November, 1939, Erskine, who was also an editorial assistant at the LSU Press, tried to interest the director in bringing out a collection of Welty's stories. "If I am successful," he wrote, "and if your MS is still available," he hoped that she would consider publication in Baton Rouge. Doubleday, Doran, however, became Miss Welty's first publisher, bringing out *A Curtain of Green and Other Stories* in 1941. Of the seventeen stories in the volume, seven had first been printed in the *Southern Review* and all but four of the others had first been sent to the *Review*, but returned as unsuitable—although Brooks admitted that they never returned one of her stories without "the feeling that we are probably making a mistake."[43]

Only one of Miss Welty's stories, "Clytie," remained to be printed in the *Southern Review*, but the association between Miss Welty and the *Review* was by no means nearing a close. Both Brooks and Warren have written some of their most perceptive critical articles on the fiction of their former contributor and Albert Erskine, at Random House, published *Losing Battles* and *The Optimist's Daughter*, two of Miss Welty's finest novels. Nor has she forgotten the editors who gave her her first start. "They were just angelic to me," she says of Brooks and Warren, and although they adamantly maintain that she scarcely needed to be discovered by the *Southern Review* or any other magazine, Miss Welty continues to believe that without their assistance and encouragement she would have remained almost totally unknown. The generosity of Katherine Anne Porter, Cleanth Brooks, and Robert Penn Warren, "their critical regard when it mattered most, not to mention the long friendships that began by letter in those days, have nourished my life."[44]

At the time of the founding of the *Southern Review*, Robert Penn

42. Brooks to Welty, August 17, 1937, and August 11, 1939, Mississippi Department of Archives; interview with Eudora Welty.

43. Albert Erskine to Eudora Welty, November 7, 1939, Mississippi Department of Archives; Cleanth Brooks to Eudora Welty, July 1, 1940, Mississippi Department of Archives.

44. Eudora Welty, "Preface," *The Collected Stories of Eudora Welty* (New York, 1980), ix.

Warren has observed, Katherine Anne Porter, unlike Eudora Welty, "was already an established writer, but not the great name she's become since." Miss Porter, in fact, could have published almost anywhere she chose, says Warren, but "she chose to publish with us." Perhaps she did so because of the other point she had in common with Eudora Welty, her southern heritage. For, although during the most productive years of her life she led a quite nomadic existence, the South to her was always "the native land of my heart."[45]

Unfortunately, however, the east Texas of her nativity was not conducive to her early artistic endeavors. In Texas, she said, "I didn't know any genuinely working artists. I think that it is because the South is a land of gentlemen and gentlemen are patrons, not artists."[46] She left the South early, then, to follow her calling in Chicago, Denver, New York, Mexico, and Europe. During the summer of 1927, while dividing her time between supporting the Obregón Revolution in Mexico and the cause of Sacco and Vanzetti in the United States, Miss Porter was living in an apartment at 27 Bank Street in Greenwich Village, the custodian of which was another young southern writer who had come to the metropolis to escape the provincial attitudes of his native region, Allen Tate. Robert Penn Warren visited there that summer on his way to his first semester at Yale, and there met Miss Porter for the first time. Despite the marked difference in their political philosophies, they began a friendship and literary alliance which became one of the most fruitful in twentieth-century American letters. Not only did their relationship as writer and editor for the *Southern Review* prove mutually beneficial in later years, but in 1938 she moved to Baton Rouge and became a major force in the literary community which orbited around Brooks's and Warren's magazine.

The recipient of a Guggenheim Fellowship in 1931, Katherine Anne Porter followed "the rule of literature" that read "one must go where one was not" and went abroad. Sailing from Vera Cruz to

45. Robert Penn Warren, quoted in Floyd C. Watkins and John T. Hiers (eds.), *Robert Penn Warren Talking* (New York, 1980), 154; Katherine Anne Porter, "*Noon Wine*: The Sources," in Cleanth Brooks and Robert Penn Warren (eds.), *Understanding Fiction*, 2nd ed. (New York, 1951), 612.

46. "Woman Writer Recalls Meeting with Reich Leaders, Work with Diego Rivera in Clubhouse Talk," Baton Rouge *State-Times*, May 30, 1939, p. 8.

Bremerhaven, she wandered about Europe for some months, carrying on a peripatetic writing career until her marriage in 1932 to Eu-
gene Pressley, a minor official in the American Embassy in Paris.
For three years, then, she worked on a number of short stories, her
novel (which went through three name changes: "Promised Land,"
"Many Redeemers," and "No Safe Harbor" before finally becoming
Ship of Fools), and a biography of Cotton Mather. In April, 1935,
Miss Porter wrote to Robert Penn Warren that she and her husband
expected to sail from LeHavre on *The City of Norfolk* on July 29.
Their reservations were made, and they expected to land in Baltimore and work their way slowly through the South, arriving for a
visit in Baton Rouge towards the end of August. "We have three
months in all," she wrote, "and I can hardly wait for July. It will be
more than five years since I left America. . . . So it's high time we
were working our way back for a good visit."[47]

The same month "The Grave," one of the first of Miss Porter's Miranda stories, appeared in the *Virginia Quarterly Review*. She had
some reason to wish that she had withheld that reminiscence of her
Texas girlhood and her sojourn in Mexico, however, for it left her
with nothing on hand when Warren wrote asking her for a contribution to the first issue of the *Southern Review*. She was, however, at
work on a short novel which she hoped would meet the editors'
deadline. "If I get *Pale Horse and Pale Rider* to you by the end of
this month," she asked, "will there be time enough for you to read
and decide—offer or no offer, you know I expect you to change your
mind if you do not care for it—and get a set of proof back to me?"
Miss Porter assured Warren that "the next thing you have from me
will be a manuscript," but nine days later she wrote: "It seems to me
now I wrote . . . that the next time you heard from me it would be to
receive my short story. I must have meant the next time but one."
An attack of bronchitis had overcome her always-precarious health,
but she promised to have the story in the mail soon enough to be in
the first issue.[48]

Katherine Anne Porter was represented in the first issue of the
Southern Review, but her contribution was another of the Miranda

47. *Ibid.*; Porter to Warren, April 1, 1935.
48. *Ibid.*

stories, "The Circus." At the end of November she had to report that *Pale Horse, Pale Rider* was not finished yet. "I have dropped all such things until the Mather book is gone," she wrote to Warren, "because that absurd project can't hang fire much longer. I'll be a confirmed neurotic if it does." Once through with the Mather biography she would work on short stories, then the novel. "That is my plan."[49] This plan, too, was soon discarded, however, for the Mather book was pushed further back on the back burner and "The Old Order" was finished and sent along to the *Review* in time for the third issue.

The cancellation of her husband's leave from the State Department and the abandonment of their plans to visit the United States was a bitter disappointment. "I keep hoping I shall get home one day soon, but I now have stopped making definite plans," she wrote to Warren in the winter of 1935. Her hopes were fulfilled in the fall of 1936 when she reported, "I am leaving Europe at last, after five years." Her husband was being transferred and, although she did not yet know where their next home would be, they would sail from France in October.[50]

Soon after returning to the States, Porter turned out two short novels, one of which she offered to the *Southern Review*. The staff quickly accepted *Old Mortality*. "I believe that 'Old Mortality' is easily one of the best things I have ever read," wrote an enthusiastic Albert Erskine, "though I am sure that my opinion would be thrown out of court as slightly prejudiced in advance. But Red and Mr. Brooks have read it now and agree with me, as I am sure most subsequent readers will, and that makes it unanimous as far as this office is concerned."[51] To that date the *Review* had printed nothing nearly so long, but the editors gladly made an exception to their short fiction policy and ran the short novel in the spring of 1937. The Brooks-Warren-Erskine opinion was indeed shared by "most subsequent readers," with *Old Mortality* being chosen for the 1937 collection of O. Henry Stories and for the 1938 O'Brien Honor Roll.

Since their return to the United States, her marriage with Eu-

---

49. Porter to Warren, November 22, 1935.
50. *Ibid.*; Porter to Albert Erskine, September 23, 1936.
51. Erskine to Porter, January 7, 1937.

gene Pressley had been breaking up, and in the spring of 1937 Caroline Gordon wrote to Warren that "Katherine Anne has cast Gene off, with a twist of the wrist as it were. She kept writing about how she was enjoying life and how it was necessary to embrace her particular demon in poverty, chastity and obedience and so on, whereupon Allen said he feared for Gene. I'm surprised he lasted as long as he did."[52] Miss Porter also gained a measure of financial independence that spring when the Book-of-the-Month Club awarded her $2,500 as "an American author whose work has not received from the book-reading public the recognition it deserved, as measured by actual sales."

The summer of 1937 she spent at the New Jersey home of her friend Glenway Wescott while working on *Pale Horse, Pale Rider*. With the fall, Wescott remembers, "She let 'Pale Horse, Pale Rider' go for another year, and turned to other work. She said *au revoir* to her New York and New Jersey friends and went to live for a while in Louisiana." Returning to Louisiana, she said "to get acquainted with my editors," Miss Porter took residence in the historic Pontalba Building at 543 St. Ann Street in the New Orleans French Quarter. Here Sherwood Anderson had lived and worked a decade earlier, and around the corner was the Pirate's Alley apartment which William Faulkner had occupied during his New Orleans sojourn. "I wouldn't live anywhere else in New Orleans but in the old quarter," Miss Porter said. According to her own account she had eloped from a New Orleans convent school and had left the South "almost for good and ever" at the age of nineteen. Her family, like so many other old southern families of the days of her youth, "felt that if one had talents they should be cultivated for the decoration of life, but never professionally," and so the many-talented convent girl knew that she must leave her native region or be regarded as a "freak": "I had to make a revolt, a rebellion, and I didn't mean living your own life, either. When I left they were all certain that I was going to lead an immoral life. It was a confining society in those days."[53]

52. Caroline Gordon to Robert Penn Warren, n.d. [1937].
53. Glenway Wescott, "Katherine Anne Porter Personally," in Lodwick Hartley and George Core (eds.), *Katherine Anne Porter: A Critical Symposium* (Athens, 1969), 35; "Always a Little Late," Baton Rouge *Morning Advocate*, September 11, 1938; Katherine Anne Porter, quoted in Archer Winsten, "Presenting the Portrait of an Artist," New York *Post*, May 6, 1937, p. 17.

Nevertheless, Porter was genuinely glad to be back in New Orleans after an absence of eighteen years. She remembered fondly "when it seemed to rain all the time and I woke up in the morning to the sound of breakfast coffee being ground, and the shouts of black Mammies clothed in faded flowered dresses, white aprons and bandannas, who were peddling all sorts of things to eat." The New Orleans that she remembered was "a uniform soot color," perhaps, she speculated, "because most of us who lived there could not afford a coat of paint, and those who could did not think it necessary." Like her grandmother, Miss Porter claimed to "yield to no one in my love of improvement" and to be "constitutionally unable to let anything, even a rented flat, remain as it is." Nonetheless, she admitted to finding the Vieux Carré "a saddish place" under the hand of progress. The old smells remained, however—"boiling molasses and brown sugar, roasting pecans and dried vertivert, and the cool odor of mold from old patios"—but mixed with them now was another smell, "the stink of political corruption which hangs nose high in air and seemes to exude like rancid sweat from the very walls." She also found the "organized Bohemia" to be "the dullest and most pretentious in America" and all political and social activity in the grip of "those who wielded alternately the battle ax and the cold chisel." In Louisiana in 1937 there was "a shameless cynicism in the administration of public affairs calculated to chill the blood." [54]

Soon after moving to New Orleans Porter offered "He" to the editors of the *Southern Review*, but they did not accept it. Nevertheless, its author did journey up to Baton Rouge in the fall of 1937, there renewing her friendship with Warren and with Cleanth Brooks and Albert Erskine, whom she had met at Allen Tate's home, Benfolly, the previous summer. While living on St. Ann Street, too, she finally finished *Pale Horse, Pale Rider*. At ten P.M. on November 16 she took a brief break from one of her furious writing spells to send Erskine the first half of the short novel and promised twenty more pages soon to follow. "I am going on in five minutes with the rest," she explained, "and it should be there in thirty-six hours." Pausing "only to catch a few hours of wakeful sleep to let the chambermaid do her chores," she finished the twenty-five-thousand-word novel in

54. Katherine Anne Porter, "Lovely Evocative Photographs," *New York Herald Tribune Books*, March 8, 1942, p. 4.

just seven days. The manuscript was greeted with great enthusiasm by the Baton Rouge editors and squeezed into the winter number despite its length.[55]

On January 12, 1938, Warren wrote to his friend Manson Redford in New Orleans that Katherine Anne Porter had recently left for Houston for a few months, but was planning to return to Baton Rouge, perhaps for good. "That prospect," he concluded, "is a source of great pleasure to all of us here." Porter did return to Baton Rouge, and on April 20, with the Warrens in attendance, she and Albert Erskine were married. The two had felt an instant rapport on their first meeting, but conscious of the twenty-one years of difference between their ages, she had resisted any serious attachment. "I honestly didn't want to get involved," she told an interviewer near the end of her life, but Erskine's mature manner and sophisticated mind tended to obliterate the years, and as he remained "so persistent, so wonderfully attentive, I simply couldn't resist any longer."[56]

"All her life," says her good friend Glenway Wescott, "Katherine Anne has been bewitched by the hope of ceasing to be homeless, of settling somewhere and getting her books and manuscripts and notebooks out of storage and within reach somehow, on shelves and in filing cabinets and in ring binders." This hope had led her to collect "an unreasonable amount of furniture and books," she agreed, "unreasonable for one who had no house to keep them in. I lugged them all with me from Mexico to Paris to New York to Louisiana." At last in Baton Rouge she saw her hope fulfilled and told an interviewer—with evident surprise—that her papers were at last in order in her own house. Formerly she traveled with a suitcase for personal effects and a steamer trunk filled with manuscripts and notes. "Always I was up to my chin in paper." In Baton Rouge she burned numerous short stories and four novels that she decided not to publish, but was left with enough material to occupy her attention for the remainder of the century. Closest to hand were notes for several novels, for the still unfinished biography of Cotton Mather, and for

55. Porter to Albert Erskine, November 16, 1937; Enrique Hank Lopez, *Fugitive from Indian Creek: Conversations with Katherine Anne Porter* (New York, 1981), 217.

56. Warren to Manson Radford, January 12, 1938; Baton Rouge *State-Times*, April 22, 1938, p. 16; Lopez, *Conversations with Katherine Anne Porter*, 227.

some forty short stories. When she came to Baton Rouge Porter turned over to the *Southern Review* the entire portfolio of her unpublished writings, telling the editors to take and use from it as they needed material. Once, in need of money, she sold "The Leaning Tower" to a slick New York journal, but when the editor started to change it she took the story back to the *Southern Review* despite the fact that it could pay only one quarter of what the New York magazine had to offer. "I chose my friends," she told Robert Penn Warren. "I like the company I keep, I won't publish in those magazines." It was more important to have the story done right, says Cleanth Brooks, than to have the extra money. "I've often been broke," she explained to Mrs. Brooks, "but I've never been poor."[57]

In Baton Rouge, for the first time in her career, Porter was working on a schedule. This new industry was due, she remarked, to the good influence of Robert Penn Warren, who amazed her "with his ability to make full use of every thirty minutes of free time. He simply goes to his typewriter," she observed, "picks up where he left off, and pounds ahead." Under the good influence of her new magazine, Porter began the revision of four short novels which she intended to publish as a collection. They should have been in by the fall of 1938, she told a reporter for the Baton Rouge *Morning Advocate*, but "somehow I just can't seem to meet a deadline." The four short novels were *Pale Horse, Pale Rider*, *Old Mortality* (which had previously appeared in the *Southern Review*), *Noon Wine* (which had been printed in *Story*), and an unpublished piece called "Promised Land," one of the early prefigurations of *Ship of Fools*. At the same time she was at work on a 10,000-word critical study of Katherine Mansfield.[58]

The collection of short novels, minus "Promised Land," appeared at last from the press at Harcourt, Brace on March 30, 1939. *Time* magazine noted that "*Pale Horse, Pale Rider* is the second book in

57. Wescott, "Katherine Anne Porter Personally," 32; Katherine Anne Porter, "Now at Last, a House of My Own," in *Vogue's First Reader* (Garden City, 1944), 290; Robert van Gelder, "Katherine Anne Porter at Work," *New York Times Book Review*, April 14, 1940, pp. 20–1; Fisher, "Conversation with Robert Penn Warren," in Watkins and Hiers (eds.), *Robert Penn Warren Talking*, 154; Interview with Cleanth Brooks.

58. Gelder, "Katherine Anne Porter at Work," 42; "Always a Little Late," Baton Rouge *Morning Advocate*, September 11, 1938, p. 13.

three weeks to come out of the new Southern literary center at Baton Rouge," the other being Warren's first novel, *Night Rider.* "That eminent patron of the arts, the late Huey Long, inadvertently started a writing colony there when he imported a group of young Southern writers to give the Louisiana State University intellectual prestige to match its new buildings." *Time* observed that Katherine Anne Porter was a newcomer to the group, and was then living in a two-room apartment on America Street in Beauregard Town, the old section of Baton Rouge. "Charming, quiet, well-liked, she cooks, sews, collects old records and music, and reads medieval documents and modern poetry." Miss Porter's well-known congeniality was perhaps a detriment to her art, but she had no desire to change her style. "There are too many bad books without me trying to turn out two a year," she said. She was, however, still hard at work on *Ship of Fools* and planning to write four books, one for each section of the country. "If they live up to *Pale Horse, Pale Rider*," concluded the *Time* critic, "the literary colony of Baton Rouge may turn out to be far more durable and important than most of Huey Long's works." [59]

In the fall of 1938 she and Erskine had "bought a little ground" which she described as "about half woods and mostly jungle" on the Old Hammond Highway near the Warrens' home. They planned to build there one day a home already named "The Cares," but in the meantime used it for a garden plot. Never mistaken for an Agrarian, Miss Porter quipped, "As usual, I'm late in joining the back to the land movement." For the spring of 1939, however, she left her beloved garden for a lecture tour, speaking at Vassar, Bennington, Olivet, and other eastern schools. Returning to Baton Rouge for the summer, she finished "The Downward Path to Wisdom," which she had promised to *Harper's Bazaar* two years earlier. Her writing was constantly interrupted, however, by more pleasing social and domestic duties. When asked if she ever intended to write about the students at LSU, she told a Baton Rouge reporter, "By the time I get around to writing about them, they'd be grandmothers and grandfathers." [60]

59. "Promise Kept," *Time*, April 10, 1939, p. 75.
60. "Always a Little Late," Baton Rouge *Morning Advocate*, September 11, 1938, p. 13; "Local Literary Scene Crowded by Announcement of Miss Porter's Book," Baton Rouge *Morning Advocate*, March 19, 1939, p. 8B.

With the publication of *Pale Horse, Pale Rider* Porter's fiction at last began to receive the credit and recognition that were its due. In April, 1940, the Society for the Libraries at New York University presented its first Gold Medal Award for "an American author revealing new and distinctive talent in the field of imaginative literature" to Katherine Anne Porter, and from New York she went on to a summer's teaching commitment at Olivet College. Her close friend Glenway Wescott remembers this, however, as "a time of cruel setbacks in her personal life." Restless and frustrated by her inability to do serious writing, she began to feel imprisoned by her marriage. The following fall, feeling the acute need for privacy to pursue her art, she moved to the upstairs apartment on the farm house at Yaddo at Saratoga Springs, New York. Yaddo, to her, was where "artists with jobs to finish [may] come, and work quietly in peace and comfort." Another of her friends observed that Katherine Anne Porter "doesn't wait for death to effect transmigration. Every now and then she stops being what she is and becomes something else. In some secluded corner of the world, she spins a cocoon, and presently comes out more brilliantly colored, with longer and swifter wings. She leaves her old life there in a tree, dry and forgotten and dead, something else she has put forever behind her." So at Yaddo in 1940 Katherine Anne Porter emerged as yet another emanation of her self.[61]

Although she did not divorce Albert Erskine until 1943, he had left Baton Rouge by December, 1941, for a job with New Directions Press, and she found an old colonial house of modified Georgian architecture near Saratoga Lake. "One day, hardly knowing when it happened," she recalls, "I knew I was going to live there, for good and all, and I was going to have a house in the country."[62]

61. Wescott, "Katherine Anne Porter Personally," 25; Porter, "Now at Last, a House of My Own," 290; Paul Crume, "Pale Horse, Pale Rider," *Southwest Review*, XXV (January, 1940), 214.
62. Porter, "Now at Last, a House of My Own," 290.

FIVE

The Baton Rouge Agrarians

They are of the South . . . and that not merely in background and accent. Which again serves to throw up the interesting fact that by far the most part of recognizable native American art at present comes up from the underside of the Mason and Dixon.

D. G. BRIDSON on the editors of the *Southern Review* in *The Criterion*

WHEN Hugh Swinton Legaré founded the first series of the *Southern Review* in 1828, he declared it among the first objects of the new magazine "to vindicate the rights and privileges, the character of the Southern states, to arrest, if possible, that current which has been directed too steadily against . . . the South . . . and to offer our fellow citizens one Journal which they may read without finding themselves the object of perpetual sarcasm, or of affected commiseration."[1] The editors of the new *Southern Review* were by no means out of sympathy with the sentiments of this prospectus. Warren was a charter member of the Agrarian movement, and Brooks, although not a contributor to *I'll Take My Stand*, was in thorough accord with the principles of the Twelve Southerners and was a contributor to the second Agrarian manifesto, *Who Owns America?* Yet the Baton Rouge incarnation of the Charleston journal was by no means so rigidly programmatic as was its namesake, and its editors chose to "vindicate . . . the character of the Southern

1. Hugh Swinton Legaré, "Prospectus," *Southern Review* (Charleston), I (February, 1828), n.p.

states" not so much with regionalistic rhetoric as with a program of excellence in the field of international letters.

As Brooks and Warren explained their position, "the name of *The Southern Review* was an expression, certainly, of regional and sectional piety . . . but the editors hoped that that piety was somewhat different from the chauvinistic variety." Certainly the editors wanted the magazine to make some contribution to the cultural life of the region, and they were youthfully ambitious enough to want it to become a kind of focus for that life. But they felt that a regional piety that pretended to be more than shallow or sentimental demanded that they relate southern problems and southern literature to the world outside the South. A problem in economics in the South could not be dissociated from the economic problems of the rest of the world, and a southern poet could not be considered without some awareness of the broad tradition of poetry and some awareness of the contemporary manifestations in, for example, France or England. At the profoundest level, "the editors felt that they could best serve their region by insisting on the highest possible standards of excellence for the magazine itself." In order to maintain those standards, the editors chose from all material available for publication without regard to the contributor's place of nativity or residence. As Malcolm Cowley commented, the *Southern Review* was even "tolerant of revolutionary opinions so long as they are expressed with force and scholarship."[2]

Warren's participation in the Agrarian symposium, *I'll Take My Stand*, together with the political philosophy reflected in his first book, *John Brown: The Making of a Martyr*, and many of his earlier essays, reviews, poems, and short stories clearly qualify him for full-fledged membership in the Nashville-based group. Much of his Louisiana work does as well. Warren's first important essay after arriving at LSU, "John Crowe Ransom: A Study in Irony," for example, demonstrates Warren's continuing loyalty to the Agrarian ideal. Here Warren gave strong support to Ransom's quarrel with the naturalism of the modern age which worships a "God Without Thunder," a God who is predictably benevolent, and a God whose

2. Brooks and Warren, *Stories from the Southern Review*, xii; Malcolm Cowley, "Partisan Review," *New Republic*, October 19, 1938, p. 312.

essence can be precisely defined by the intellect. Rejecting this simplified deity, Warren agreed with Ransom that the true God is inscrutable, that his nature is unpredictable, and that his essence transcends all rationalist attempts to apprehend it.

"The way of life congenial to the terms of the myth of rationality is called industrialism," wrote Warren, and the deity of this myth has given his faithful "a machinery, a technique, and gospel of production" which will provide them a maximum of efficiency and the gratification of all desires. Yet, as Warren analyzed it, two major problems existed with the new creed. First, from his mid-Depression viewpoint, Warren observed that the goods and services which the God of reason dispensed became the property of a relatively small number of his believers. And second, he believed that "the very superiority in efficiency may brutalize desire, for reason, pure and simple, dictates an immediate gratification without let or irrelevancy." In a system dedicated to the gratification of appetites by the most direct and "rational" means, mere production becomes the ideal human conduct. Warren concluded, however, that in order to be human at all, man must have something that will stop action and allow him time to reflect. This something "cannot possibly be reason in its narrow sense. It is sensibility." And only in an agrarian society would man have fuller opportunity to experience his native sensibility, or in other words, to experience his proper humanity. "The essential qualities" of the agrarian society—"order, tradition, stability—are merely aspects of that sensibility."[3]

Close to the end of his tenure at LSU some six years later, Warren continued to defend the South against northern imperialism. In a radio broadcast debate with James B. Trant, progressive dean of LSU's College of Commerce, Warren condemned the South's enduring colonial status within the United States and the fact that the wealth from southern resources too often found its way into northern pockets while its rightful owners went uncompensated. "We were always a colonial section," he maintained. "We fought a war against English colonialism, and then we fought a war against

3. Robert Penn Warren, "John Crowe Ransom: A Study in Irony," *Virginia Quarterly Review*, X (Winter, 1935), 93–112.

northern colonialism. We won the first, swapped the devil for the witch, and then fought against the witch. We're still fighting against the witch to my mind." Dean Trant attempted to point out that "when our oil goes out, something else comes back in place of that oil or in payment for it. It may be machinery, it may be automobiles . . . it may be shoes, it may be flour, it may be any of the good things of life that we so much enjoy." Warren protested, "They made me pay for my automobile!"[4]

In 1956, at a Vanderbilt reunion of the Fugitive group, Warren recalled what the Agrarian cause had meant to him in the 1930s. Just before the United States entered World War II, he said, "there was a period of unmasking of blank power everywhere." Thinking of Stalin, Hitler, Mussolini, and, to no small degree, of Huey Long, Warren saw that the seizure of power by the few made one feel that "all your work was irrelevant" and "that the de-humanizing forces had won. And that you had no more relevance." Even in "this so-called democratic state" Warren saw "no individual sense of responsibility and no awareness that the individual has a past and a place." This sense of the disintegration of the individual in modern society impelled him into the Agrarian camp with its emphasis upon the human being as individual. This notion, says Warren, became fused with his personal sentiments and sentimentalities, and the myth of the southern past was such an element. To him it represented "a heroic story—a parade of personalities who are also images for these individual values." Unlike some of his fellow Agrarians, Warren made no claim to be an economist. The movement to him, rather, was a protest against "a kind of de-humanizing and disintegrative effect on [his] notion of what an individual person could be in the sense of a loss of [one's] role in society."[5]

Yet, when he was asked by the *Partisan Review* in the summer of 1937, "Do you find . . . that your writing reveals any allegiance to any group, class, organization, region, religion, or system of thought," Warren's reply was an unqualified, "God knows I don't." Already

4. Robert Penn Warren, "Industrialization: The Old South Fades," in Robert Heilman (ed.), *Aspects of a World at War: Radio Forum of the Louisiana State University* (Baton Rouge, 1942), 119.
5. Purdy (ed.), *Fugitives' Reunion*, 208–10.

Warren was backing away from the political and economic remedies of the Agrarians. "The danger of regionalism," he declared in 1939, "lies in the 'ism.' Meaningless as a fad, it is not a cure-all and gives the writer no substitute for talent and intelligence."[6]

Cleanth Brooks arrived too late at Vanderbilt to participate in *I'll Take My Stand*. During his undergraduate career, however, he did establish close philosophical and critical ties with Ransom, Davidson, and Warren, and while doing graduate work at Oxford in 1931, visited the Ransom family in Devonshire. In April, 1932, Warren made a similar visit to his old Vanderbilt mentor, and together they discussed Brooks's close reading of *I'll Take My Stand*, his intelligent sympathy with the group's principles, and the excellent potential that he displayed as a possible contributor to a future Agrarian symposium.

Brooks has written essays on the South and literature and on the South and religion which show an affinity with the Agrarian philosophy, and at various times he has given his voice directly to the defense of the doctrine, as in his contribution to *Who Owns America?*, the second Agrarian manifesto. His first published monograph, *The Relation of the Alabama-Georgia Dialect to the Provincial Dialects of Great Britain*, was written, Brooks says, "with the mingled purpose of justification, defense, and, if need be compromise."[7] Thus Brooks, who like many of his fellow southerners had grown weary of the hick-baiting and amused condescension of northern commentators on "the Sahara of the Bozart," set out to demonstrate the validity of the southern pronunciation within the tradition of the language of Elizabeth, Shakespeare, and Marlowe. Some of his most interesting critical pieces, moreover, printed in his first collection of essays, *Modern Poetry and the Tradition*, deal with the relationship between the Fugitive poets and their native region, and certainly his personal relationships with Warren, Ransom, Davidson, Tate, and the other Agrarians served to strengthen his regional bias. Equally significant is the fact that Brooks's most

6. Robert Penn Warren, "The Situation in American Writing, Part II," *Partisan Review*, VI (Fall, 1939), 113; Robert Penn Warren, "Some Don'ts for Literary Regionalists," *American Review*, VIII (December, 1936), 142.

7. Interview with Cleanth Brooks, New Haven, Connecticut, May 16, 1979.

sustained effort of criticism of a single author is his explication and evaluation of the works of William Faulkner.

Yet Brooks, like Warren, was never so doctrinaire through the 1930s as were his Nashville friends. Unlike most of their Agrarian colleagues, neither Brooks nor Warren ever thought that Agrarianism had any *political* possibilities. Their best hope was that the movement might affect a long-range philosophical change in the South and in the nation. "If society is sick," Brooks has recently commented, "the poet may well be the one who tells us the nature of the illness. He gives a useful diagnosis of the malady. Of course this act has a very real connection with remedying the situation, for a good diagnosis may facilitate finding a proper remedy. I think, however, that when the poet or the novelist actually goes out on the hustings to argue for a specific remedy, it is very likely that he will move out of literary art into some kind of practical rhetoric."[8] As far as Cleanth Brooks was concerned, the Agrarian movement was important insofar as it helped to create a consciousness in the South of itself and its traditions by which the intellectual might operate. It brought positive attention to the region as a literary mecca for the first time since the days of Thomas Jefferson. Brooks perceived, as too many of his fellow southern intellectuals did not, that redemption for the South lay neither on the highway to an industrialized and modernized New South nor on the retrograde path to the vanished glories of the Old South. Rather the region's survival as a cultural reality lay in the practice of letters. Unlike Donald Davidson and the more rigid of the Agrarian brotherhood, he saw that the only way in which regionalism could have a lasting impact on the world of letters was to refuse to confuse the region with the historical, geographical, social, and political province. In order that regional writing might be understood as a work of art, and not merely as a documentation of local color, Brooks perceived that it was essential that the reader be able to judge any work of art by a universal standard. Having established a common definition by which art might be known, then southern writers might be judged by the

8. Warren, "Conversation with Cleanth Brooks," in Simpson (ed.), *The Possibilities of Order*, 8.

same standard as the northern or western literary artists and receive commendation commensurate with their talent and energy.
Of all the Agrarians who became New Critics, therefore, Brooks has
emphasized most heavily the virtue of close textual analysis and the
precept that an inside knowledge of literature is a precondition of
enjoying its real benefits.

At the time that Brooks and Warren came to Baton Rouge there
was much talk in the Agrarian camp of founding or capturing a little
magazine to be completely under the editorial and financial control
of the group. As Richard M. Weaver, a Brooks and Warren graduate
student, observed, "Undoubtedly the Agrarians would exert an immensely greater influence if they held some city or some university;
if they had a concentration of forces which would serve as a radiat-
ing center of impulse—if they had a Rome, as it were."[9] The considerable Agrarian contribution to the *Southwest Review* under the energetic editing of the Baton Rouge wing of the movement held out
some hope that the Nashville-based group had found a house organ
despite the antipathy of senior editors Smith and McGinnis, and
this hope burgeoned with the founding of the *Southern Review*.

Allen Tate observed that "the index of *The Southern Review* . . .
would be a roll call of the best Southern writers of the century,"
and Malcolm Cowley referred to the editors as "a group of de-
reconstructed rebels." Indeed, the *Southern Review* served as an
outlet for scores of articles by agrarians of all persuasions. In the
first volume alone a total of twenty-two articles, reviews, stories, and
poems from the pens of the Twelve Southerners appeared, and
much more work of the like-minded men and women whom Davidson described as "two dozen of the most fertile and productive minds
that ever arose out of a common nucleus of ideas and more or less
common concerns" appeared alongside that of the original twelve.[10]

Desmond Hawkins, writing in T. S. Eliot's *Criterion*, agreed that
the *Southern Review* was "the best kind of alliance between re-

9. Richard M. Weaver, "The Tennessee Agrarians," *Shenandoah*, III (Summer,
1952), 9.
10. Allen Tate, *Memoirs and Opinions: 1926–1974* (Chicago, 1975), 194; Cowley, "Partisan Review," 312; Donald Davidson, "The 'Mystery' of the Agrarians," *Saturday Review of Literature*, XXVI (January, 1943), 6–7.

gional interests and specialist literary activity." The function of the *Review*, he explained, "is to define the highest kind of civilization congenial to its locality, to expand its *genius loci*," and to maintain what in Hawkins' opinion was "much the best equipped school of literary criticism in America." In the spirit of Eliot's tradition-oriented magazine, Hawkins further observed, "*The Southern Review* has no money on the Liberal horse, and perhaps for that reason is ready to get on with its own affairs." M. D. Zabel pointed out that the magazine's essays on regionalism "require no unthinking agreement," though whoever disagrees with their point of view must do so "on a level of intelligence and sanity, not of provincial bias of the customary intolerant violence of propagandist causes." From New Orleans, Hamilton Basso echoed Zabel's approval of the *Review*'s sense of balance, maintaining that it "wisely avoids too great a preoccupation with the purely regional and includes within its range subjects of national and international interest." [11]

Brooks and Warren opened the pages of their review to contributions by writers who held beliefs not shared by the editors but who developed their positions with acuteness and depth. Margaret Marshall, writing in *The Nation*, found it piquant not only that the *Review* "comes out of Huey Long's bailiwick, but that both contributors and subjects often veer to the left." [12] Although frequently accused by their detractors on the left of acting as "window dressing" for a right-wing take-over in America, the Agrarians were consistently more vigorously antifascist than anticommunist, and especially after 1939 they became more vocally so. In a Baton Rouge radio broadcast entitled "Contrasting World Orders," for example, Brooks spoke out strongly in favor of "'the rule of law,' which has as its basis the idea that we try to make our laws conform to a set of general rules of general applicability, something quite different from a decision on an immediate law which might rest on an intuition of a particular moment." Mindful, perhaps, of the impact of the late Huey Long on the state of Louisiana, Brooks issued a forceful warning against tendencies toward totalitarianism in the United

11. Hawkins, "Periodicals: American," 405–406; Zabel, "Recent Magazines," 51; Hamilton Basso, "Books in Brief," *New Republic*, September 25, 1935, p. 195.
12. Margaret Marshall, "Notes by the Way," *Nation*, January 4, 1941, p. 22.

States. "I think it's highly important," he told his audience, that in view of the visible similarities between many American institutions and their counterparts in Nazi Germany we should "discuss basic ends, I should say, even matters of creed, matters of ultimate belief, particularly because one does find Fascistic elements in our country, and one can see that the temptation on certain levels in our own civilization to imitate the totalitarian regimes is here and has to be guarded against." Answering the moderator's question as to whether the firmness of democratic traditions would prevent any fascist element from gaining power in America, Brooks was far from optimistic.

> I don't know that I would agree that it would prevent, though let us hope that it would be a strong stay. I think that the essential permanence and strength of that Jeffersonian tradition would make us bitterly regret having gone in a totalitarian direction after we had done it. On the other hand I think it's only fair for us to admit that there are certain things in our folkways and traditions which would make totalitarianism attractive to us. Even in the South, which has this Jeffersonian tradition strongly imbedded, there are factors which might render the temptation to imitate totalitarian methods very strong.[13]

So receptive were Brooks and Warren to ideas and manuscripts which did not correspond to their own ideal of literary and political thought that in August, 1938, former *Broom* editor Matthew Josephson wrote to Brooks that "either I am blind or *The Southern Review* hardly seems agrarian at all."[14] This detente with non-Agrarian writers caused some consternation among the ranks of the Twelve, with Donald Davidson especially berating Brooks and Warren for being too generous with the left and center. He felt that the *Southern Review* should be a purely Agrarian organ and devote no space to its opponents. He laid down this position in letters to the editors and to their former Nashville colleagues, yet Brooks and

13. Cleanth Brooks, *et al.*, "Contrasting World Orders," in Heilman (ed.), *Aspects of a World at War*, 43–50.
14. Matthew Josephson to Cleanth Brooks, August 29, 1938.

Warren continued to offer a forum to all shades of political opinion so long as it was well thought out and forcefully written. Nevertheless, the *Southern Review* remained the single most important outlet for Agrarian opinion throughout its run.

Neither Brooks's nor Warren's relation to Agrarianism is easily charted, but 1936 saw the climax and then decline of their enthusiasm for the cause. One of their first efforts of 1936, for example, heartily promoted the ideas of the Agrarians. During the spring, Brooks and Warren had placed with the *American Review* their first jointly authored publication, a defense of southern traditions and values entitled "Dixie Looks at Mrs. Gerould." The catalyst for this Agrarian-oriented essay was an article printed in the previous month's *American Mercury* by Katherine Fullerton Gerould, "A Yankee Looks at Dixie." Brooks's and Warren's essay was a witty and tempered yet devastating counterblow to Mrs. Gerould's attack on their native region, which the two southerners took to be a "dilution of fashionable ideas and attitudes, a pre-digested pap" which represented "a journalistic sensibility functioning at a very low temperature."

In her literary critique of the South, Mrs. Gerould had condemned the South as callous, bigoted, ignorant, and slothful and traced these evils to the South's agricultural way of life. "Whatever one may think of the brutalizing effect of machines," she had philosophized, "no one, I believe, will deny that a certain callousness has always gone with the cultivation of the soil. Humanitarianism, one suspects, was born in towns." Brooks and Warren, however, did deny her criticisms. First, they replied that it was "a bit rough on Robert Frost, who used to write poems after he had been cultivating his moral callousness all day in the hayfield," and quite as rough on Robert Burns, the shepherd Psalmist, and Jesse Stuart. Then, to her second pronouncement, that humanitarianism was born in towns, Brooks and Warren answered that it "makes it seem odd that Nazareth was a country village, and the manger of Bethlehem not a tool locker in a Ford garage."

They were no less ready to argue with her statement that "agricultural civilizations . . . have never tended, in themselves, to foster psychological sensitiveness" because "neither growing of crops, nor

the hunting of foxes, nor the breeding of horses encourages it."
While granting that the practices of agriculture might not "in themselves" foster "psychological sensitiveness," Brooks and Warren
asked, in turn, how much sensitivity one derived from the activities
of an industrial society. Neither running an advertising agency nor
"screwing on Bolt 38" in an assembly line, they countered, "in
themselves" encouraged sensitivity.

In conclusion, Brooks and Warren went on to point out that the
basic assumption of Mrs. Gerould's essay was invalid. "The true an-
tithesis of an agricultural society," they reasoned, "is not urban as
such, for agricultural societies have always had cities, including
Periclean Athens, the Rome of Cincinnatus, the Jerusalum of Sol-
omon, Elizabethan London, and Concord, Massachusetts of the
'golden day.'" Even Chartres, "an agricultural market town of thirteenth century France," erected a cathedral which captured the
imagination of Henry Adams, "a citizen of New England itself."
Rather its opposite is an industrial society which need not be exclusively metropolitan. "There may be a wheat factory as well as a
wheat farm," they pointed out.[15]

Such a pointed and well-argued reply delighted Brooks's and
Warren's Agrarian friends. Andrew Lytle, for example, could not
conceal his glee in a letter of congratulations to his Baton Rouge colleagues. "I read the reply you and Cleanth made to that nasty
woman," he wrote to Warren in his "Uncle Micajah" dialect, "and it
war a real beaut. I didn't know her before, but I'm sure I wouldn't
know her now, for as far as I can tell she's completely demolished."[16]

In April, 1936, the two men were able to travel to Nashville to
what George Marion O'Donnell termed a "veritable convention of
the Agrarian group around the table at Petrone's." Besides himself,
Brooks, and Warren, also in attendance were Allen Tate, Caroline
Gordon, Andrew Lytle, John Crowe Ransom, Donald Davidson, and
Frank Owsley, and "great was the gaiety of the assemblage, particularly after Warren had finished his fifth bottle of ale."[17] The immedi-

15. Cleanth Brooks and Robert Penn Warren, "Dixie Looks at Mrs. Gerould,"
American Review, VI (March, 1936), 585–95.
16. Andrew Lytle to Robert Penn Warren, April 1, 1936.
17. George Marion O'Donnell to Richmond C. Beatty, spring, 1936, quoted in
Young, *Gentleman in a Dustcoat*, 261.

ate outcome of the evening's festivities was Ransom's agreement to write an essay on O'Donnell's poems which were to appear in the spring number of the *Southern Review*. Brooks and Warren, however, seem to have come away from Petrone's with more than a hangover and Ransom's promise. Zeal for their common cause was rekindled, and the warmth of that fire produced the largest outpouring of Agrarian writing since the 1930 advent of *I'll Take My Stand*.

Disappointed by the limited impact of the 1930 book, the Agrarians sought to broaden the field of their influence, and with the urging of charter Agrarian Allen Tate and newcomer Herbert Agar, former London correspondent of the Louisville *Courier-Journal* and Pulitzer Prize winning historian, an alliance was struck between the southern Agrarians and the English Distributists to produce a critique of Western capitalism. Unlike *I'll Take My Stand*, however, *Who Owns America?* was not to be the product of close collaboration among its various contributors; rather, Tate and Agar were to serve merely as editors of a very loosely joined group of essays.

In the spring of 1935, Warren wrote to John Gould Fletcher concerning the new venture. "Has Ransom talked with you any about the projected second *I'll Take My Stand*?" he inquired. Warren then informed Fletcher that Tate was in Nashville, and that the two of them had "managed to generate a certain enthusiasm in each other" for the proposed volume. In fact, Warren speculated that he was probably more excited than Tate, who was "sunk in the middle of his book," *The Fathers*.[18]

Meanwhile in Nashville, Tate and Agar were attempting to piece together the loosely related essays into a single framework. The more conservative wing of the Agrarian party was none too pleased with the alliance from the start, and their sniping at the book's progress caused Tate to snap back at Davidson, "If . . . the ghost of Huey Long wants the honor of editing, he is damned welcome to it." As the season went along, however, the snarls of editing began to untangle themselves, and by the end of November Brooks wrote to Agar that "the news of the symposium is fine, and I feel greatly honored to be included in the list of contributors." Brooks reiterated to Agar the desire of the *Southern Review* to use several essays from

18. Robert Penn Warren to John Gould Fletcher, May, 1935.

the forthcoming book in the spring issue which he hoped would be out in early March.[19]

By the time the spring issue of the *Review* came out, Tate and Agar had all of the essays in hand, and on March 5 Frank Owsley was able to inform Brooks that Herbert Agar and Agar's wife Eleanor Chilton, Allen Tate and Caroline Gordon, John Donald Wade, and Andrew Lytle had all visited him on the previous weekend to read proof for *Who Owns America?* "Three or four of us read each essay," he wrote. "I wish that you and Red might have been here."[20] The book was released on April 30, 1936.

Cleanth Brooks's contribution to *Who Owns America?* was an essay entitled "The Christianity of Modernism," which he delivered to Agar on January 3, 1936. With characteristic modesty, Brooks explained to his editor that his article was a hasty job, and he gave Agar "*carte blanche* with regard to it. . . . If it won't do, please don't hesitate to throw it out." He went on to explain, however, that although the essay "doesn't say anything, of course, that we don't know already . . . I hope that you may think it good strategy to attempt to get a hearing from the group whom I am particularly addressing."[21]

Despite all of these *caveats*, Brooks's essay, first published in the *American Review* for February, 1936, was one of the strongest in *Who Owns America?* As Crane Brinton observed soon after the book's release, although Brooks's essay "seems at first to be a bit off the main line taken by his colleagues," he in fact "gets down to the ultimates that lie behind this book with a precision attained by none of the other contributors."[22] As in many of his essays in literary criticism, Brooks observed that science is at feud with art and religion and that, in the case of the Protestant churches, the war is over. The Protestants have been worse than defeated: they have been con-

19. Allen Tate to Donald Davidson, September 28, 1935, in Fain and Young (ed.), *The Literary Correspondence of Donald Davidson and Allen Tate*, 294; Cleanth Brooks to Herbert Agar, November 19, 1935.
20. Frank Owsley to Cleanth Brooks, March 5, 1936.
21. Cleanth Brooks to Herbert Agar, January 3, 1935.
22. Crane Brinton, "*Who Owns America?*", *Southern Review*, II (Summer, 1936), 18–19.

Major Troy Middleton, James Monroe
Smith, and Huey P. Long.
Courtesy of Arthur Scouten.

Cleanth Brooks in the 1940s.
Courtesy of Cleanth Brooks.

Robert Penn Warren at LSU, *ca.* 1935.
Courtesy of the LSU Office of Public Relations.

Charles W. Pipkin, *ca.* 1935.
Courtesy of the LSU Office of Public Relations.

Eudora Welty, *ca.* 1945.
Photograph by Kay Bell, courtesy of Eudora Welty.

Katherine Anne Porter, *ca.* 1940.
Photograph by Eudora Welty and reprinted with her permission.

Paul M. Hebert, 1939.
Courtesy of the LSU Office of Public Relations.

Campbell B. Hodges.
Courtesy of the Department of Archives and Manuscripts, Middleton Library, LSU.

verted. In their attempt to remain "relevant" the Protestant churches have constantly altered their goals and their very definitions of their own meaning. To Brooks's mind, they could not undergo further reformation without being reformed totally out of existence.

In its emphasis on the social gospel, protestantism, according to Brooks's point of view, had so far secularized itself as to have completely compromised its commitment to Christianity in favor of its concern for the conditions under which men live. Although by no means out of sympathy with the impulse to better the living conditions of one's fellow man, Brooks saw the Protestant churches' preoccupation with worldly reform as a means of competing with science for the attention of their congregations, when in fact, he believed, the churches have a far more solid claim to their communicants' loyalties than do the technocrats and social scientists. For science, Brooks maintained, "has nothing to say about values." Rather, the scientist must always preface his prescriptions with a qualification: "*If* you want this result, then take this means." To Brooks, science was "the technician-in-chief to civilization," defining the means by which man might obtain his various ends. But science could never be the pilot. Science could not name the objectives, for that is the function of religion.

Religion, which Brooks roughly defines as "that system of basic values which underlies a civilization," is more worthy to determine that civilization than is the economic order into which we have drifted. "If the Christian assumptions are valid," he argued, "then the Christian theologian and pastor, whatever the world may think, can hardly have a more important vocation." On the other hand, if the liberal wing of the Protestant churches remains ascendant, then the churches become "merely humanitarians in search of a social program" and "hardly Christian in any historical sense of the term." Thus, Brooks concluded, "unless Liberal Protestantism is prepared to be a religion, it is a superfluity, and it had better allow itself to be absorbed into one of the movements which puts the material well-being of man first, willing to implement this through collectivization, the liquidation of certain classes, and whatever else may be necessary."[23] Brooks's essay, therefore, related to the Agrarian cause

23. Cleanth Brooks, "The Christianity of Modernism," in Allen Tate and Herbert Agar (eds.), *Who Owns America?* (Boston, 1936), 323–33.

by admirably demonstrating that the truths which the group held were not the truths of science and were in no sense new but the traditional truths of Western civilization.

Warren's contribution to *Who Owns America?*, "Literature as a Symptom," is a double-barreled blast at would-be writers who, having no deeply felt convictions of their own, merely adopted the currently fashionable stance of either the regionalist or the proletarian as a position from which to exercise their talents. Warren attacks with equal vigor the novelists and poets of the right who attempt to argue themselves into a right relation with nature, the land, and local tradition and those who, from the left, attempt to reason themselves into an appropriate relation to a social class by condemning religion, patriotism, the ownership of property, and other relics from the past.

Although himself a stout traditionalist, Warren has no use for either type's conception of literary theme as a mere instrument, an element in a novel which the writer may adopt and discard at need. "A commitment made on these grounds is nothing more than the final demonstration of a writer's fatuity and emptiness," Warren argues. Such a superficial commitment "does nothing to enlarge the experience and mind of the writer as a man or citizen," he says; for literature then becomes only "a function, not a cause, of life."[24]

Crane Brinton contended in his *Southern Review* notice of *Who Owns America?* that "recent years have not diminished the strength or the prestige of the group still known as the Southern Agrarians," and in fact, the new book seemed at first to have some political impact. Copies of the manifesto were distributed to Franklin D. Roosevelt and other such prominent New Dealers as Harold Ickes, Cordell Hull, and Henry Wallace; and President Roosevelt's speech at his second presidential nomination heartened the Agrarians. According to Agar, the president's address "came right out of *Who Owns America?* Now let him act on it."[25]

The new book as a whole, however, was a disappointment to its contributors. It was an even more loosely knit symposium than *I'll*

24. Robert Penn Warren, "Literature as a Symptom," in Tate and Agar (eds.), *Who Owns America?*, 264–79.
25. Brinton, "*Who Owns America?*", 15; Edward S. Shapiro, "American Conservative Intellectuals, the 1930's, and the Crisis of Ideology," *Modern Age*, XXIII (Fall, 1979), 373.

Take My Stand had been, and it formed no integrated pattern nor presented a well-built platform. Rather, each of its twenty-one contributors, gathered from all shadings of Agrarianism and Distributism, "carved out of his own stone," and thus the symposium followed no general order but went only where the individual essayists chose to take it. With the publication of the unfocused joint venture, Donald Davidson and others of the Agrarian persuasion claimed that it had displaced another symposium which they had discussed and to some extent projected, as a sequal to *I'll Take My Stand*.

Hard on the heels of *Who Owns America?* followed another Agrarian-Distributist attempt to bring its program before the public, this time in the form of a journal of commentary of the sort that many of the charter Agrarians had hoped the *Southern Review* would be. On June 4–5, 1936, a meeting of the Agrarian and Distributist groups was held in Nashville for the purpose of creating a "Committee for the Alliance of Agrarian and Distributist Groups." Attending were Herbert Agar, Ralph Borsodi, Chard Powers Smith (a New York lawyer, paleontologist and poet), and Agrarians Tate, Davidson, Ransom, Lanier, Wade, and Owsley, plus Brooks, Warren, and Pipkin. The committee drew up a statement of principles strongly condemning fascism, plutocracy, and communism, praising decentralization of ownership of agriculture, industry, and trade, and urging the revival of family farming. Their statement argued that American liberties were threatened by the growth of giant corporations and by excessive urbanization: "In politics we are losing our freedom. In economics we are losing our independence. In life we are losing our proper sense of values." As the best means of propagating these ideas, the committee chose a weekly magazine which was to be jointly financed and edited by the two conservative groups. "The need of such a publication to represent our program in the South and West is overwhelming," they decided, and believed that such a publication "would capture within two or three years a large portion of the audience that reads *The Nation* and *The New Republic* because it cannot get anything else."[26]

26. "Minutes of Convention Held by the Committee for the Alliance of Agrarian and Distributist Groups at Nashville, Tennessee, June 4–5, 1936," Andrew Lytle Papers, Vanderbilt University (quoted in Shapiro, "American Conservative Intellectuals, the 1930's, and the Crisis of Ideology," 374).

In the first issue of *Free America*, Herbert Agar, the chief organizer of the journal, stated the magazine's editorial policy. In accordance with Agrarian principles, Agar contended that the journal would stand for "individual freedom" and the belief that such freedom "can exist only in societies in which the great majority are the effective owners of tangible and productive property . . . in which group activity is democratic . . . and society, ownership . . . and government" are decentralized.[27] He also predicted that the magazine would build on the work, not only of the Agrarians, but also of the Borsodi homestead movement, the "Independent Americans" of New York, the National Catholic Rural Life Conference, the cooperative movement, and the survivors of the Henry George single-tax crusade.

While the broad base of support for the journal might, at first, have been helpful, it was soon to prove the undertaking's downfall. The earliest hint of dissent occurred when Agar approached Cleanth Brooks for a contribution to the magazine's first issue. Although Brooks agreed to send one, Caroline Gordon wrote to Brooks in January, 1937, asking him to withhold it. "Dirty work at Times Square," she explained. Although Gordon did not know the full story of the dispute, she reported that the gist of the matter was this: "The New York crowd, manipulated, we think by Borsodi, has organized to publish a bigger and better magazine, one that pays. They are incorporating, and the Agrarians will have only one representative on the board while the Catholics, Single Taxers, and Cooperatives will predominate." Lytle and Tate, believing that Agar had been taken in by the other parties of the alliance, had written to him stating that the Agrarians would not consent to minority status. Feeling Agrarian doctrine diluted by so many other "isms" would not have much force, Tate had stipulated that either the Agrarians must control the magazine or have no representation at all. Gordon further expressed Agrarian fear of being sucked "into the insatiable maw of New York."[28]

Although Warren had received this news, he was nevertheless surprised to learn when Agar wrote him in February that he believed himself in trouble with the Nashville Agrarians. Agar's side of

27. Herbert Agar, *Free America*, I (January, 1937).
28. Caroline Gordon to Robert Penn Warren, January, 1937.

the story corroborated Gordon's, but did show the non-Agrarians in a much better light. Agar claimed to have attempted to act as a liaison between the various camps and thought that "when Nashville withdrew . . . the effort being made in New York was worth what little support I could give it." Agar was sure that his efforts had not only failed to prevent the breakup of the conservative alliance but had cost him the personal goodwill of the Agrarians, a situation which he very much regretted. "It seems to me important," he concluded, that "the few of us who are trying for the same basic reformation in America shouldn't have beastly internal squabbles, like a lot of Communists."[29]

In his reply to Agar, Warren assured him of his and Brooks's continued personal friendship and protested that he knew of no general Agrarian ill will toward him. As for their feelings about the magazine, however, Warren confessed that it was not what he and Brooks had wanted to see. They had hoped that in any coalition of Agrarian and other groups, the Agrarian group would be dominant for several reasons. First, it was numerically larger and had had a longer existence. Second, its principles seemed more fundamental and inclusive. Warren excepted the Catholics, of course, as Catholics, but felt that in any alliance between Catholic-Distributist or Catholic-Agrarian groups in the United States at least, "the emphasis would definitely have to be on the Agrarian side of the hyphen."[30]

Although the Agrarians ultimately reconciled their differences with *Free America*, with Tate serving briefly as book review editor and Davidson, Lytle, and Tate all contributing reviews and essays, Brooks's and Warren's names do not appear among the list of contributors, and their absence from the formal ranks of the Agrarian cause dates from this period. Significantly, when the Agrarian old guard met the North Carolina "Planners" in formal debate at the Nashville meeting of the Southern Historical Association in November, 1936, their ranks were thinner due to pressures of academic and editorial responsibilities and Depression era economics, and by the absence of the Baton Rouge wing.

Even more unwholesome to Agrarian dogma than northern industrialists were native southerners who, in the words of Rich-

29. Herbert Agar to Robert Penn Warren, February 15, 1937.
30. Robert Penn Warren to Herbert Agar, April 15, 1937.

ard M. Weaver, "have accepted completely the doctrine of progress, and who have their entire investment of substance, position, and prestige in it. They are the ones who want more factories, more of everything which would make the South a replica of Lowell and Schenectady and Youngstown with a consequent swelling of bank deposits and payrolls. Not all of them are disingenuous: some are simply unable to see an alternative."[31]

The Agrarians rated the Planners of North Carolina chief among the "collaborationists" of the New South in the 1930s. The high point of the 1936 Southern Historical Association Convention was John Crowe Ransom's debate with Progressive champion W. T. Couch, director of the University of North Carolina Press. According to Donald Davidson, who witnessed the event, Couch

> picked out minute contradictions in various Agrarians' doctrines as they appeared at various stages and capped all with some nasty implications as to the integrity, honesty, and sincerity of agrarians in general, and of Ransom, Tate and Lytle in particular. Taking a quotation from Ransom's *God Without Thunder* out of its context, he demonstrated that "knowledge is sin." And in the light of the agrarian argument that benefits come from the soil, he proved, by a wonderful chain of syllogisms, that since the negro hand works the soil, he receives more benefit than his planter boss, who is removed from the soil by the distance of a horse's legs; and therefore the negro laborer is proved to be, by "agrarian" reasoning, a being superior to the planter who, as an upholder of white supremacy, has crankily insisted on the negro's inferiority.[32]

Of course, the Agrarians were outraged at this twisting of their arguments and Ransom, himself, immediately rose "shaking with rage" to defend his work and his character. As Caroline Gordon remembered Ransom's speech, he insisted that it "did not require a high degree of intelligence or perseverence to master *God Without Thunder*," which Couch had attacked as being unintelligible. "Fur-

31. Weaver, "The Tennessee Agrarians," 8.
32. Donald Davidson to Robert Penn Warren, November 29, 1936.

thermore," Ransom argued, "Mr. Couch has misquoted me and has mispronounced some of my words." The next day, Ransom was "somewhat shamed" to remember his exchange with Couch. "I am mortified to think how I behaved," he told his friends, but Caroline Gordon, for one, believed that "the brethren all enjoyed it very much."[33]

The Baton Rouge Agrarians enjoyed this lively exchange only from a distance, however. After the failure of *Who Owns America?* and *Free America* to make any discernible political impact, Brooks and Warren demurred from a serious role in the Agrarian/Planner contest and concentrated their time and energies on the literary work which was their primary responsibility. Although they were by no means out of sympathy with the Vanderbilt core of the group and certainly maintained a lively interest in the political and philosophical debate being waged by shadings of the American political rainbow, especially where that debate involved the South, Brooks and Warren were increasingly concerned with strictly literary pursuits and the publishing of an excellent magazine as a means toward personal, regional, and national salvation.

Writers and critics are often an irascible tribe, even among friends, and Brooks and Warren on more than one occasion were engaged in editorial controversy with their Agrarian comrades. In 1937, for example, Brooks and Warren had to choose between friendship and personal obligation on the one hand and strict editorial honesty on the other when John Crowe Ransom submitted to their journal an essay entitled "Shakespeare at Sonnets." In his *Memoirs* Allen Tate recalls that Ransom "had been reading Donne, and had derived a formula for 'metaphysical' poetry that raised Donne above Shakespeare the sonneteer." Ransom contended that although "it is not likely that John Donne could have written Shakespeare's plays," it is completely impossible that Shakespeare could have got into the plays the equivalent of Donne's lyrics. Although Ransom's "formula" was strictly rational in crediting Donne with a coherent center which Shakespeare lacked, Brooks and Warren attempted to get Ransom to repress the essay or at least to tone it down. Their re-

33. Caroline Gordon to Robert Penn Warren, n.d.

quest at first greatly annoyed Ransom, who complained to Tate, "The boys dealt pretty pedantically with my poor paper." When Ransom refused to change the essay, however, except insofar as to qualify his position by explaining that he intended "throwing a few stones at Shakespeare" only "out of respect to the intelligence of the editors and readers of a serious literary publication," the editors felt honor bound to print it as it read. Ransom was appeased and his pique quickly passed, but the essay brought him a great deal of adverse attention, brought no credit to the *Southern Review*, and at least briefly strained the relations between Brooks and Warren and their Vanderbilt mentor.[34]

Unfortunately quarrels within the Agrarian ranks could not always be so easily patched up and forgotten. The friendship between Brooks, Warren, and Ransom was an old and solid one based on mutual respect and shared habits of mind. Not so were some of the other Agrarian alliances which too often proved to be marriages of convenience. Stark Young, for example, whom W. J. Cash refers to as "an Agrarian by remote control," had been recruited by Tate and Davidson in 1929 as a contributor to *I'll Take My Stand* largely on the strength of his reputation. In many ways, however, he epitomized "the high caste Brahmins of the Old South" that the Fugitives had always fled.

Young had thought little enough of the Agrarian splinter at Baton Rouge from the beginning, and had chosen neither to attend the LSU Writers' Conference in 1935 nor to contribute any of his material to the *Southern Review*. When in 1936 Randall Jarrell reviewed Young's book *Feliciana*, real strain developed. Jarrell, in 1936, was a brilliant but brash young man with a fine critical sense but as yet little social sense or charity. Of the author, Jarrell had written, "Sometimes Mr. Young is snobbish, sometimes sentimental—[a flaw which Allen Tate had noted in a letter to Davidson as early as November 9, 1929]—sometimes he shows a disquieting admiration for moral perceptions or stylish effects which do not seem to the reader admirable at all. Mr. Young is too often, as one of his charac-

34. Tate, *Memoirs and Opinions*, 43, 44; John Crowe Ransom to Allen Tate, November 4, 1937, and November 17, 1937, quoted in Young, *Gentleman in a Dustcoat*, 294, 295.

ters says about himself, 'myself strutting in my own procession.'"
But "at his best," Jarrell conceded, Young "is decidedly worth reading," and the reviewer found "the most exquisite pleasure" in Young's
sketch "Echoes of Livorn."[35]

The editors requested that Jarrell "pull in his horns" somewhat,
but with some misgivings published his review in the fall number.
"I haven't seen what the review said of me, and probably never will,"
Young wrote to Allen Tate, but he nevertheless attacked Tate, Jarrell, and the *Southern Review* for what he considered an unjust attack on Ellen Glasgow's *Vein of Iron* in the same omnibus review.
Glasgow had never been an Agrarian favorite. Tate had confided to
Davidson that "she writes an abominable prose style, and that she is
one of the worst novelists in the world." An even worse damnation
from the Agrarian if not the New Critical point of view was Tate's
opinion that she represents "everything that I have learned to detest
in the transformation of the Virginia character—the feeble and of-
fensive assumption of past superiority" while hypocritically using as
her novels' heroes men whom she would not allow in her house.
Nevertheless, Tate had asked her to write an essay on "modern
Woman" for *Who Owns America?*, which she declined to do on account of her health and her lack of interest in "'modern woman' as
contrasted or divided from modern humanity."[36]

Glasgow complained to her friend Young in a letter dated March
11, 1936, that Tate had written to her "with great enthusiasm" of
Vein of Iron and had promised to review it in "that Southern Magazine (I have never seen a copy) that they publish in Baton Rouge."
In fact, Jarrell rather than Tate wrote the review and in it pointed
out "the heaviness of her style," which he characterized as "commonplace." "She is fond," accused Jarrell, "of the most obvious and
familiar rhetorical devices, and these are most evident in important
scenes. . . . In general her style is a good, average, useful style, but
when one compares it with a first-rate one, both its inadequacies

35. Randall Jarrell, "Ten Books," *Southern Review*, I (Fall, 1975), 405.
36. Stark Young to Allen Tate, March 21, 1936, in Pilkington (ed.), *Stark Young*,
I, 684; Allen Tate to Donald Davidson, December 12, 1929, Fain and Young (eds.),
The Literary Correspondence of Donald Davidson and Allen Tate, 243; Ellen Glasgow
to Stark Young, March 11, 1936, in Pilkington (ed.), *Stark Young*, I, 685.

and ornaments become obvious." Jarrell concluded by observing that *Vein of Iron* "was intended to be a great book . . . and yet the texture and details are too commonplace, the words of the characters too often have the value of something overheard in the street or over the telephone—no more." [37]

Warren agreed with Jarrell's assessment of Glasgow's work, writing to him soon after receiving the review with compliments "on some very astute remarks" concerning *Vein of Iron.* The author herself, however, was not pleased and began a series of outraged letters to Stark Young protesting "that vicious attack on me" in the *Southern Review.* Young, in turn, began to barrage Allen Tate with attacks on Jarrell's review in particular and on the *Review* and its editors in general. When Tate, seeking to avoid a quarrel, attempted to defend the *Review* by pointing out that as it was understaffed Brooks and Warren had perhaps erred in printing Jarrell's piece, Young snorted back, "I'd think a few people could deal with a *quarterly.* Or else drop it. Nobody compelled them to start it." [38]

Tate's retort was a stronger defense of his LSU friend's magazine, to which Young replied in terms of the utmost peevishness: "I agree with you that [the *Southern Review* is] the best literary critical journal, I suppose, which is saying little. As to a lot of critical writing I keep finding myself with the prayer that none of these Yankees see it." Specifically, Young attacked Ransom's piece, "The Tense of Poetry," in the summer, 1936, issue, the only issue which he had read, as "that imminence of sound and wind, Southern style" but concluded his pettish diatribe with the observation that "the number is at least dignified, which is ahead of anything now in New York." [39] The bitterness aroused over Jarrell's review effectively ended Young's involvement with the Agrarians. Although he invited both Brooks and Warren to contribute to his 1937 anthology, *A Southern Treasury of Life and Literature,* and called on Brooks in Baton Rouge some time after the incident, there remained but lit-

37. *Ibid.*; Jarrell, "Ten Books," 397.

38. Robert Penn Warren to Randall Jarrell, October 16, 1935; Ellen Glasgow to Stark Young, March 11, 1936, in Pilkington (ed.), *Stark Young* I, 685; Young to Tate, March 21, 1936, *ibid.*, 638–84.

39. Stark Young to Allen Tate, May 4, 1936, *ibid.*, 696.

tle cordiality between Young and his collaborators on *I'll Take My Stand*, and he formally disavowed any personal commitment to the Agrarian cause by 1940.

The most severe and bitter break in the *entente cordial* between the *Southern Review* and former Agrarians occurred in the winter months of 1937–1938 when John Gould Fletcher broke with his former friends over the editorial policy of the Baton Rouge journal. Fletcher, who had lived in England for twenty-five years, returned to his native Arkansas in 1933. Although a Fabian socialist through most of his years as an expatriate, Fletcher, who had contributed to *I'll Take My Stand*, joined the Agrarian group with alacrity, considering that its "defense of the culture of the Old South was in a way an answer to a prayer" that he had cherished since going abroad in 1908. Agrarianism gave him hope that "some part of America might in some way be delivered from the incubus of the machine."[40]

Fletcher was a friend of his fellow Arkansan Charles Pipkin, as well as of Warren, and while LSU was helping to underwrite the financial and editorial responsibilities of the *Southwest Review*, he was asked to serve on the board of editors by the Baton Rouge staff. Further evidence of the good will that existed between Warren and Fletcher may be found in the review that each did of the other's poetry. In 1932 Warren reviewed Fletcher's *Preludes and Symphonies* in *Poetry* magazine. In his article Warren stated that "these poems represent, to my mind, some of the most suggestive experiments in the resource of English verse made in the century of experiment." Although the review was not entirely commendatory, the effect was generally quite favorable, and ended with Warren's pronouncement that Fletcher's "work would be important, if for no other reason, on account of the extension of rhythmical possibilities of the language and the peculiar care bestowed upon the richness and variety of verse texture."[41] Fletcher responded in kind in 1935 in an article on "The Modern Southern Poets" in *Westminster Review*. In this eval-

40. John Gould Fletcher, quoted in Virginia Rock, "The Making and Meaning of *I'll Take My Stand*" (Ph.D. dissertation, University of Minnesota, 1961), 484–94.
41. Robert Penn Warren, "A Note on Three Southern Poets," *Poetry*, XL (May, 1932), 106.

uation of the work of Ransom, Davidson, Tate, and Warren, Fletcher found them to be as "important for the history of American poetry as Robinson or Frost of the Mid-Western poets."[42] He found Warren's verse promising—a happy combination of Tate's probing with Davidson's "facing-up." Warren's "Kentucky Mountain Farm," "Pondy Woods," and "The Return" were cited for special commendation.

Despite a sizable legacy from his father, Fletcher was "considerably hard up" by 1935 when he began to bombard the *Southern Review* office with manuscripts, requests for books to review, and demands for payment for previously published material. Notwithstanding his strained circumstances, the tone of Fletcher's letters was haughty and condescending in the extreme, and on many occasions he presumed to lecture Brooks and Warren on the way a little magazine should be properly run.

Nevertheless, on April 29, 1935, Warren commissioned Fletcher to review the plays of William Butler Yeats, and on November 8, he was asked to review S. Foster Damon's biography of Amy Lowell. Warren, with the greatest courtesy, explained that "there is no one better able to speak of this general subject than you, and we shall consider ourselves fortunate if you will undertake this task." In the same letter, however, Warren returned Fletcher's "Three Poems on Trees," which the *Review* had received on September 25. "About the poems, which we have had so long," Warren wrote, "we have decided not to use these. I do like very much the central section of 'Liveoak,' but neither Brooks nor I believe that these three, taken as a group, are among your best or most representative pieces." This rejection seems not to have impaired the friendship, for on March 20 Warren wrote again to his contributor assuring him that "I have the greatest personal esteem for you and have admired your work for a long time," and on December 13, Fletcher replied with a letter highly commendatory of the *Southern Review*'s first three issues. "Almost the only criticism I can make is that you devote a little too much space to controversy concerning poetry. The public is not interested in such controversy and it also does not read very far. Print

42. John Gould Fletcher, "The Modern Southern Poets," *Westminster Review*, XXIII (Winter, 1935), 229–51.

as much good poetry as you can, but don't let the magazine become a battleground for potential theorists," he advised.[43]

Fletcher's review of Yeats's *Wheels and Butterflies* was printed in the *Review*'s first issue, and the review-essay on Amy Lowell appeared in number four under the title "Herald of Imagism." But on November 2, 1937, Brooks and Warren returned Fletcher's article on a writers' conference in New York which he had attended the previous summer, with the explanation that "the general topic is one to which we have devoted a great deal of space in the past." Warren took pains to assure Fletcher that he did not mean to imply that his piece did not "bring freshness to the discussion," but explained that "the pressure on our space is greater every day."[44]

Fletcher's reaction was immediate and severe. "I have just received from you my article in defense of regionalism, which was called forth by my attendance at the American Writers' Conference . . . and by my hearing there the long paper attacking all Southern writers, which B. A. Botkin of the University of Oklahoma presented to that congress," he wrote to Warren on the 10th of November.

> I am sorry that you were not able to accept this paper, but the fact that you found it interesting enough to keep for so long emboldens me to send the enclosed. These poems are the fruit of my trip across the country from New Hampshire to Kansas last September. They are a series, and yet no doubt some of them are better than others. As I note in your review that you are continuing the admirable habit of giving every poet accepted considerable space, I am wondering whether you consider these poems—or some of them—worthy to appear alongside of others you have printed. . . . If the decision goes against me, I will accept it as final.[45]

The verdict was not to Fletcher's liking. On January 15, 1938, Cleanth Brooks returned a Fletcher short story, "The Harmonica," with the consolation that "the decision has not been easy to make,

43. Robert Penn Warren to John Gould Fletcher, April 29, 1935; Warren to Fletcher, March 20, 1935; Fletcher to Warren, December 13, 1935.
44. Warren to Fletcher, November 2, 1937.
45. John Gould Fletcher to Robert Penn Warren, November 10, 1937.

but we finally decided that in view of heavy commitments for the future we are having to send it back." Four days later Brooks also returned Fletcher's poems. "We have considered these poems long and seriously," he explained, "and though we may be making a mistake, we have finally decided not to use them."[46]

On the very day that his poems came home to Little Rock, Fletcher fired off a long and vitriolic letter to Pipkin attacking his junior editors. He complained bitterly of the editorial decisions of Brooks and Warren, claiming they showed a lack of sound critical judgment by refusing his verse. He further castigated them for running the poetry section "in the interest of a little clique—engaged in proving that Donne was a better poet than Shakespeare!—and that T. S. Eliot and his imitators are the only modern American poets worth reading." For his part, he concluded, "*I have resolved to have nothing more to do* with *The Southern Review*." Pipkin's only reply to Fletcher's tirade—"This morning your letter was received"—certainly gave Fletcher no satisfaction, although for several years he continued to send the *Southern Review* offices letters and proposed contributions. After his attempt at circumventing Brooks and Warren through Pipkin, none of Fletcher's poems were published and the only thing he succeeded in doing was driving away two loyal and talented friends.[47]

"It is sad," wrote Frank Owsley to Warren in February, 1938, "to be practically the last rose of summer or the last leaf of autumn." After 1938, he reported, he and Davidson would be the only Agrarians left in Nashville. Lytle, he said, was "more or less a commuter to Cornsilk," Allen Tate and Caroline Gordon were at the University of North Carolina at Greensboro, Ransom was gone to Kenyon, Wade to Georgia, Warren to LSU, and Herman Clarence Nixon "has gone Communist." Owsley reconciled his lonely lot with the memory of Jesus' commission to his disciples to go to the corners of the earth to preach the gospel, and in that connection also recalled that

46. Cleanth Brooks to John Gould Fletcher, January 15, 1938; Brooks to Fletcher, January 19, 1938.

47. John Gould Fletcher to Charles Pipkin, January 22, 1938; Pipkin to Fletcher, January 24, 1938.

"there were twelve apostles and one was named Judas Iscariot—is that Nixon's first name?" he asked Warren.[48]

By 1941, even the most unreconstructed of the group, Donald Davidson, wrote to Brooks that he was just about used up on the subject of the South. Brooks had requested that Davidson review W. J. Cash's *Mind of the South*, and although Davidson supplied the review, he made the observation that "times being what they are, I don't imagine that many more books about the South, of this type, will be written, or desired. The New Order is coming right down on us, fast, no less here, by domestic promotion than from the hostile region abroad." "I am feeling," he had recounted in another letter, "just as John Ransom says he is feeling—worn out with polemics."[49]

Although the political phase of their careers was largely over, the inner cadre of the Twelve Southerners and their closest followers maintained warm personal friendships and their work together was far from over. They continued to make contributions both as individuals and as the group somewhat loosely regarded as the southern New Critics.

48. Frank Owsley to Robert Penn Warren, February 17, 1938.
49. Donald Davidson to Cleanth Brooks, May 18, 1941; Donald Davidson to Robert Penn Warren, November 29, 1936.

SIX

A Southern Harvest

ROBERT PENN WARREN had first come to national attention as a promising poet—the junior member of the Fugitive group in Nashville—but the Fugitives turned away from the writing of verse to the defense of southern tradition as Agrarians, sweeping Warren along. "Briar Patch," Warren's contribution to *I'll Take My Stand*, and his Agrarian-oriented biography *John Brown: The Making of a Martyr* therefore obscured fine early poetry. Nevertheless, throughout his graduate career Warren continued to write imaginative literature, publishing his first piece of fiction while still at Oxford in 1931 and completing two early novels which were never published. His first love, however, remained poetry.

"Writing poetry is more pleasant than prose," he jokingly told one interviewer. "You can lie on your back and mumble longer before you have to get up and go back to the typewriter." This approach to composition is only somewhat tongue-in-cheek, for "poetry is really sound," Warren explained, and "you compose it out loud as you pace the floor mumbling."[1] By the time Warren arrived

1. Hal Boyle, interview with Robert Penn Warren, "A Correspondent's Notebook," Baton Rouge *Morning Advocate*, November 9, 1949.

at LSU he had composed a great deal of it. Besides the seventeen poems that he had contributed to *The Fugitive*, Warren's verse had appeared in the *Sewanee Review*, the *Saturday Review of Literature*, the *New Republic*, and *Poetry*, among many others. Between May, 1934, and January, 1935, Warren placed half a dozen poems in various little magazines, some of which remain among his best-known work. By the time of his move to Baton Rouge in September, 1934, Warren was reaching his full maturity as a poet and was committed to the writing of serious major poetry.

Not long after his arrival at LSU Warren began looking for a publisher to issue a collection of his works. Several years before, the firm of Brewer, Warren, and Putnam had announced a volume of Warren's poetry, but he withdrew it before they set it in type. "Since that time," he wrote to John Gould Fletcher in December, 1934, "I have made little effort towards publication." Warren felt that "the time was inauspicious," and that no publishing house would risk the publishing of his poems. Further, he wanted to get out a better selection than he might have offered prior to his prolific seasons in the first years of the 1930s. With a new crop of poems, however, he told Fletcher that he was "now on the verge of taking up the matter actively to see what can be done."[2]

Warren's search for a publisher led him to the Alcestis Press, which, in February, 1935, brought out his first volume of verse, *Thirty-six Poems*. The depth of the Depression bore out Warren's observation to Donald Davidson that "I don't imagine it's a good time to have anything knocking around the bookstores now," but the new book did bring considerable critical recognition to its author's talents. John Crowe Ransom, for example, sent a letter of congratulations, swearing that "the *Thirty-six Poems* are much the biggest literary event lately, and the best 'first' volume ever published probably." And the Poetry Society of South Carolina demonstrated its approval by awarding Warren the first of his three Caroline Sinkler Prizes. Most of the critical attention given to *Thirty-six Poems* centered on their pedigree. Reviewers pointed out Warren's debt to

2. Warren to John Gould Fletcher, December 13, 1935.

the Nashville poets and to T. S. Eliot, but the more astute of them noted, too, that he was passing beyond the formidable influences of his apprenticeship and beginning to demonstrate an independence of style which marked his as "one of the most serious and gifted intelligences of his generation."[3]

Between 1935 and 1937 most of the *Thirty-six Poems* were placed in a number of prestigious little magazines. The *Virginia Quarterly Review*, for example, took "Resolution" and "History"; Ransom at the *Kenyon Review* considered "Love's Parable" "quite a feature to get hold of"; *Poetry* presented its Helen Haire Levinson Prize "to Robert Penn Warren of Baton Rouge, for 'The Garden' . . . and for earlier works printed in this magazine"; *The Nation* ran "Crime"; and the *Southern Review* published "Ransom" and "Letter from a Coward to a Hero," the only poems that Warren ever submitted to his own magazine.[4] During that same period, however, only seven new poems joined them in print—a testament to Warren's passion for exacting craftsmanship and his flat refusal to submit a line which was not as finely honed as his effort and talent could make it.

Warren took leave from LSU tne summer following the publication of *Thirty-six Poems*, first to visit his old graduate school friends at Berkeley and then to teach at two writers' conferences. The first half of July he spent teaching at the University of Montana. He then moved to the University of Colorado, where he joined Robert Frost and Thomas Wolfe for a three-week teaching assignment at Boulder. Only two months earlier Warren had reviewed Wolfe's newest novel, *Of Time and the River*, which he had criticized as merely "an attempt to exploit directly and naïvely the personal experience and self-defined personality in art." Far from taking offense, however, Wolfe sent his most promising protégé, Thomas H. Thompson, to LSU to study with Warren. Warren "could make friends with

3. Warren to Donald Davidson, July 13, 1936; John Crowe Ransom to Warren, February 15, 1935; Morton D. Zabel, "Problems of Knowledge: *Thirty-six Poems*," *Poetry*, XLVIII (April, 1936), 37.

4. Ransom to Brooks, February 10, 1940; "Announcement of Awards," *Poetry*, XLIX (November, 1936), 104–106.

anybody," observed his student Robert Lowell, "even showy writer giants that [he] had slaughtered in a review."[5]

As if his duties as teacher, editor, and poet were insufficient, Warren was also becoming a dedicated writer of prose fiction. "I stumbled onto fiction rather late," he once remarked. "For years I didn't have much interest in fiction, that is in college. I was reading my head off in poetry, Elizabethan and the moderns, Yeats, Hardy, Eliot, Hart Crane," but in the spring of 1930, while he was still at Oxford, Paul Rosenfeld who, with Van Wyck Brooks and Lewis Mumford, was editing the *American Caravan*, wrote to Warren asking for a long story. Rosenfeld, Warren recalls, "had had the patience one evening to listen to me blowing off about nightrider stories from my boyhood," and had become convinced of Warren's talent as a storyteller. "So Oxford and homesickness, or at least back-homeward looking, and Paul Rosenfeld" conspired to make him write "Prime Leaf," a novelette which appeared in *American Caravan IV.* "I remember playing hooky from academic work to write that thing," he told Ralph Ellison, "and the discovery that you could really enjoy trying to write fiction. It was a new way of looking at things, and my head was full of the way objects looked in Kentucky."[6]

Warren's academic work, his poetry, criticism, and Agrarian writing kept him from any more fiction for a number of years, but by 1933 he had completed the manuscript of a novel. Despite the best efforts of Allen Tate and others of Warren's friends the book was never published, so Warren had been in Baton Rouge for more than a year and a half before his second piece of fiction appeared in print. This time, however, he placed two short stories in the quarterlies in rapid succession. The March–April 1935 issue of *The Magazine* ran "Testament of Flood," a piquant story of the pain and innocence of first love, and the April, 1935, *Virginia Quarterly Review* published "Her Own People," a story recounting the insensitivity of both the white and black communities of a small Tennessee town to the plight of a lonely Negro girl.

5. Robert Penn Warren, "A Note on the Hamlet of Thomas Wolfe," *American Review*, V (May, 1935), 191–208; Robert Lowell, "Louisiana State University, 1940," *Day by Day* (New York, 1977), 25.
6. Warren, in Cowley (ed.), *Writers at Work*, 191.

Even with a full teaching schedule Warren committed himself to writing six days a week. The pace that he set for himself was a grueling one, but the pleasure of creation together with "some prospect of pleasure at the day's end, like carrots held out in front of a donkey," made him stick to it. All that he required was "a place to put a typewriter, a lot of cigarettes, something to lie down on (grass will do)—to pretend you're thinking—and no sound of the human voice." Warren's method, too, was a demanding one. "I try never to depend on later revision," he said. "Don't leave a page until you have it as near what you want as you can make it that day." As for his "place to put a typewriter," former Warren graduate student Thomas H. Thompson remembers seeing the small outbuilding where Warren did his writing. There "his typewriter stood on an inch-thick carpet of paper scraps yellowed and decaying into the mat." No less spartan than the pace that Warren set for himself, they were "absolutely desolate surroundings," Thompson recalls.[7]

Such diligence and hard work paid off. Warren's next short story, "When the Light Gets Green," a fictionalized memoir of the author's boyhood in western Kentucky, won an honorable mention in the Edward J. O'Brien Short Story Collection of 1937 and the high praise of many of Warren's friends and colleagues. To Caroline Gordon, for example, "When the Light Gets Green" was "one of the finest—I believe the most perfect—story written by a contemporary."[8] Better news yet, however, came on the night of June 13, 1936, when Robert W. Linscott, an official of the Houghton Mifflin publishing company, announced the awarding of the $1,000 Houghton Mifflin Literary Fellowship to Robert Penn Warren on the basis of his tale of the Kentucky "Black Patch War" of 1905, "Prime Leaf." With the cash prize came a contract for Warren's yet unwritten first novel.

As early as January, 1936, Warren had indicated to Herbert Agar that he was "trying to get the novel started." His busy schedule, however, left him little time for fiction. At the end of the spring semester Warren took leave of his teaching duties at LSU and moved

7. R[oland] G[elatt], "The Author," *Saturday Review of Literature*, June 24, 1950, p. 11; Thompson to author, November 21, 1979.
8. Caroline Gordon to Warren [1936].

to a single-room building near Amite, Louisiana, which had once been a creamery. There he spent the first part of the summer working on *An Approach to Literature*, the first of the famous Brooks and Warren textbooks, and whiling away his afternoons attending the murder trial of an old Negro who had shot a young companion. The old man was popular with the white citizens of Amite, and all were relieved when, at the last moment, he entered a plea of "guilty of manslaughter," thus saving himself from hanging. He had hung doggedly to his plea of "not guilty" because he felt no guilt over killing a man "for talking meanness against his baby-girl daughter." This incident later found its way into Warren's 1964 novel *Flood*.[9]

From Amite, Warren returned to Boulder for his second term at the Colorado Writer's Conference. From mid-July through the first week in August, Warren gave two or three talks per week and a public lecture, participated in two round-table debates with other members of the staff, and read scores of manuscripts and conferred with their young writers. Leaving Boulder, Warren went on to Nashville to visit Ransom, Davidson, and Owsley and to gather background information for his projected novel. "I never saw him take notes," recalls Thomas Thompson, "and he advised me against it." Outlining "impedes the imagination," he warned. Instead, says Thompson, "he carries everything around in his head."[10]

Warren agonized over the book for nearly a year without being quite able to come to grips with it. Then, in January, 1937, after spending Christmas vacation in Mexico, Warren received from Ferris Greenslet of Houghton Mifflin a request for several chapters by May 1. "That, as you may guess," Warren wrote to Frank Owsley, "caused some consternation in my bosom." Warren told his old friend that "the thing had been on the verge of getting started for several months," but that he "couldn't find the exact center for it somehow." To his obvious relief he could report in March that he was underway with "some two chapters, rather long ones, already finished." As to the quality of the manuscript, however, the fledgling

9. Robert Penn Warren to Herbert Agar, January 19, 1936; Warren, in Cowley (ed.), *Writers at Work*, 205.
10. Interview with Thomas Thompson, November 21, 1979.

novelist was less certain. "One day," he told Owsley, "when I read over what I have done, I get rather complacent; the next I get suicidal." By April 15 he was able to report a hundred finished pages, but saw that the complete novel "promised to be rather long." He decided to do no teaching in the summer of 1937 and so hoped "to be able to break the back of the thing then." With an optimism born of his recent creative spurt, Warren planned "to finish it by January at the latest." [11]

Rather than return to Boulder in July, Warren resigned his position on the staff of the writers' conference and resolved to devote all summer to the novel "even if I eat wild honey and locusts." John Crowe Ransom was signed up as a member of the Boulder faculty, and Warren regretted not being able to join his friend and mentor there, but, as he explained, he was "pretty steamed up" about the novel and "must have a long period of uninterrupted work." The Warrens for a while toyed with the idea of taking advantage of the favorable rate of exchange and spending their summer in Mexico, but decided instead to accept Howard and Dorothy Baker's invitation to join them in a long working vacation in northern California. [12]

Driving first to Nashville, Warren was able to see his former teacher after all. Appropriately, Warren represented the *Southern Review* at a dinner honoring John Crowe Ransom "for long and distinguished service to literature." After a brief return to Baton Rouge the Warrens drove west to California, reaching Oakland on July 27. The next day they and the Bakers departed for Clear Lake, in a remote part of northern California where they were to spend the rest of the summer. Dorothy Baker was at work on her first novel, *Young Man with a Horn*, and Warren managed to finish about 80,000 words of his novel. "But," he lamented to Herbert Agar, "I am nowhere near the end. The scale of the thing has turned out to be much larger than I had anticipated, and I am not near the middle yet." [13]

11. Robert Penn Warren to Frank Owsley, March 22, 1937; Owsley to Warren, April 15, 1937; Warren to Herbert Agar, October 20, 1937.

12. Robert Penn Warren to Frank Owsley, March 22, 1937; Warren to John Crowe Ransom, February 24, 1937.

13. Warren to Herbert Agar, October 20, 1937.

At the end of October he wrote again to Agar that he had not "been able to get seriously at the thing" since his return from the West, but that he had "been able to complete a couple of poems." One of these, "Bearded Oaks," is one of the few Warren poems which show a definite relationship to the poet's Louisiana environment. Inspired by the grounds of the Grace Episcopal Church in St. Francisville, a mile or two from Oakley Plantation where John James Audubon lived and painted, Warren remembers the time, "in Louisiana, up in West Feliciana, long ago, when I used to go there and stand in the silence of the moss-draped oaks of the old graveyard." Most memorable to the poet was "that palpable silence, the never-violated shadow of the spreading live oaks and the windless gray garlands of moss, [which] seemed to absorb everything into a Platonic certainty—even human pain." [14]

Ransom, responding to "Bearded Oaks" and some work in progress which Warren had sent to him, including an early draft of "The Ballad of Billie Potts," saw these recent poems as "the clearest sort of evidence that Warren's is about the best-techniqued talent we have today." Regarding Warren's novel in progress, Ransom commented that he should "think the Muses are at civil war if the fiction leads you to stop the poetry," but felt that if the recent poems were any indication, "they are going to accommodate their rivalry." Ransom had not yet seen any of the novel and admitted that he tended "to think of Warren as Warren the poet. But it is easy," he concluded, "to compound a definition if we have to." [15]

In November it became necessary to further compound the definition of Warren as teacher-critic-poet-novelist-short story writer-and editor to include anthologist, for in that month Houghton Mifflin released his collection of short stories by southern writers, *A Southern Harvest*. Dedicated to Ransom, the volume included stories by a number of Warren's contemporaries. Not only had Warren chosen stories by a number of his fellow Agrarians, but he had selected contributions from Katherine Anne Porter, William Faulkner, Thomas

14. Robert Penn Warren to Herbert Agar, October 20, 1937; Robert Penn Warren, *Who Speaks for the Negro?* (New York, 1965), 10.
15. John Crowe Ransom to Robert Penn Warren, November 17, 1937.

Wolfe, Lyle Saxon, Roark Bradford, and a number of others. Ransom quickly mailed his thanks and congratulations to the editor. "It is certainly a distinguished book," he wrote, "and it is pretty fine to be a dedicatee. I relish the honor and the friendly action both." As for the volume itself, Ransom felt it to be "a most unusual sort of book; more alive, more contemporary, with more stuff in it than other books" of its type. Warren's friend Howard Baker was even more commendatory toward *A Southern Harvest*, calling it "the best collection of American short stories there is." And the Agrarians were in universal agreement. "The *Southern Harvest* does you and the region proud," wrote John Peale Bishop. Davidson added that "just such a collection has a real place" as a counterweight to the progressive, anti-traditional southern anthologies of "Caldwell and Company," and Caroline Gordon's only complaint was that Warren had not included his own story "When the Light Gets Green." [16]

Although generally well received by the metropolitan critics, *A Southern Harvest* was occasionally attacked for presenting stories of unequal value or for its editor's "regrettable omissions." The principal objection to *A Southern Harvest*, however, came from the Marxist critics, who objected to the volume's regional bias and to Warren's Agrarianism. Eleanor Clark, for example, sensed a "defensiveness" in Warren's introduction, "as if the 'Renaissance' which he describes, when forced to appear outside its special meeting-place, were not quite sure of its values." She saw nothing unique or exclusive about writing in the South: "We can only deduce," she wrote, "that what does belong to them 'exclusively' is nothing but a hypersensitive resistance to Marxism, and in spite of this resistance many of them are so much more of their time than of their region that their work forms part of the general direction of writing everywhere." [17]

Warren had gone on record numerous times defining regional literature. In his essays "Not Local Color" and "Literature as a Symp-

16. John Crowe Ransom to Warren, November 17, 1937; Howard Baker to Warren, November 13, 1937; John Peale Bishop to Warren, November 24, 1937; Donald Davidson to Warren, December 3, 1937; Caroline Gordon to Warren, n.d.
17. Eleanor Clark, "No More Swans," *Partisan Review*, IV (March, 1938), 56–58.

tom" he explained that art "cannot be achieved without consideration of both time and place in a very special sense." Mere local color,
however, the quaint or picturesque for its own sake, is particularly
distasteful to the writer who bases his art on a tradition such as that
of the Old South. The writer who exploits local color merely for its
own sake, Warren maintained, produces a product that is "incom-
plete and unphilosophical." He does not "provide a framework in
which human action has more than immediate and adventitious
significance." In such writing "manners tend to be substituted for
value, and costume and *decor* for an essential relationship between
man and his background, both natural and social." Although he admitted that he "should be the last to disparage the [writer's] agrarian
pieties," he insisted that "if poetry of the soil is to be written," that
soil must serve as the clay from which the brick of a philosophical structure is made and not be used solely for the sake of "lyric
glibness."[18]

In his own fiction Warren continued to draw from scenes of his
Kentucky boyhood but endowed those memories with themes of
universal significance. In his next short story, "Christmas Gift," for
example, he examined the growth of mutual respect and friendship
between an improbable pair of people, a small-town doctor and a
small boy from a family of sharecroppers. Although this story was
selected for the O. Henry Memorial Award collection of 1937, Caroline Gordon, one of Warren's staunchest partisans and most out-
spoken critics, chided him for his too-facile writing technique and
challenged him to tasks which would be more demanding of his talent. "You have written one short story that is as good as any in the
Dubliners," she wrote to him, but she continued that he had written
still others "that are of the kind that Joyce was too smart to write."
Although Warren shared in large measure Joyce's talent for fine
craftsmanship in short story writing, Gordon charged that "technique [is not] worth a damn if passion [does not] infuse every detail
of the stories with life." In Warren's inferior short stories, she com-

18. Robert Penn Warren, "Not Local Color," *Virginia Quarterly Review*, VIII
(January, 1932), 154; Robert Penn Warren, "Set in a Silver Sea," *Poetry*, XLVI (September, 1935), 346–49.

plained, one is too aware of the method and short-changed on genuine emotion. Rather than continue to waste his talent on mediocre
short stories, Gordon insisted, Warren should get on with his novel.[19]

Whether because of Caroline Gordon's advice or his own sense of
where his true interest lay, Warren did give up the short story for
four years and return to his abandoned novel. "I write very few"
stories, Warren informed Lambert Davis at Harcourt, Brace. "My
real interest in fiction is in the novel. . . . So stories are out, or at
least, out for years to come. I only write them when I get a special
itch."[20] The itch was to strike but once more while Warren was in
Baton Rouge. His last story there did not come until the winter of
1941 when he placed "Goodwood Comes Back," the narrative of the
rise and fall of a big-league baseball player from a rural Kentucky
community, in the *Southern Review*.

At about the same time that "Christmas Gift" was going to press
and *A Southern Harvest* was appearing in the bookstores, Warren
wrote to Owsley that he was "running so far behind on my novel
that I see no hope for me if I do not take full advantage of the
[Christmas] holidays for work. I did manage to get a lot done this
summer, up to some 80,000 words, but the fall has been so cluttered
that I have done only a chapter and a half since my return." Warren
limited his critical writing in 1937 to one brief review for *Poetry*, a
rather curt commentary on Robinson Jeffers' *Solstice and Other
Poems*, and by the end of the year was able to report that he was
feeling somewhat better about his saga of the Black Patch War and
the personal struggle of Percy Munn, his novel's protagonist. "Mr.
Munn is still with me," he wrote to his friend Bertrand Bronson at
the University of California. "The whole thing has been getting
much longer. I grievously miscalculated the scale of the thing. I still
have some four or five chapters to do, but I am approaching them
with some renewed energy, for yesterday I got a report from Houghton Mifflin on the first ten. They state their pleasure in terms that

19. Caroline Gordon to Warren, n.d.
20. Robert Penn Warren to Lambert Davis, December 17, 1941.

raise hopes for a slight commercial success. And Lord knows that wouldn't hurt my feelings any."[21]

Warren's novel "was a tremendously complicated book to write," said his Baton Rouge neighbor, Katherine Anne Porter, but, she observed, he "went through it as though he was simply making notes for a journal," snatching every available odd moment to add a line or a paragraph. Writing on such a schedule and sharing his time with so many other projects, Warren might never have finished the novel had he not, with the end of the spring semester, taken leave from LSU, and, on the twenty-eighth of May, 1938, set sail from Savannah, Georgia, on a freighter bound for Italy. There he would write and study Italian at the University for Foreigners at Perugia. "Everybody who writes," Gertrude Stein had once observed, "is interested in living inside themselves in order to tell what is inside themselves. That is why writers have two countries." Warren took this belief both metaphorically and literally. "I like to write in foreign countries," he said, "where the language is not your own, and you are forced into yourself in a special way." Hearing regularly only a foreign tongue, Warren felt that he could reserve his own language more effectively for purposes of composition, and even if Italy offered little by way of seclusion, "at least the distractions are different," he observed. When he returned to Baton Rouge in the fall the novel was complete and he had written a few poems besides. By October he had heard from his editor, Robert Linscott, that Houghton Mifflin was beginning to set up the proofs for the novel and an early spring publication was assured.[22]

At the end of the fall semester the Warrens made a trip North, he to read a paper at the convention of the Modern Language Association in New York the last week in December, and Mrs. Warren to visit with the Ransoms while her husband was away. Warren spent five days in Gambier on his way back to Baton Rouge, carrying on

21. Robert Penn Warren to Frank Owsley, November 30, 1937; Robert Penn Warren to Bertrand Bronson, January 14, 1938.

22. Katherine Anne Porter in Robert van Gelder, *Writers and Writing*, 42–43; Gertrude Stein, quoted in Frederick J. Hoffman, *The 20's* (New York, 1965), 43; Robert Penn Warren, "Some Important Fall Authors," 10.

what Ransom called "the best conversation I've had since Tennessee." Waiting for Warren in the *Southern Review* office when he returned was Ransom's lengthy and thoughtful critique of the novel. Ransom had finished reading the manuscript after the Warrens had left and found the last part to be "mighty fine." "The novel," he concluded, "is a philosophical one," and he compared Warren's protagonist to "my Lord Hamlet" and the dilemma which he confronts. He also found points of comparison between Warren's themes and those treated by Allen Tate in his 1938 novel, *The Fathers.* "The Ravage of civilization," he wrote, "is of course the pale cast of thought induced in sensitive people; it's man looking for his lost motives." Although Tate and Warren treat common themes, Ransom saw their approaches as quite different. "In Tate," he wrote, "one man doesn't lose his motives, though they are ineffective ones; another man does and he's a goner." [23]

Ironically, Ransom's chief complaint with Warren's book was the "certain sense of oddness in the materials." As he told Tate later in the month, he wished that the material were "*conventionally* heroic instead of being about the odd and isolated Kentucky night riders." Ransom confessed to probably being "very sensitive about localism" since leaving Tennessee for Ohio, but thought that "those ungainly readers from Houghton Mifflin" would undoubtedly expect such a "strange" story to be so only for strangeness' sake and thus forget to look for more. "That," he was convinced, "will be a usual stumbling block for the general run of readers." Although Ransom stressed this point rather strongly, he told Warren, "I'm far from feeling dogmatic about this," and concluded that the novel "is about the smoothest best-sustained piece of narrative I've seen in many a day. God bless it." [24]

More good news awaited Warren's return to Baton Rouge, for on January 24 he learned that Eyre and Spotswood had purchased the English rights to the new novel, an excerpt from which, entitled

23. Ransom to Warren, January 4, 1939.
24. John Crowe Ransom to Allen Tate, January 31, 1939, quoted in Young, *Gentleman in a Dustcoat,* 329–30; John Crowe Ransom to Robert Penn Warren, January 4, 1939.

"How Willie Proudfit Came Home," ran in the winter number of the *Southern Review*. Willie Proudfit's tale is of the early days of the American frontier, and in the context of the complete novel strikes an effective counterpoint to the terrorism in turn-of-the-century Kentucky with its idyllic theme of the freedom and innocence of a simpler era. Howard Baker, especially, responded heartily to the narrative of Willie Proudfit's adventures. Feeling that Warren had successfully recovered from the lapse of emotional involvement with his material, Baker found in Warren's prose "the power of emotionally grasped material to express reflective significance . . . perfectly realized." Although "rich in elemental feelings and language," the tale "teaches the limitations of feelings," Baker concluded.[25] Warren's California friend was but one of the story's many fans, and Edward O'Brien selected it for his 1939 collection of *Best Short Stories*.

Night Rider appeared on March 14, 1939, to a hail of critical acclaim. The plot of the novel is a thrilling one, dealing with the Black Patch Tobacco War, the same material that Warren had worked before in "Prime Leaf." The "war" pitted the members of the Tobacco Trust against the American Tobacco Company buyers, non-trust farmers, and, ultimately, against the federal troops who were sent in to quell the violence. The novel's principal character, a young lawyer named Percy Munn, is essentially an idealistic liberal whose initial peripheral involvement with the farmers' union draws him deeper and deeper into a cause for which he has but little genuine sympathy and toward his inevitable doom.

The regional flavor of *Night Rider* is strong and true, illustrating Warren's contention that "art cannot be achieved without consideration of both time and place in a very special sense." Christopher Isherwood found that *Night Rider* "reconstructs an entire world." Warren's ability to re-create the world of his boyhood for Isherwood, "a foreigner, without previous knowledge of the social background, is a measure of his great success."[26]

25. Howard Baker, "In Praise of the Novel," *Southern Review*, V (Spring, 1940), 793.

26. Christopher Isherwood, "Tragic Liberal," *New Republic*, May 31, 1939, p. 108.

The author went to great pains, however, to emphasize his conviction that *Night Rider* was not a piece of historical fiction. "The events belong to my early childhood," he told Ralph Ellison. "I remember the troops coming in when martial law was declared in that part of Kentucky. When I wrote the novel I wasn't thinking of it as history." In fact, he told the members of the Baton Rouge Quota Club, although "many of the incidents included in the book happened before I was able to write" they were the product of a still lively oral tradition in Kentucky and northern Tennessee where he had gleaned them "from conversations at the village store and under the maple trees where groups gathered on Sunday afternoons."[27]

Warren's Nashville friends had great praise for *Night Rider*. Davidson was the first to send his congratulations to Warren, calling it "a genuinely fine novel" which "stirred me (sated novel-reader that I am, too) right down to the bone-marrow. Hurrah for Red and his novel." Davidson passed his copy along to Frank Owsley, who wrote that "there have been few books—novels—that have gripped me as much as this one did. The action was powerful, filled with suspense and was marching like a well organized army to the end." Still profoundly committed to the Agrarian cause, Owsley predicted, as had Ransom, that *Night Rider* would never achieve the status that it deserved due to the cultural myopia of the North and the economic bondage of the South. "This book, despite its fine artistry," he ironically remarked, "should be a best seller—except for one thing: the jews who buy the books and the yankees who buy the books do not know a tobacco stalk from a rag weed; nor do they know that there exist any such powerful, rugged 'bastards' as our southern countryside produces." If the South "were a free people," he concluded, "and owned our own country and its wealth and could afford to buy books, you would sell half a million copies. As it is, the city bastards will probably not buy over fifteen or twenty thousand copies of the best novel that has come out in God knows when in the English language."[28]

27. Warren, in Cowley (ed.), *Writers at Work*, 187; Baton Rouge *State-Times*, May 31, 1939, p. 15.

28. Donald Davidson to Robert Penn Warren, March 19, 1939; Frank Owsley to Warren, March 20, 1939; Owsley to Warren, April 13, 1939.

Despite Owsley's and Ransom's dire predictions that the north-east literary establishment would ignore the book or, worse, misunderstand it, Warren's novel proved his own dictum that good literature is always exportable whatever its setting. Critics for the New York *Times'* "Books of the Times" and all of the other New York weekly book review supplements agreed *Night Rider* was the most distinguished novel of the season and among the best first novels ever. Isherwood and Baker both commented at length on the novel's thrilling action scenes and its author's wonderful talent for writing believable dialogue—what Isherwood called the "literary virtue of making people talk." These virtues did not escape the notice of Hollywood, and on April 2 Warren told a Baton Rouge newspaper reporter that negotiations for the movie rights to *Night Rider* were underway but still "up in the air."[29]

To Warren's disappointment, movie negotiations for *Night Rider* failed to materialize, but he was compensated by the award of $2,500 in March, 1939 by the John Simon Guggenheim Memorial Fellowship committee. Warren was one of sixty-nine recipients that year, others being Richard Wright for *Uncle Tom's Children* and John McGrady, a twenty-seven year old New Orleans painter, for "Swing Low Sweet Chariot," a collection of scenes of Negro life in the Deep South. With the Guggenheim award money Warren planned to write his second novel, this one of life in the South during the boom and depression of the 1920s, "a period of reordering of social objectives and social ideals."[30]

Since his days at Vanderbilt Warren had seen the decade of the twenties as a crucial one in American history and especially in the history of the South. The shifts of values that took place with the urbanization and industrialization of the upper South had inherent in them the sort of drama he wished to treat in terms of personal reactions to the political and economic issues of the era. The locale of the novel was to be that of a southern city much like Nashville, and the characters were to include a college football player, hired by a broker because of his athletic ability, a group of academic people, a

29. Isherwood, "Tragic Liberal," 108; Baton Rouge *Morning Advocate*, April 2, 1939, p. 8.
30. "Second Southern Novel," *LSU Alumni News*, XV (March, 1939), 3, 4.

teacher in a Negro college, a wealthy banker who is also a breeder of fine horses, the father of the football player (a small farmer), and a young geologist working for the banker. The newly published novelist got off to a swift start on his second novel, tentatively titled "And Pastures New" from Milton's "Lycidas" and, he told an interviewer from the Baton Rouge *Morning Advocate*, "as it looks now, it will be a long book, and I couldn't say when it will be finished."[31]

Warren spent June of 1939 in middle Tennessee and Kentucky gathering material for the novel and visiting with Donald Davidson. The Guggenheim Fellowship took the Warrens to Italy in the summer, where they met John E. Palmer, then a Rhodes scholar at Oxford. The three moved to a villa on the Sirmione Peninsula, where Catullus had lived and worked 2,000 years before and not far from Mrs. Warren's ancestral home of Brescia. When England declared war on Germany on September 3, Palmer was recalled to Oxford and the Warrens moved down to Naples. The international situation was explosive, and nowhere was the tension more palpable than in Italy, but, as Warren later recounted, "We could not have got passage if we had tried, so we remained." The Warrens did, in fact, arrange tentative booking on the *Excambrion*, which was to sail from Genoa on October 18, but Italy clung feebly to its neutrality, and so, making virtue of necessity, the Warrens settled down to await developments. After the first few weeks the excitement died away, Warren said, and "things went along pretty much as usual."[32]

If the Warrens felt "settled" in precariously neutral Italy, their friends in the States were considerably less comfortable about their safety. "Do you know whether Red has been torpedoed, bombed, or is suffering from undernourishment somewhere in Italy?" Owsley asked of Cleanth Brooks on October 12. Brooks's reply mentioned the Warrens's tentative sailing date and their plans to remain if Mussolini stayed out of the war, and in answer to a similar question from Donald Davidson later in the month Brooks said that although he had had little word from Warren due to the strict censorship of

31. Baton Rouge *Morning Advocate*, April 2, 1939, p. 8.
32. Baton Rouge *State-Times*, September 5, 1939, p. 12; Robert Penn Warren, untitled statement in *Wilson Library Bulletin*, XIII (June, 1939), 652.

the mails, he tended to believe that they would stay, "for conditions seem more auspicious for continued peace in Italy at this time than when Red wrote over a month ago."[33]

Through the fall and winter of 1939 Warren worked on a play, his novel, and a few poems while Russia invaded Finland, Lithuania, Latvia, and Estonia. With the coming of spring, Germany overran Denmark and Norway, but still France and England remained calm and Italy remained neutral. Then, on May 10, 1940, the quiet of the "phony war" was shattered as Nazi panzer divisions knifed across the Low Countries. Four days later, with the Dutch Army surrendered and the Belgians routed, the Germans crossed the Meuse into France. That same day Lincoln Fitzell wrote to Brooks that he was worried about his old Berkeley classmate. "From this morning's radio report it appears that Italy is about to 'enter the whirlpool,'" he wrote. "Consequently we are becoming very anxious." Brooks's reply was somewhat reassuring. Although he had had no direct report from Warren for some time, he told Fitzell that he was sure in his own mind "that the advice of the State Department to all Americans in Italy has moved him out or will have him out in a few days."[34]

The next word from Warren was that he was indeed leaving Italy as soon as possible. In a message postmarked Rome, May 13, Warren indicated that he and his wife would be sailing from Naples on the fifteenth aboard the *Conte de Savoie*. By the end of the month, however, no further word had been received, and Brooks wrote to Davidson expressing his fears. "All of us here warned Red as well as we could before he set off to Italy that we felt it was going to be a gamble to hope to find peace and security in that country at the present time." The last specific word that Brooks had had from Warren was that his passport would expire on May 15 and must be renewed. "My hope," wrote Brooks, "is that the government refused to renew it, and that he is now nearing the shores of this country."[35]

33. Frank Owsley to Cleanth Brooks, October 12, 1939; Brooks to Owsley, October 16, 1939.
34. Lincoln Fitzell to Cleanth Brooks, May 14, 1940; Brooks to Fitzell, May 22, 1940.
35. Brooks to Donald Davidson, May 29, 1940.

With the drastic censorship of the Italian press, Warren had not been able to tell until late spring what part Italy would play in the spreading European war. Then, on June 10, 1940, Mussolini threw in his lot with Hitler and invaded crippled France. When it could no longer be doubted that Italy would become a part of the Central European Axis, the Warrens, with the aid of their friend P. M. Pasinetti, an Italian national and contributor to the *Southern Review*, secured passage on the *Washington* and finally started on the way back to America. "Thank goodness we heard from Red this morning," Fitzell wrote to Brooks on June 14. "He is safely back and temporarily residing in North Bennington, Vermont." The passage had been an interesting but safe one. "We came over with refugees from Holland, Belgium, and Norway," Warren reported, and British authorities stopped the ship at Gibraltar and removed a number of individuals reported to be enemy agents. Still the ship was quite packed, "but the officers handled the crowd very well indeed and within the first twenty-four hours had everything settled down very nicely."[36]

After their landfall in New York the Warrens went to Bennington to confer with Francis Fergusson, drama critic and director, about Warren's play, and from there to Olivet College where Warren joined Katherine Anne Porter, John Peale Bishop, and Sherwood Anderson on the staff of the summer writers' program. From Olivet Warren moved on to Colorado to reclaim his old post on the University of Colorado's writers' conference from July 22 through August 9. Only after a stop at Gambier to visit Ransom did Warren return to Baton Rouge, having been away for so long that, with the frantic building program still going on, he claimed hardly to recognize the place.

Back in Baton Rouge after their Italian interlude, the Warrens purchased a new home in the country south of town and were nearly "turned grey" by their remodeling efforts during the period of wartime rationing restrictions. Set beside a bayou and surrounded by fifteen acres of live oaks, this was the home in which Warren thought to live out his days. "I loved it there," he later commented,

36. Lincoln Fitzell to Brooks, June 14, 1940; Baton Rouge *State-Times*, September 17, 1940, p. 2.

but after only a single semester at LSU he again took leave, this time to serve for a semester as visiting lecturer in fiction at the University of Iowa's School of Letters.[37] The period from his return from Italy through the spring of 1942 became Warren's most prolific period of critical writing to that date. Not only was he much involved in work on the third of his and Brooks's influential textbooks, *Understanding Fiction*, but during this time he also turned out a number of significant book reviews and critical essays.

Through the Baton Rouge years Warren had done a great many book reviews and a fair number of critical articles, leading Morton D. Zabel to remark in 1939 that as a critic he "is developing toward the size and weight of first rank importance." Among the most significant critical efforts of this period are his articles on *Of Time and the River* ("A Note on the Hamlet of Thomas Wolfe"), Katherine Anne Porter ("Irony with a Center"), and John Crowe Ransom ("Pure and Impure Poetry"), this last being his *Measures* lecture to the Creative Arts Program at Princeton. Although encouraged to submit a collection of his critical work to Harcourt, Brace in 1941, Warren felt that his critical output was not yet of sufficient volume or worth to merit being issued in a single volume. "Some day I may put together some essays," he told his editor, "but not soon." Not until 1958 did Warren's *Selected Essays* appear, with three of its ten essays emanating from the LSU period.[38]

As Warren began the fall semester of 1940 his new novel was nearing completion. The basic plot, setting, themes, and characters were little changed from the plan that he had begun with the spring of 1939. The new novel was laid in the period of flamboyant and unstable prosperity of the 1920s and ended with the coming of the Depression. It involved university life, but that part of the plot did not constitute its basic material. The setting, Warren said, "is merely the South," that is, "it could be any one of several places." Warren called the story "an attempt to get the spirit of that period

37. "America's Dean of Letters," *Newsweek*, August 25, 1980, p. 67.
38. Morton D. Zabel, "Condition of American Criticism: 1939," *English Journal* (College Edition), XXVIII (June, 1939), 417; Warren to Lambert Davis, December 17, 1941.

and dramatize some of the forces that were operating at that time, and which, for that matter, have not ceased operating."[39]

During the summer of 1941 the Warrens took an extended vacation to Mexico, where, despite a rather serious automobile accident, work on the novel progressed toward an end. By the end of 1941 the manuscript was completed and Warren had a contract with Houghton Mifflin to bring it out early in 1942. Richard Mealand, story editor for a Hollywood studio, informed Warren in October, 1941, that he was very much interested in reading the new book to see if it had possibilities for a motion picture. "As you probably know," he said to the author, "we had a great deal of enthusiasm for *Night Rider*, but unfortunately nothing materialized insofar as a movie sale. I am hoping that *And Pastures New* will be something we can use."[40] Although Warren himself admitted that he did not "expect any big sale" for the book, his fame as a writer of prose fiction was now on a par with his renown as a poet, editor, and critic.

The novel did not appear until 1943 and then under the title *At Heaven's Gate*, with many changes from Warren's original outline and first draft. The novel's strongest character is Bogan Murdock, the powerful and corrupt head of Meyers and Murdock. Ruling a corporation which owns bank stock, real estate, and lumber companies, Murdock is ruthless in his manipulation of business and government officials and even members of his own family to achieve his ends. He and his associates, including the governor, practice their influence with the legislature, causing it to buy land they hold at a premium price. Murdock also is involved in the switching of securities, which allows him to drain capital from companies that he controls. Once this fraud becomes apparent he seeks to avoid prosecution by bribing a World War I hero to perjure himself on his behalf. Failing in that tactic, Murdock resorts to the blatant use of political power and the exploitation of public sympathy caused by the death of his daughter to escape the punishment that he deserves.

Although Warren had for years protested that the novel was set

39. *Louisiana Leader*, VII (October 1940), 5.
40. Richard Mealand to Warren, October 23, 1941.

in no particular place and with no particular real people in mind, Bogan Murdock's career brought immediately to mind that of Colonel Luke Lea of Nashville. By 1921, the year Warren entered Vanderbilt, Tennessee, like much of the upper South, was in the midst of an important socioeconomic transition. Urbanization and industrialization were gradually creating new power bases at the expense of the farmers and rural-oriented small-town merchants and professionals. Especially in Nashville, industry and population were expanding rapidly, and during the twenties, Tennessee's capital city was noisy and brawling with a spirit reminiscent of the old West. This process of urbanization concentrated the power of Tennessee politics into the possession of a few people, and the most colorful, most controversial of these was Colonel Lea.

Founder and owner of the Nashville *Tennesseean*, Luke Lea was a former United States senator and had served as a colonel in the American Expeditionary Force during World War I. According to one biographer, Lea was an "intelligent, charming man with an extraordinary ability to manipulate people. . . . He also had a gift for the dramatic and was a bona fide war hero."[41] But this Tennessee king-maker's flaws were apparent also. His attitude toward the law was one of strict observation of the letter while ignoring the spirit. Further, he was an ambitious man with a taste for power and a recklessness of hazard in its pursuit. Having helped to establish Henry Horton as governor of Tennessee in 1929, Lea had access to the highest councils of government and a thick batch of political IOU's.

Lea's banker was Nashville businessman Rogers Caldwell, with Lea, the principal prototype for Warren's Bogan Murdock. Caldwell and Company was an early-day conglomerate, operating everything from banks to baseball teams. In the 1920s it was the most powerful financial institution in the South, with interests and investments extending from Texas to Georgia. Lea's political sagacity and Caldwell's money made the pair a formidable force in Tennessee. Soon the two were accused of using their influence with the legislature for personal gain as state officials began throwing contracts to Caldwell and Company enterprises.

41. David D. Lee, *Tennessee in Turmoil* (Memphis, 1979), 21, 81.

On November 7, 1930, Caldwell and Company collapsed. Its Bank of Tennessee went under, taking $3,418,000 in state deposits with it. By the fourteenth of the month Caldwell and Company, the South's greatest financial empire, went into receivership. Within a matter of days, Tennessee's state government, at the onset of the nation's worst depression, had lost $6,659,000. Luke Lea and Rogers Caldwell were financially destroyed and the state was in fiscal shambles. On June 5, 1931, a move to impeach Lea's puppet governor failed, but the Lea machine maintained power only until being overcome the next year by that of "Boss" E. H. Crump of Memphis.

Bogan Murdock, is, of course, neither Luke Lea nor Rogers Caldwell, nor is he an exact replication of a melding of their two careers. But these two Tennessee power brokers are personalities who suggested the character of Bogan Murdock as surely as Huey Long provided the suggestion for Willie Stark, and, to paraphrase Warren himself, if he had never gone to live in Tennessee and if Luke Lea and Rogers Caldwell had never existed, the novel never would have been written. The use of fictionalized avatars of actual contemporary or historical persons was to recur through Warren's next four novels. Not only does Long provide the prototype for Willie Stark in *All the King's Men*, but Jeroboam O. Beauchamp becomes Jeremiah Beaumont in *World Enough and Time*, two sisters whose names are now lost to history become Amanda Starr of *Band of Angels*, and Floyd Collins is transformed into Jasper Harrick in *The Cave*.

Even at the methodical pace at which he wrote poetry, and despite his major commitment to fiction, by the end of 1941 Warren had many poems on hand and more under way. Earlier in the year the Cummington Press had approached him about a collection for a series which would begin in the spring of 1942 with R. P. Blackmur's *The Second World*, but Warren agreed to let New Directions, where Albert Erskine was then an editor, print the best of his work since *Thirty-six Poems*. "I don't want to publish every damned line I write," he told Lambert Davis, "for as it is I throw away a lot of stuff." [42] But Warren sent to New Directions eleven of the poems he had done in the last six years which he thought worthy to survive.

42. Robert Penn Warren to Lambert Davis, December 17, 1941.

The new volume, *Eleven Poems on the Same Theme*, appeared in February, 1942, in the Yale Younger Poets Series, was dedicated to Cleanth Brooks and Albert Erskine, and won for its author the 1942 Shelley Prize for poetry.

The common theme of these eleven poems is that of much of Warren's work in verse and prose, the problem of knowledge of good and evil and the obsession with history as a source of meaning. As Cleanth Brooks has observed, modern man is haunted with a "consciousness of the past which drives us back upon history in search of meanings. The absolutes are gone—are dissolved, indeed, by our consciousness of a plurality of histories and meanings."[43] Warren's characters, therefore, are of two types, those who, out of ignorance of the past, are strong, brave, and resolute but doomed to failure by their ignorance and those who are rendered incapable of any meaningful activity by their knowledge of the near impossibility of sorting certainty from all of life's pluralities and shadings. Types of the former are the "Hero" for Warren's 1935 poem "Letter from a Coward to a Hero," Bill Christian in *Night Rider*, Bogon Murdock in *At Heaven's Gate*, and Willie Stark in *All the King's Men*. These are men incapable of fear, but incapable also of asking themselves the proper questions by which to learn the truth.

The avatars of the second side of Warren's dilemma are his most frequent protagonists, the tragic liberals who are frozen in inactivity or who act through no conviction except the compulsion of "the cause." The "Coward," Percy Munn, Gerald Calhoun, and Jack Burden are examples of the type from Warren's early novels and poetry. The irony of American volunteers fighting first with the Russians in Spain and then against them in Finland before the United States entry into World War II, all for the good of the same cause, struck Warren as a paradigm for the condition of modern man. Treated in "Terror," one of the eleven poems, this illogical impulse serves as evidence that since modern man can find no long-range meaning in life, he "seeks meaning in mere violence."[44]

43. Cleanth Brooks, *Modern Poetry and the Tradition* (Chapel Hill: University of North Carolina Press, 1939), 86.
44. Robert Penn Warren, "Notes," in Kimon Friar and John M. Brinnin (eds.), *Modern Poetry, American and British* (New York, 1951), 542–43.

The Warren hero, and he is rare, must sift through all of history's ambiguities and forge truth from a fusion of seemingly unreconcilable opposites. He is neither the conventional man of action, cutting through all obstacles along the shortest route to a preselected goal, nor is he the merely contemplative denizen of the ivory tower, unwilling to take any action in a universe where no action can be absolutely right. As Jack Burden learns following the death of Willie Stark, "History is blind, but man is not." He must, therefore, "go out of the house and go into the convulsion of the world, out of history and into history and the awful responsibility of Time."

The notion of a verse drama had first begun to take shape in Warren's mind one autumn afternoon in 1937 while he was sitting on a porch with one of his graduate students. The conversation had turned to the possibility of incorporating into a play Warren's philosophical concept of man's condition: his imperfect knowledge of his world and the imperfect tools with which he was forced to deal with it, his mandate to act and his responsibility for the consequences of his actions despite the fact that the best intended acts might easily go astray and lead to evil ends. In Warren's philosophy the "unfairness" of the human condition led the individual first to disillusion and then to a desire to escape the awful responsibility of acting in time and of contributing to history.

This theme, dealt with in *Thirty-six Poems* and in *Eleven Poems on the Same Theme* as well as in *Night Rider*, was to be buttressed in the proposed play by a setting and plot suggested by Warren's observations of political life in Louisiana during and immediately following the consulship of Huey P. Long. As Warren explained to his student, the plot would be based on the career of a southern politician "who achieved the power of a dictator, at least in his home state, and who was assassinated in the Capitol which had been the scene of his triumphs."[45]

Warren began writing exploratory fragments that winter, and by the spring of 1938 he had begun to feel that he had discovered the means by which to relate the main theme of the play to the plot and

45. Robert Penn Warren, "A Note to *All the King's Men*," *Sewanee Review*, LXI (May, 1952), 477.

setting. In the shade of an olive tree in a field near Perugia in 1938 Warren wrote the first lines of the play he was to call "Proud Flesh." By stealing moments from *Night Rider* and from his poetry, he expected to be finished with it by the end of the fall semester in 1939. The first draft of the play was completed during the summer of 1939 while Warren was in Italy on his Guggenheim Fellowship. "Between watching the troops in the streets and listening to radio reports of the war," the novelist-turned-dramatist was able to turn to his play in good earnest. Through the fall and winter, with the "boot heels of Mussolini's legionnaires clanging" on the Roman pavement, Warren completed the bulk of the play. The first draft was finished in Rome at Christmas, but Warren "felt too close to it to undertake a revision," and so mailed the play off to some friends in the States. He was aware that "Proud Flesh was not yet a finished product, but felt that rewriting would best wait for the criticism of Brooks, Erskine, Heilman, and some other trusted readers and for his own "more detached inspection."[46]

Francis Fergusson, former drama critic for the *Bookman* and then professor of drama at Bennington College, had heard of the work in progress as early as February, 1939, and had urged Warren to send him a copy of the manuscript and perhaps to undertake an amateur production at Bennington. Warren's first stop on his return from Italy in the spring of 1940, therefore, was at Bennington, where he did some rewriting under "the subtle criticism and inspiring instruction" of Fergusson. "But still," says Warren, "the play was not to my mind finished." Returning to Baton Rouge in September, Warren told a reporter for the *Louisiana Leader* that although a first draft of the play was completed, he would "probably work on it for another five or six months." The play, he stated, was a mixture of prose and verse, "and, as to content," he would "simply say that it is political and contemporary."[47]

46. Robert Penn Warren, "How a Pulitzer Prize Novel was Created," *Chicago Sunday Tribune Magazine of Books*, May 11, 1947, p. 14; Warren, "A Note to *All the King's Men*," 476; Warren, "Pulitzer Prize Novel," 14; Warren, untitled statement in *Wilson Library Bulletin*, 652.

47. Warren, "A Note to *All the King's Men*," 477; *Louisiana Leader*, VII (October, 1940), 5.

Rather than set about an immediate revision of "Proud Flesh" at that time, Warren laid it aside and picked up the threads of "And Pastures New," the novel that he had put away in the spring of 1939. The play was never too far from Warren's attention, however, simmering on a back burner until December, 1941, when he responded to a request for material from Harcourt Brace. "Proud Flesh," he told editor Lambert Davis, "needs a thorough reworking, and won't be ready for some time." The author admitted that he should work with his "dramatic mentor," Francis Fergusson, but told Davis that, at worst, he hoped to have the play finished within the year. Warren also mentioned that he had forwarded "a considerable section" of the play to Houghton Mifflin, but that the Boston publishing house had been "very vague and, to me, unsatisfactory" about the manuscript. They wrote him "a very nice letter," he said, which enclosed a copy of the reader's report which saw "Proud Flesh" as traveling in "'the true direction of American drama', etc. etc." Although the report contained some enthusiastic comment, the publishers "got cagy" and did not want to publish the play until it had been produced. The Atlantic Monthly Press had also expressed some encouraging interest in the play, but had not taken it, so Warren was happy for Davis to see the play, although his only complete copy "doesn't incorporate much of the late work on the thing and needs some editing and sharpening very badly." [48]

Harcourt, Brace, as well, chose not to publish the play, and Warren did not attempt further revision until the winter of 1942–43 after he had left Louisiana State University for the University of Minnesota. The 1943 version was "more realistic, discursive, and documentary in method (though not in spirit)" than its predecessors, Warren maintains, for he was then far from Baton Rouge and the "world in which the story had its roots." Warren, freed from the literal and factual arena of the story's genesis, "was ready to be absorbed freely into the act of imagination." [49]

As early as December, 1941, Warren had indicated that he had

48. Robert Penn Warren to Lambert Davis, December 17, 1941.
49. Warren, "*All the King's Men*: The Matrix of Experience," 163.

plans to write two or three novels and that he had done "a considerable amount of work on one of them by way of preparation, the one
based on Long." When the revision of the play went slowly, therefore, due to what Warren called his "ignorance of the practical
stage," it was easy for him to shift his energies from drama to prose.
In Minneapolis in 1943 Warren suddenly saw his play as a novel
"simply because, half unknown to me," he recalls, "the conviction
had been growing that in the story of my man, Willie Stark, the context that invites power is as important as the personal genius for
power; and a novel gives more air and space for the development of
such an idea." In the expanded context of the narrative a new voice
and a new point of view was required, so Jack Burden, who had
been a nameless newspaper reporter in the drama version, became
the focal character and the consciousness through which the reader
views each of the characters, who "in greater or lesser degree," find
in Willie Stark "some fulfillment of the self unfulfilled in his actual
life." The resulting novel was, of course, *All the King's Men.*[50]

The play was finished not long after the novel was published in
1946 and had received the Pulitzer Prize for literature in 1947. In
the winter of 1946 Warren sent a copy of his manuscript to Eric
Bentley, who passed it on to the producer of the University of Minnesota Theatre, Frank Whiting. Whiting's students presented the
play in April of 1947, and Bentley enthusiastically reviewed the production in *Theatre Arts* in November of that year. Robert Penn
Warren, Bentley reported, "has combined two styles: the tough realism of American fiction and the poetic modernism of T. S. Eliot."
Bentley's review was highly reminiscent of the first notices of *Night
Rider.* "How good a play is *Proud Flesh?*" he asks rhetorically. "In
moments of enthusiasm, or straining after slick superlatives, one
might exclaim: 'Here at last is the American Play.' On the lowest
estimate, it is very brilliant and meaty and suggestive. It shows that
Warren, potentially at least, is as much a playwright as he is a poet
and novelist. As a first play it is astonishing. I know of no single fact

50. Warren to Davis, December 17, 1941; Warren, "Pulitzer Prize Novel," p. 14;
Warren, "A Special Message to Subscribers," n.p.

that gives me more hope for American drama."[51] The play was first produced professionally by Michel Bouche, Arnold Brockman, and Iris Michaels at the East 47th Street Theatre in New York on October 16, 1959, and was published by Random House in 1960, retitled *All the King's Men: A Play*. Warren dedicated his only work of drama to his "dramatic mentor," Francis Fergusson.

Too many readers of *All the King's Men* believe that "Warren came to Louisiana about the time of Long's assassination, listened to lurid tales, and with quick opportunism cashed in on widespread interest in the Kingfish by writing a thinly concealed biography of the popular hero-villain in the form of a novel." To Diana Trilling, for example, *All the King's Men* is "not the first novel to draw inspiration from the career of Huey Long"—John Dos Passos' *Number One* and Hamilton Basso's *Sun in Capricorn* being two of several others. She does, however, note that "Mr. Warren would seem to stay closer to his original." However she may find Warren's alleged adherence to the facts of Long's biography, she abhors the conclusion which she draws from the novel—that it is "difficult *not* to infer from Mr. Warren's novel that a Willie Stark's absolute power is justified by such public benefaction as the fine hospital that he builds." Orville Prescott, too, found *All the King's Men* to be merely "another interpretation of the career of Huey Long and the looting of Louisiana," and he too found strongly objectionable what he sees as "Mr. Warren's refusal to consider Huey Long as the American variety of fascist he really was, instead of just a mixture of idealism and corruption."[52]

Warren has gone to great lengths to show that *Proud Flesh* and the novel which grew out of it are no more "historical" than was *Night Rider* or *At Heaven's Gate*. "When I am asked how much *All the King's Men* owes to the actual politics of Louisiana in the '30's" the author later wrote for the *Yale Review*, "I can only be sure that if

51. Eric Bentley, "*All the King's Men*," *Theatre Arts*, XXXI (November, 1947), 72–73.
52. Arthur H. Scouten, "Warren, Huey Long, and *All the King's Men*," *Four Quarters*, XXI (May, 1972), 23; Diana Trilling, "Fiction in Review," *Nation*, August 24, 1946, p. 220; Orville Prescott, "Outstanding Novels," *Yale Review*, XXXVI (Autumn, 1946), 192.

I had never gone to live in Louisiana and if Huey Long had not existed the novel would have never been written." This, however, is far from saying that Warren's state is Louisiana or that his politician is Huey P. Long. The "Boss" could as easily be identified with Mississippi's scandalous Theodore Bilbo, Benito Mussolini, Adolph Hitler, or, so Warren maintains, any of "a thousand dictators which the era spawned."[53]

As is the case with all good writers of fiction, Warren was "more concerned with the myth than with the fact, more with the symbolic than the actual." An LSU student of the period states that he can "never remember seeing Warren get excited or worked up about Huey. What absorbed Warren's curiosity and concentration was the political and financial corruption in Louisiana after Long's death." Poet and publisher Alan Swallow declared that although "Willie Stark's resemblance to a well-known southern politician . . . is obvious . . . the book is no more than a study of him than *Richard III* is a history of Richard III and no more a study of the South than *Hamlet* is a study of Denmark." What the author of *Proud Flesh* did gain from his closer observation of Louisiana politics during and after the Huey Long regime "was a line of thinking and feeling" which eventuated in the play and novel. That line was not one which ran parallel to Warren's own philosophy but closer to perpendicular to it, so that, as the author states in a recent introduction to *All the King's Men*, "my book represents an intersection of Louisiana, Huey P. Long, and me." The strength of the novel bears out Dr. Johnson's observation that "comparison is better in proportion as the lines converge from greater diversion."[54]

Warren had seen and heard Long but once in his life and had "never spent five minutes in anything that might possibly be called research," he says. "I simply lived in the world in which his legend took shape." The foreground materials of *All the King's Men* are derived from his own section, and to that degree Warren may be said to be a regionalist, but his basic materials are the state of civilization

53. Warren, "*All the King's Men*: The Matrix of Experience," 161.
54. Scouten, "Warren, Huey Long, and *All the King's Men*," 25; Alan Swallow, *U.S. Quarterly Booklist*, II (December, 1946), 283–93; Warren, "*All the King's Men*: The Matrix of Experience," 162; Warren, "A Special Message to Subscribers."

and, yet more basically, the human forces and needs which have produced, and in turn attempt to come to grips with, that state. Besides Huey Long the influences on Warren's novel are many, and most profound among them, perhaps, is Shakespeare. As he has explained:

> At LSU I taught, among other things, an advanced course in Shakespeare, and month after month, year after year, I was soaking myself in his plays and always seeing more and more the germs of the issues and problems of our modernity in those plays. And reading those plays in Louisiana was, certainly, not like reading Shakespeare in Tennessee—and even less like reading him in the dreamy settings of Yale or Oxford.[55]

Not only Shakespeare absorbed him. During this period he was deeply engrossed in Dante, Machiavelli, Guicciardini, and the history of the later Renaissance. Machiavelli, in fact, is quoted in the novel's epigraph and appears in the meditations of Jack Burden. William James and American history, too, were fascinating to Warren and figure heavily in his drama and novel.

In the original version of the verse play the name of Warren's dictator was not Willie Stark but Willie Talos from the brutal, blank-eyed "iron groom" of the Knight of Justice in *The Faerie Queen.* Even as Warren's conception of the character grew wider than this two-dimensional servant of abstract law, much of Talos remained. The Talos/Stark character represents, to his creator, "the kind of doom that democracy may invite upon itself." Neither the play nor the book, however, was ever intended to be "about politics." Politics, Warren maintains, "merely provided the framework story in which deeper concerns, whatever their final significance, might work themselves out."[56]

To many critics, however, suggestion meant identification, and the journalistic relevance of the piece of fiction was far more important than its merits as a work of art. When *All the King's Men* ap-

---

55. Warren, "A Special Message to Subscribers."
56. Warren, "A Note to *All the King's Men*," 476.

peared in print more than ten years after the murder of Senator Long in Baton Rouge, his renown, both in his native state and beyond its borders, "was yet green in pious tears, anathema, and speculation." The consequent equation of Stark with Long led some critics to view *All the King's Men* as a "not-so-covert biography" of the late senator and even as an apology for his excesses. Perhaps the most vehement reviewer of this camp was Robert Gorham Davis, who saw Warren as nothing less than a hired propagandist for the yet-powerful Long machine.

Despite Warren's protest that he had "no desire to whitewash whatever may need whitewashing in Long's human frailty, arrogance, self-absorption, cowardice, vanity, and cynical use of his all too corruptible tools," Davis contended that the novel "must be judged in political as well as literary terms, for its total effect is to justify Long and the intellectuals who played ball with him." Davis believes that the ethics of collaboration with a dictator was the central theme of *All the King's Men*, and certainly this is a main consideration of the novel. Davis maintains, however, that Warren saw himself as a type for Adam Stanton, a young idealist given a university and a journal rather than a hospital with which to do some good at the tactical level while masking a vile and bloody dictatorship at the strategic. Further, the reviewer thinks that Warren, out of a misguided sense of gratitude or an attempt at personal justification, simplifies and alters Long's career "almost in the spirit of Parson Weems." Davis professes no surprise that Warren "should assume that Long's program would economically benefit the mass of people, despite evidence to show that, through squandering money, lowering wage rates and imposing indirect or hidden taxes, Long made their situation worse. But it is surprising that *All the King's Men* never really faces the threat of men like Long to the democratic process itself." [57]

Warren's own reaction to such reviews in which he is cast as "a base minion of the great man" has been merely fatalistic. In a num-

57. Warren, "A Special Message to Subscribers"; Davis, "Dr. Adam Stanton's Dilemma," 3, 24.

ber of essays and interviews he stressed the point that even if he had wished to make Stark a projection of Long he would not have known how to go about doing so. "For one reason," he says, "I did not and do not know what Long was like, and what were the secret forces that drove him along his violent path to meet the bullet in the Capitol." Nevertheless, reviewers continued to make the identification of Stark and Long and to cast Warren in the role of Dr. Stanton or of the Boss's "intellectual gunman," Jack Burden.

Then too, Warren has observed, there are those who interpreted the novel as "a rousing declaration of democratic principles and a tract for the assassination of dictators." This reading too, although closer to Warren's personal political views, is far removed from the author's actual meaning. But each time he disclaimed the notion that Willie Stark *was* Huey Long, or anyone else but Willie Stark, the disclaimer was "almost invariably greeted by something like a sardonic smile or a conspiratorial wink, according to what the inimical smiler or the friendly winker took my motives to be—either I wanted to avoid being called a fascist or I wanted to avoid a lawsuit." Warren at last decided that "there is really nothing to reply to this kind of innocent bone-headedness or gospel-bit hysteria." Readers who do not realize from the text that the author was trying to create a fable which could serve as a frame for his own ideas "cannot be expected to abandon their preconceptions, prejudices, or convenience because of any statement of mine." Warren has often quoted Louis Armstrong's observation that "there is some folks that if they don't know, you can't tell 'em." [58]

With "And Pastures New" and "Proud Flesh" fermenting and *Eleven Poems on the Same Theme* recently published in 1941, Warren was ready to set afoot several other ambitious literary projects. By cutting down on his outside work and saving summers, Warren thought he could "do a novel about every year and half or two years," but, as he told Davis, "I do not want to feel that pressure is being put upon me to produce only novels and textbooks. I intend to

58. Warren, "A Note to *All the King's Men*," 479–80.

go on writing poetry, and shall probably do another verse play before too long." One thing he wanted to do was to bring out a book including the best work from the *Thirty-six Poems* and the *Eleven Poems* plus some new work still in manuscript. "I am in no immediate haste about it," he wrote in December, 1941, "but I do not want to wait too long." Houghton Mifflin had already made a verbal promise to issue such a collection after the publication of "And Pastures New," thus catching the "carry-over force" of such attention as the novel should attract, but failed to publish either the poems or the novel.[59] In 1943, therefore, at the urging of Allen Tate, Warren gave his novel manuscript to Davis at Harcourt, who published it that year as *At Heaven's Gate* and followed in 1944 with Warren's *Selected Poems: 1923–1943*. By that time, however, Warren was no longer at Baton Rouge.

59. Robert Penn Warren to Lambert Davis, December 17, 1941.

SEVEN

Teachers and Students

Who else, except of course the equally astonishing Mr. Warren, would have thought of . . . addressing so many words, with such seriousness, probity, and profundity, so much kindly patience to exemplify and elaborate, to the forlorn purpose of making freshmen and sophomores articulate?

JOHN EDWARD HARDY
on Cleanth Brooks

IN 1912 William A. Read became chairman of the English department at Louisiana State University. Read had earned his B.A. degree in 1888 at King College in Tennessee and had done graduate work at the University of Virginia from 1892 to 1894. On leaving Virginia he matriculated at the University of Göttingen for one year and then spent two more years at the University of Heidelberg, where he received the traditional German Ph.D. After graduating from Heidelberg, Read returned to the South to teach for a brief period and to do postdoctoral work at Johns Hopkins. From 1899 to 1902 he was professor of English and modern languages at the University of Arkansas; he then moved to LSU, "where he spent the rest of his career reading the volumes of the *Oxford English Dictionary* as they appeared." A linguist who could claim some national and even international reputation in his field, Read is remembered by former students as a charming gentleman as well as an erudite scholar who "knew all that then was known in the field of phonology and most of the field of philology." [1]

1. Heilman, "LSU Forty Years After," 139; Arthur H. Scouten to author, September 23, 1979 (in possession of the author).

The four professors who served under Read in 1932 were, like their chairman, well trained by the standards of the era, but highly traditional in their outlook and methods. Their approach to literature was almost purely historical and biographical, and none of the four had done much academic publishing. Earl Lockridge Bradshear wrote western novels under a pseudonym and Earle Uhler's racy potboiler about student life at LSU, *Cane Juice*, served only to get him fired from the LSU faculty. Women from upper-class Louisiana families who had earned Master's degrees after attaining some experience teaching high school usually conducted lower division classes. These women were generally quite competent at teaching grammar and composition but had little in the way of scholarly training.

With the growth of the university during the early 1930s, the English faculty more than doubled in size. Besides Brooks and Warren, four new Ph.D.'s joined the staff in 1935: Nathaniel Caffee from the University of Virginia, Arlin Turner from the University of Texas, Robert Heilman from Harvard, and Thomas Kirby from Johns Hopkins. Typical of the new Ph.D.'s being turned out of American English departments of the time, all were well trained in their respective specialties but none then knew or cared much for criticism.

To augment the staff charged with teaching composition and rhetoric to freshmen, the department began the near-wholesale hiring of teaching assistants. Thanks once again to Senator Long's largesse, the university could offer promising graduate students a small stipend in addition to free tuition, a luxury few other state universities could afford during the Depression. Thus a great many first-rate graduate students were attracted to Baton Rouge prior to World War II, including the *Southern Review*'s two managing editors, Albert Erskine and John E. Palmer.

Cleanth Brooks joined the LSU English faculty in 1932 with the idea that literature as literature was a proper subject for a college curriculum and that it could be taught intelligently. Too often, he knew, a non-reader of poetry—either a young instructor "with the grad-school grave smell" still about him and "like Frankenstein's monster at an early stage, a bit helpless and mechanical," or else a "grey-suited unpromotable" capable of telling a class that "Ode to a

Nightingale" is a very beautiful poem, but none too resourceful in the face of "Prufrock" or "The Garden"—taught poetry to freshmen and sophomores.[2] Such courses, quite naturally, remained curricular poor relations in a league with remedial composition.

Brooks wished to return students' attention to individual poems by concrete and inductive study in opposition to those who taught paraphrase, biography, history, inspiration, or didactics. His was the *explication de texte* method, adapted from John Crowe Ransom and I. A. Richards, and during the years that he and Warren taught at LSU their work triggered a profound shift in the university study of literature across America. In the words of one former student, the Brooks and Warren approach was aimed at "Professor Readywit rather than Miss Beautyseeker," and it shot down all scholarly excuses for the study in literature classes of that which is not literature.[3]

William Read, though himself a traditionalist by temperament and training, encouraged Brooks's aesthetic approach as an alternative to the strictly historical approach that was then being taught at LSU and in almost every other English department in the country. Although dedicated to subverting and exploiting the concepts of poetry Read held, Brooks himself was also a talented linguist whose first book compared the dialects of Georgia and Alabama to those of the southwest shires of England. Nevertheless, his principal contribution to his new department was his course "The Aesthetics of Poetry." This course, which was based on a survey of English critical doctrine from the era of Sir Philip Sidney to the 1930s, stressed critical definitions, the problems of value, and the relation of poetry to science. Such innovations were new to Brooks's colleagues at LSU and were the source of much misunderstanding and some ridicule when he introduced them in the fall of 1934.

Also new was Brooks's course in twentieth-century poetry. In it Brooks's students studied the principal English and American poets from Thomas Hardy to Hart Crane, examining their break with Victorianism, their general intellectual background, and their critical

2. Hugh Kenner, "Omnibus Review of Poetry Textbooks," *Poetry*, LXXXIV (April, 1954), 47.
3. Scouten to author, September 23, 1979.

ideas. Brooks's third class each week was a course in the nondramatic literature of the seventeenth century exclusive of Milton. Taught each fall semester, the course stressed the school of Donne, the transition to the Age of Reason, and the poetry and prose of Dryden. This course alternated in the spring with the poetry and prose of John Milton. Also on Brooks's twelve-hour-per-week teaching schedule was a two-semester course in English composition.

Despite the raised eyebrows of his new colleagues, a *corps d'elite* of the most gifted of LSU's students soon began flocking to Brooks's classes. But exciting and challenging as he was to the department's most talented students, he never gave up on the less promising. Robert Heilman remembers that "it was a matter of the common report that, if a student's recitations were even faintly capable of being interpreted to the student's credit," Brooks invariably interpreted them so. In the words of one undergraduate, "he tried to pull the student in rather than put him down."[4] With this tactic Brooks was not lowering his own lofty standards but attempting to gain a foothold on the student's terrain from which to lead him to higher ground.

So eager was Brooks to communicate to his students the value of English literature that on at least one occasion he recommended to his colleagues that they take a lesson from the coaching staff of the football-crazy university. Surveying the scene at LSU and at other American universities, Brooks concluded that the only thing well taught was football. He did not mean, he insisted, to make a sneering jibe at the overemphasis on athletics in the average American university but insisted that any English or history teacher might take the coach's achievement quite seriously and try to learn something from it. According to Brooks, athletic coaching differed from academic teaching in several pertinent ways. First, the coach was not hobbled by the necessity for letting the average player determine the level of his coaching. Second, he could teach his subject as a discipline, not as a collection of data, and thus textbooks, lectures, and factual information fell into their normal place. And finally, the coach could reserve his mark of distinction for those who

4. Heilman, "Cleanth Brooks," 135–36.

really deserved it. As Brooks pointed out, the coach "is on the alert for unusual talent, the special case . . . his goal is to develop special potentialities to the full." From his observations of teaching in the English department, Brooks concluded, "The average university is somewhat more temperate in its enthusiasm for turning out the best possible group of scholars."

Elaborating on his point that the coach could teach his subject as a discipline, Brooks said that "everybody knows that it is absurd to try to develop a fine halfback by having him merely read histories of football, study blackboard diagrams and write term papers on the 'Theory of the Delayed Cross Buck.'" Although the training of a scholar and an athlete are obviously on different levels, the coach seldom committed the common academic error of "trying to cram the student's gizzard with information which is never intimately related to any intellectual discipline mastered by the student." Every teacher, Brooks was sure, could think of dozens of instances of students being taught to parrot information which they had not assimilated, and of which they had no real understanding. The student too often could quote other people's opinions by rote, but could not form one of his own. "The man who has made his letter can usually be counted on to know the sport for which he holds it. But the man who has made two letters in his university, his B.A., his B.S., his M.A., stands in a different category."[5] This appalling inability of university graduates to "read, write and reckon" was to Brooks a concern of equal magnitude with his work in literary criticism and the promotion of modern poetry. The testaments of his commitment to remedy the situation include not only his and Warren's great pedagogical books, *An Approach to Literature*, *Understanding Poetry*, and *Undestanding Fiction*, but also dozens of former undergraduate and graduate students whose substantial contribution to the world of letters stems from the teaching and inspiration of Cleanth Brooks.

One of the highest compliments paid to Brooks as a teacher came from his former mentor at Vanderbilt, John Crowe Ransom. In the pages of the *Kenyon Review*, Ransom declared that "parents may be

5. "Teachers May Take Lesson from Football Coaches," Baton Rouge *State-Times*, April 30, 1940, p. 8.

advised, if they ask advice, that they need not fear to entrust the good young men . . . to him at the university if they can qualify for the courses. They will be acquainted among other things with the soul of man, and even the soul of modern man, and that is something which is in store for them anyhow, one time or another."[6]

In 1934, another dedicated teacher came to LSU when Robert Penn Warren joined the English faculty. Although he had already made a deep and abiding commitment to the writing of imaginative literature, Warren has professed never to have felt competition between his teaching and the writing which occupied most of his non-classroom hours. During the thirties and forties he may well have needed the teaching income in order to write, but even after the sale of movie rights to *All the King's Men* and the Literary Guild selection of *World Enough and Time* in the 1950s gave him a comfortable income, he continued to put in about five months of each year on a college campus. "For a person who wants to write," Warren believes, "the advantages of pedagogy . . . outweigh the disadvantages. And this seems to be the greatest advantage: a teacher is forced to clarify—or to try to clarify—his own mind on certain questions which are necessarily involved in the business of writing."[7]

Warren's teaching assignment at LSU included his famous creative writing class, an undergraduate course in Shakespeare, and a two-semester graduate seminar on the nondramatic literature of the sixteenth century. "His chief interest over those years was in Jacobean tragedy," one former graduate student recalls. Arthur Scouten, a distinguished teacher and critic himself, vividly remembers how excited Warren became in discoursing about Webster's play *The White Devil*, "explaining how a certain character in the play was a part of another character in the play, and how Prince Hal . . . spoke of Hotspur as being a factor of himself." Scouten speculates that Warren's primary concern was with the techniques and ideas displayed in Jacobean tragedy, and that Warren's own fiction was an attempt to shape modern subject matter into a similar psychological mold. "Few teachers could be more affable and courteous to students," Scouten recalls, but Warren had little time for small talk. He

6. Ransom, "Why Critics Don't Go Mad," 147.
7. Warren, statement in *Wilson Library Bulletin*, 652.

was possessed by an imperative urge to translate onto paper the creative and critical ideas within him, and went about his business on campus at top speed. "A familiar scene to us students," says Scouten, "was the appearance of the two men, absorbed in earnest conversation, hurriedly crossing the broad lawn from a classroom building to *The Southern Review* office . . . Brooks having to trot to keep up with Warren's long, jerky stride."[8]

Soon after Brooks's and Warren's reunion at LSU, Morton D. Zabel noted in a *Poetry* magazine essay that "there are projects afoot in literary and critical pedagogy (at the University of Chicago, Kenyon College, Louisiana State University and Harvard College) which are of the greatest moment in the coming years."[9] Several circumstances conspired to cause the two former Rhodes scholars to undertake one of these projects, a new textbook and a new method of teaching literature in the college classroom which resulted in a change so great that the "revolution in literary studies" has become an historical cliché. First, the partnership welded by working together on the *Southwest Review* and the *Southern Review* allowed a collaboration of talents which could scarcely be matched in any other English department in the country. Second, from their work in criticism and the classroom, Brooks and Warren agreed that the need was as great for a major reformation in the teaching of literature as for a reordering of the English poets. During his two years at Berkeley, Warren had been as appalled by the poor quality of teaching in the English department as Brooks had been at Tulane.

In 1935 LSU was using the McCallum *College Omnibus* as the text for introductory courses in literature. Like all texts of its day, the McCallum book was biographical in its approach, with no critical apparatus by which the teacher and student might approach the stories and poems aesthetically. An example of McCallum's attempt at criticism is in his comment on Keats's "Ode to a Nightingale": "The poem is sheer magic."[10] John T. Purser, one of Brooks's graduate students, complained to Brooks of the method in McCallum and together they began work on a text inspired by the work of Richards and Ransom.

8. Scouten, "Warren, Huey Long, and *All the King's Men*," 23, 24, 26.
9. Zable, "Condition of American Criticism," 417.
10. James Dow McCallum (ed.), *The College Omnibus* (New York, 1934).

The resulting book, *An Approach to Literature*, was a natural outgrowth of the classroom work of its three authors. As such, "its dominant motive," says Brooks, "was not to implant newfangled ideas in the innocent Louisiana sophomores we faced three times a week," but "to try to solve a serious practical problem."[11] Although Brooks, Warren, and Purser each used other approaches as well and at several different levels, the one set forth in their book was an attempt to bring into the college classroom some of the critical insights developed since the work of Coleridge and to set these insights in a context of literary and social history.

During the spring semester of 1935, the collaborators used mimeographed poems and critical questions in their own classes. Warren's reputation at this time was only beginning to make itself felt, and Brooks and Purser were unknowns. The Depression, also, was at its worst that year, and on top of all else McCallum's *Omnibus* was still fresh and had become the standard text across America. Brooks, Warren, and Purser interested their friend Marcus Wilkerson, director of LSU's new press, in the project. Wilkerson took the textbook ideas to James Monroe Smith, who also favored the idea and promised university support. The fact that John Purser was a close personal friend of Governor Allen no doubt did the venture no harm, and Brooks had to take aside his enthusiastic young colleague and discourage him from seeking political influence.

The printers began to set up the book by mid-July, 1936, just as Warren was leaving Louisiana to teach at the University of Colorado's summer writer's conference, but with the help of Albert Erskine doing design work, *An Approach to Literature* was off the presses in time for use in LSU classrooms in September. The approach "was not received by the English Department with deafening cheers," Brooks recalled. Its method was new and somewhat difficult for teachers whose training was in literary history and biography. The new book did not sell well at first and was criticized for its antitraditional approach, the validity of some of its interpretations, and its heavy reliance on southern writers.[12]

11. Cleanth Brooks, "Forty Years of *Understanding Poetry*," an address delivered to the 1979 meeting of the College English Association, typescript courtesy of *College English Association Critic*, Texas A&M University.
12. *Ibid.*

Clearly the book was not long on biographical and historical background, nor did it convey the editors' "warm pulsing feelings" about the poems under consideration. These calculated omissions were taken by critics of the traditional academic school as proof that Brooks and Warren had no use for biography and history, and that they were "cold-blooded analysts who found no pleasure—certainly no joy—in literature." "Yet," asked Brooks, within the length of a single textbook "how much commentary do you have space for? We were trying to apply the grease to the wheel that squeaked the loudest. Besides, the typical instructor, product as he was of the graduate schools of that day, had been thoroughly trained in literary history, or so we assumed." [13] The editors believed that he could be relied on to provide whatever historical or biographical information the situation called for.

The Agrarians *were* well represented, with poems, stories, and essays from Donald Davidson, John Donald Wade, Andrew Lytle, and Allen Tate filling many of the anthology's pages. Many other pieces were reprints of recent *Southern Review* selections, and William Faulkner, Erskine Caldwell, and other southerners helped to fill the remaining pages. 1936 had been a big year for the Agrarians—the biggest since the publication of *I'll Take My Stand*—and the Baton Rouge splinter of the group was not in this instance backing away from its commitment to the cause. Believing that the South's colonial mentality was not merely manifested in the field of economics, Brooks and Warren were making an attempt to remove their native region from the educational imperialism which had been its lot since *McGuffy's Reader*, *Webster's Dictionary*, and the Yankee schoolmarm invaded the South in the nineteenth century. Warren lamented that southern educators "tend to tail a kite after the kite has been pulled to the ground elsewhere, and new kites have gone up." [14] Southern teachers were too eager to imitate the methods being developed elsewhere instead of doing their own pioneering. *An Approach to Literature* was very consciously a pioneering effort in education from south of the Ohio. Ironically, the English departments of the University of Maine and the University of

13. Cleanth Brooks, "The State of Letters: The New Criticism,' *Sewanee Review*, LXXXVII (Fall, 1979), 593.
14. Warren, "Industrialism: The Old South Fades," 128.

New Hampshire were among the first outside of the authors' own to adopt it.

Although not a single commercial publisher would even read the manuscript in 1935, by 1939 most major textook companies wanted the book's copyright. Teachers had learned to appreciate the new critical approach, and the LSU Press was able to sell its plates and rights to the book to F. S. Crofts, a small but highly selective text-book company, for 2 percent of future royalties—one of the Press's best deals of all time. Dozens of similar texts were written during the next decade, but *An Approach to Literature* remained highly popular and by 1975 had gone through five editions.

Hardly had the first copies of their first textbook come off the presses before Brooks and Warren were hard at work on a second, an endeavor which would be primarily effective, if not ultimately causative, in bringing about a revolution in the teaching of poetry in the American college classroom. Built upon what its authors had learned from writing the poetry section of *An Approach to Literature*, the new volume was an attempt to incorporate methods drawn from their experience of teaching poetry and particularly modern poetry. In their classrooms, they had seen students, "many of whom had good minds, some imagination, and a good deal of lived experience," who were incompetent at handling matters of attitude, emphasis, symbolism, and figures of speech in even the simplest poems. Consequently, Brooks and Warren designed their text to meet these problems rather than merely to try out on their students a special theory for teaching poetry. The authors aimed to return the student's attention to the individual poem by concrete and inductive study and to win it away from those critics who were interested primarily in the historical and didactic interpretations as the reason for studying poetry. As a graduate student from this era recalls, his two professors took the leadership in a movement to "outlaw certain forms of professional posing, hokum, and hanky-panky—a movement that has so far succeeded . . . that there is hardly an English professor in America now who . . . will any longer dare to go into one of his classroom routines of 'This man can write!'" [15]

15. Brooks, "The New Criticism," 593; John Edward Hardy, "The Achievement of Cleanth Brooks," in Louis D. Rubin, Jr., and Robert D. Jacobs (eds.), *Southern Renascence: The Literature of the Modern South* (Baltimore: Johns Hopkins Press, 1953), 414.

Rather than evade the basic aesthetic questions posed by each poem, Brooks and Warren hoped to present the student, in proper context and after proper preparation, some of the basic problems with the aim not of making technical critics, but merely of making competent readers of poetry. In their manifesto, the "Letter to the Teacher" which prefaces the volume, Brooks and Warren quote Louis Cazamian's position that "much more fruitful than the problems of origins and development are those of content and significance. What is the human matter, what the artistic value of the work?"[16] In other words, if poetry is worth teaching at all, it is worth teaching as poetry. It must never be used as an excuse for something else.

A twenty-five-page introduction sets forth the critical faith of the editors. Here Brooks and Warren explain how poetry should not be read and here they pose their cardinal tenet: that the poem is an organic whole and as such must be judged as good or bad insofar as the poet did, or failed to do, what he intended. Beyond the "Letter to the Teacher" and Introduction, *Understanding Poetry* is divided into seven sections. These deal with (1) Narrative Poems, (2) Implied Narrative, (3) Objective Description, (4) Metrics, (5) Tone and Attitude, (6) Imagery, and (7) Theme. These divisions are not logically exclusive; they inevitably overlap. Throughout the book the editors often refer to the danger of studying a poem exclusively for its metrics, or imagery, or theme. To them the poem is simply organic structure. They applied this idea to 238 poems ranging from old ballads to Allen Tate and Hart Crane, and they follow 37 of the poems with elaborate prose criticism.

As early as November, 1936, the two professors wrote to Donald Davidson asking that he read a few sections of analyses. At the time they informed him that the manuscript was scheduled to go to Holt in early December, and so were asking him and others "to check any grievous blunders and to make suggestions."[17] They did not meet their first deadline, and in March, 1937, Warren informed

16. Cleanth Brooks and Robert Penn Warren, *Understanding Poetry* (New York, 1938), iv–xv.
17. Cleanth Brooks and Robert Penn Warren to Donald Davidson, November 4, 1936.

Frank Owsley that since Christmas he and Brooks had been trying to push the book to completion in January. Eight months later the two collaborators were still struggling with the manuscript. It had been completed and submitted to the publisher during the summer, but Holt had considered it too long and asked Brooks and Warren to cut it down somewhat. Holt had in fact miscounted the number of pages, and the manuscript was well within tolerance, but its two authors became dissatisfied with their work and took more time for further revision. This work they finished in November.

Brooks and Warren wanted to name their new book "Reading Poems," but Henry Holt thought such a title too modest and so changed the name to *Understanding Poetry*. The new text appeared under that title on May 21, 1938, but still Brooks and Warren were not completely satisfied with their efforts. The authors had no expectations of leading a pedagogical revolution and admitted that they would be pleased to interest as much as 20 percent of college English teachers in their approach. Of this modicum, they expected an even smaller group of converts. Shortly after the new book appeared, Brooks wrote to F. O. Matthiessen of his fears that his and Warren's efforts had fallen short. Although Matthiessen was a leader of the historical and biographical school of criticism, Brooks hoped that Matthiessen's opinion of the book would be favorable. Nevertheless, he asked the older critic for perfectly candid comments. "I am sure that there are plenty of mistakes in the book—many of which can't be written off as printers' errors," he concluded.[18] The two collaborators need not, however, have put themselves to so much worry. Matthiessen not only approved of *Understanding Poetry* but immediately adopted it and profited by it in his own classroom.

He was not the only one to approve, for reviews of the text were generally quite favorable. John Berryman and John Crowe Ransom, for instance, were very enthusiastic, with Ransom noting especially the book's fresh analyses of old poems. "What can this mean," he asked in the *Kenyon Review*, "but that criticism as it is practiced now is a new thing?" As *Understanding Poetry* pointed out to him,

18. Cleanth Brooks to F. O. Matthiessen, June 14, 1938.

"We need the new critics for the classics even more . . . than we need them for securing our possession of the strange moderns." [19] Even reviewers who were not totally convinced by the book's approach were willing to admit some merits.

One of the most prophetic reviewers was R. L. Morris in the *Sewanee Review,* who predicted that "*Understanding Poetry* will not be the only book of its kind. . . . But it will be a model difficult to follow." The truth of Morris' statement may be found in the now general belief that *Understanding Poetry* has been one of the truly revolutionary books of our times. It has had a host of imitators in both poetry and prose concerns, but none has been so good or so influential as the original. It has been the single most important influence upon a whole generation of teachers in college English departments; it has changed the teaching of literature in American colleges. This change, believes former Brooks and Warren student Alan Swallow, has been mostly to the good. "It has brightened up the college English courses in many respects; it has provoked the student to some thought he otherwise might not have had; it has made him 'see' literature more carefully than did his counterpart" prior to *Understanding Poetry.* Assessing the impact of Brooks's and Warren's textbook in 1957, Swallow saw some bad results as well. "As the young teachers 'fell into line,' a new kind of academic unimaginativeness has been created. And the second generation has been on the whole, pretty poor." [20]

Understanding Poetry was Brooks's and Warren's last jointly written book while the two of them were at LSU. Together they worked on a book on Shakespeare as poet which was never completed, and Warren declined Brooks's offer to join him in a companion volume to *Understanding Poetry.* In December, 1941, Warren told his editor at Harcourt Brace that he had "no intention of doing a lot" of textbooks because such writing took too much time away from his fiction. "In fact," he continued, "I am not much inclined to

19. John Crowe Ransom, "The Teaching of Poetry," *Kenyon Review,* I (Winter, 1939), 81.
20. R. L. Morris, "Can Poetry Be Taught?" *Sewanee Review,* XLVII (January, 1939), 93–94; Alan Swallow, "The Careful Young Men: Tomorrow's Leaders Analyzed by Today's Teacher's," *Nation,* March 9, 1957, pp. 209–10.

any except in so far as it grows directly out of the work in the classroom." Brooks, he assured Lambert Davis, felt much the same way. Warren, therefore, asked to be excused from "the textbook angle" unless he and Brooks should happen into a topic into which they could put their best interests.[21]

For most of LSU's English faculty, *An Approach to Literature* and *Understanding Poetry* were "a baptismal experience" in the detailed objective analysis of poetic method and quality of the type offered by Brooks and Warren. According to Robert Heilman, they did not see these changes as part of an educational revolution but thought of them as not much more than "procedural innovations introduced by amiable and talented colleagues who did not look or sound like revolutionaries." Brooks and Warren were strongly convinced of the worth of their approach, but were by no means dogmatic. Heilman recalls that they were always willing to listen to arguments against their methods and were often willing to make adjustments. Never doctrinaire or absolutist, Brooks once admitted that applying the new critical approach to Wordsworth was like "manicuring an elephant."[22]

This amiability and good humor went far to prevent the formation of mutually antagonistic factions within the English department. Brooks, especially, is remembered for his beguiling, gentlemanly persuasion when attempting to convert colleagues to the Brooks and Warren method, and was able to speak the language of the traditional scholar as well as any at LSU. As author of one work on dialectical pronunciation and as an editor of the Thomas Percy letters, publications characterized by a rather small ledge of text sitting atop a double column of small-type footnotes, he had well established his scholarly reliability. Warren, too, was notoriously interested in history, and although he agreed with Brooks that it was more important that English students know critical methods and be able to apply them in specific judgments than to possess a wide knowledge of English literature as a historical sequence, he dumbfounded at least one graduate student who thought he had Warren's

21. Robert Penn Warren to Lambert Davis, December 17, 1941.
22. Heilman, "LSU Forty Years After," 130–39.

mind perfectly categorized. In a comprehensive oral examination for the Master's degree, Warren asked the hapless candidate, who was expecting to be asked to cite examples of irony in John Donne, to name instead the two biographers of Robert Browning. Like most other students who have attempted to categorize Warren, he erred in believing Warren uninterested in scholarly research.

Warren's regard for his graduate students was remarkably high. Even in comparison with the exceptionally high quality of students he had associated with at Vanderbilt, Berkeley, Yale, and Oxford, Warren was quite satisfied with the members of his seminars. After four years at LSU Warren wrote to A. T. Johnson, his former department head at Southwestern College in Memphis, "Every year the quality of the graduate students here is getting better and better, at least in our department."[23]

John E. Palmer recalls how the excitement generated by the work that Brooks and Warren were doing at Baton Rouge attracted him back to Louisiana. Palmer, a native of Gibsland, Louisiana, took his Bachelor's degree with honors from Louisiana Polytechnic Institute with a triple major in French, English, and political science. Upon graduation in June, 1935, he accepted a fellowship to Columbia University and flew to New York for his first semester as a graduate student. No sooner had Palmer registered for his summer courses than someone showed him a copy of the first issue of the *Southern Review*, then less than a month old. So excited was Palmer that something so good was coming out of his home state that he immediately called Baton Rouge, and, by virtue of having edited the undergraduate newspaper at Louisiana Tech, received a fellowship in the journalism department. "I just wanted to be where the *Southern Review* was happening," he recalls.[24]

Palmer finished his second Bachelor's degree in 1937 and, having taken a number of classes with the editors of the *Southern Review*, became a graduate student in the English department. During the year that it took him to earn his Master's degree, Palmer became close friends with Albert Erskine, with whom he worked as

23. Robert Penn Warren to A. T. Johnson, October 6, 1938.
24. Interview with John E. Palmer, May 16, 1979.

an editorial assistant at the LSU Press. With the strong recommendation of Brooks and Warren, Palmer, in September, 1938, won a Rhodes scholarship and sailed to England to begin work on his degree as a Bachelor of Literature. He stayed with the Warrens in Italy during the summer of 1939 until the war in Europe abbreviated his vacation and he was recalled to England. Palmer finished his work at Oxford in 1940 and returned to Baton Rouge as an instructor in the English department. For two years he shared a house belonging to the Warrens with Robert Lowell, Jean Stafford, and Peter Taylor, who served as his graduate assistant.

Palmer was paid $175 per month that year to teach five sections of freshman composition, and so he continued to moonlight as editorial assistant and designer for the LSU Press until December. That month Albert Erskine left Baton Rouge to take a position with New Directions and Brooks and Warren were happy to hire Palmer as Erskine's replacement. The managing editor's position allowed him to drop two of his sections of composition and he continued with the *Southern Review* until accepting a Naval commission in 1942. After the war, Palmer returned to Baton Rouge as an assistant professor, and there he remained until 1946, when he was offered the editor's post at the *Sewanee Review*. After eight years, he left to become editor of the *Yale Review*, where he was once again reunited with Brooks and Warren.

Brooks's and Warren's reputations drew students to Baton Rouge from all over the nation. Alan Swallow is one example. Born on February 11, 1915, in Powell, Wyoming, he had while still in high school abandoned his early ambition to become an engineer in favor of becoming a poet. At the same time, he discovered the publications of the Haldeman-Julius Company, a little press which printed the Little Blue Book Series, and sold them at ten or twenty for a dollar. Swallow read 250 of the series during the summer of his sixteenth year, and began to think more or less seriously about the publication of quality literary material in an inexpensive format for widespread distribution.

During his high school and undergraduate years, Swallow began working toward his goals. He began sending out verse while a senior in high school and had his first acceptances in two or three little magazines. His sophomore year at the University of Wyoming, he decided to start a little magazine. *Sage*, as it was named, published local talent and went through several issues before its demise. Swallow stayed busy with numerous literary projects while at Wyoming. Upon graduation, he and his new wife considered taking over a small weekly newspaper to realize his ambitions. A letter from LSU changed his immediate plans. Robert Penn Warren had been the judge of a poetry contest sponsored by *College Verse* and had been impressed by Swallow's entry. Correspondence between the two followed, and not only did Warren arrange for Swallow's appointment to the graduate school with a reading fellowship, but also saw that Mrs. Swallow was hired as secretary at the *Southern Review*.

Although something of a leftist politically, Swallow got along very well with his Agrarian instructors. He finished his Master's degree work in one year, writing his thesis on "The Method of Composition in the Poems of Sir Thomas Wyatt," and applied to the English department at Berkeley to do his Ph.D. under Warren's former teacher Willard Farnham. Warren again gave his young student a strong recommendation, writing to Farnham, "He strikes me as a first-rate man. His reading has been wide; his development this year has been unusually rapid; he has a good philosophical and critical bent."[25] Berkeley turned down Swallow's application, and what Warren considered the California school's loss became LSU's gain. Swallow stayed on in Baton Rouge, working toward his Ph.D. and picking up his publishing career where *Sage* had left off.

Swallow later remembered that "in those days there were young writers arriving from all over the country to study under Brooks and Warren. One day two of them suggested that it would be a shame if some of the better student work was lost because there was nobody to print it." Having never forgotten his early ambition to become a publisher, Swallow took the job upon himself. During the fall of 1939, he borrowed $100 from his father and purchased a used hand press, some type, and furniture, and taught himself to print. He set up the press in the garage of his Dalrymple Drive apartment. "To

25. Robert Penn Warren to Willard Farnham, February 24, 1938.

my good fortune," he says, "the library of LSU had good holdings in the areas of history of type, of printing and of typography. I read all of these books I could so as to learn as much as possible in a short time about these materials, and then set out to print." The first book was called *Signets: An Anthology of Beginnings*, and Swallow's method was to set one page of type at a time, print the copies on the hand press, and then distribute the type back in the cases. "I don't object to setting the type," Swallow admitted years later. "In fact I rather like it."[26] But when he published *Signets*, he insisted that each of its contributors come by at the end of the day to help distribute the type in its cases.

The volume was finished by March, 1940, and was the first to carry the Swallow imprint. Although Alan Swallow was solely responsible for publication, the two students who first suggested the idea, Frederick Brantley and Sheila Corley, were charged with the editorial duties. In the book's foreword, they observed that "the introduction of young writers who are just beginning or who have had perhaps one or two pieces of work published is a task not often undertaken by the anthologist. Such a collection is usually cast aside because of a lack of marketability or less frequently because the basis of selection is too arbitrary to justify itself."[27] Although *Signets* is by no means one of the forgotten treasures of American literature, one of the twelve young writers of poems and short stories represented there, Swallow himself, went on to attain a well-deserved niche in the pantheon of twentieth-century literati, and several others—poet Thomas McGrath, Pulitzer Prize winning journalist Thomas H. Thompson, and Poe biographer and university professor Robert D. Jacobs, for example—have earned respect in their individual fields. Coeditor Frederick Brantley left LSU to do graduate work at the State University of Iowa, where he continued publishing his short stories in *American Prefaces*, a little magazine which he edited upon completion of his Master's degree.

Alan Swallow's second venture into publishing, the first of the

26. Richard Ellman, "Publisher for Poets," *Saturday Review*, July 22, 1961, pp. 33–34.
27. Sheila Corley and Fredrick Brantley, Foreword to *Signets: An Anthology of Beginnings* (Baton Rouge, 1940), n.p.

Swallow Pamphlets series, was also printed in his off-campus garage. This offering was called *First Manifesto* and consisted entirely of the poems of another of Warren's students of creative writing, Thomas McGrath. Swallow recalls as one of the most exciting days of 1940 the one in which Frederick Brantley told him of a new student on campus who was writing verse and had published a few things in the magazines. McGrath, a new M.A. candidate, was, like Swallow, a leftist in the midst of conservatives. Brantley brought Swallow some of McGrath's manuscripts, and the novice publisher "sat down by the wall of the garage and read them through. Reading them it was a great shock to think that we had such a fine and exciting talent."[28] Swallow immediately set about meeting the new poet and soon resolved to print a small collection of his poems.

"The reason for the pamphlet idea," said Swallow, "was that I still had the notion . . . that good literature ought to be put out at a very inexpensive price, and these pamphlets were projected at 25¢ each. I still had in mind that a primary reason for getting the equipment for printing, and gaining the experience in printing, was to be able to have a little magazine." About that same time, Swallow conceived the idea that would become the hallmark of all his future publishing. While at work on McGrath's manuscript, he came to believe that "in the realm of book publishing there was a need for an effort analogous to that of the 'little' magazine in the magazine world; that is, the effort would be non-commercial and would provide labor and editorial dedication, with the thought of quality without regard to the commercial or sales aspect of the matter."[29] Although Swallow never abandoned the idea of publishing a literary journal, his ideas on book publishing began to solidify and to take over the main part of his energies. Chiefly he was interested in responding to the problems of poets on the matter of publishing. Swallow resolved by 1940 that he would put his own labor into producing work rather than pay printers' expenses, thus reducing the out-of-pocket expenditures to such an extent that he could sell enough to pay back that expense and leave enough to pay his author's royalty and to support his family.

First Manifesto appeared in April, 1940, one month after *Sig-*

28. Alan Swallow, "Story of a Publisher," *Wyoming Library Roundup*, XXI (September, 1966), 34.
29. *Ibid.*, 34–35.

nets. Swallow had worn his type rather badly and had to replace it with a better series, but he had learned much about the printer's trade. During the year, he read even more about printing and typology and, through Willmore Kendall, a member of LSU's political science faculty, began correspondence with a Chicago typographer who advised him on the selection of type. This man was doing the layout for a magazine which Swallow became determined to publish and which appeared in the fall of 1940 under the title *Modern Verse.*

Fall of 1940 was also the projected date of publication for the Swallow Press's first full-length book of poems. "In thinking about a first full book of poetry to offer on the market, I asked Robert Penn Warren if he knew any good poets who had remained unpublished in book form," Swallow recalled.[30] Warren suggested his old Berkeley roommate, Lincoln Fitzell, whose work Swallow had seen in the *Southern Review* and admired. Swallow contacted Fitzell, and in May, 1940, the poet and the printer entered into a publishing contract. With his course work and qualifying examinations completed, Swallow packed his printing equipment and returned to Wyoming for the summer to finish his dissertation and to begin work on Fitzell's book, *In Plato's Garden.* The printing job, which Swallow always felt was one of the best he ever did, was finished and the book issued in the fall of 1940 when the printer moved to Albuquerque to begin full-time teaching at the University of New Mexico.

In the meantime, the magazine *Modern Verse* began publication that fall and drew heavily upon Swallow's former LSU fellow graduate students to fill its pages. Thomas McGrath contributed eleven poems to the first volume, and E. Shirley Forgotson sent in one. Lincoln Fitzell and Yvor Winters also placed poems in the first issue. Swallow's editorial policy reflected well his philosophy of publishing. "A magazine such as this," he told his readers, "edited, printed and published by one person—all these labors contributed without remuneration—can afford the luxury of an individual editorial policy. The editor may choose for publication . . . those poems which he regards worth his labors. . . . His only responsibility to the readers . . . is that he keep his standard of selection catholic and broad."[31]

30. *Ibid.*, 35.
31. Alan Swallow, "Editorial," *Modern Verse*, I (January–October, 1941), 25.

Modern Verse ceased publication with the bombing of Pearl Harbor, when its editor, printer, and publisher joined the U.S. Army Medical Corps, but Swallow's contribution to letters continued after World War II. As a professor of English at the University of New Mexico, Western State College, and the University of Denver, Swallow followed in the footsteps of his LSU mentors, Cleanth Brooks and Robert Penn Warren, as a strong advocate of the modern critical revolution which they had helped to launch. Yet valuable as the teaching methods were which Swallow learned from Brooks and Warren and passed on to students of his own, Swallow's principal contribution to literature was in the field of publishing and editing. Here, too, his skills and his inspiration were gleaned largely from his association with the editors of the *Southern Review*. The editor, printer, and publisher of Swallow Press might well have been quoting Brooks or Warren when he wrote that the one great virtue of his profession was "in the estimation of new work, where the matter of critical judgment becomes paramount." What Swallow learned from his exposure to the *Southern Review* and its editors was that although the judgment of a commercial press may be blunted by many factors, including the possible economic picture for the book, the publisher of the little magazine can assert his own judgment and taste. In Swallow's words, "he need not compromise so much. And although no one taste can do the whole job . . . if his taste is strong, he will bring to light some excellent work."[32]

When Herbert Lyons of the *New Republic* wrote to Robert Penn Warren in September, 1941, asking him to recommend some "promising unknowns" for the magazine's "writers under 30" supplement, Warren responded with the names of seven of his most promising graduate students and Baton Rouge friends. Among them were three he recommended with "special enthusiasm": Peter Taylor, Jean Stafford, and Robert Lowell. Lowell, one of *the* Lowells of Massachusetts, had attended, as had his father, St. Mark's school before going on to Harvard. During his second year at the university, Lowell "was getting quite morose and solitary" and so took the advice of his psychiatrist, former Fugitive poet Merrill Moore, to go study with

32. Alan Swallow, *An Editor's Essays of Two Decades* (Denver, 1962), 7.

John Crowe Ransom at Vanderbilt. Lowell made the move against his family's wishes. They would "rather have had me a genial social Harvard student," he said, "but at least I'd be working hard this way. It seemed to them a queer but orderly step."[33]

Lowell left for the South in the spring of 1937, just as Ransom was leaving Vanderbilt for a position at Kenyon College, with a summer's sojourn between as instructor at the University of Colorado's writers' seminar. With little to occupy him that summer, Lowell took up Ford Madox Ford's casual invitation to visit him at the home of Allen Tate and Caroline Gordon in Tennessee. In what Lowell later regretted as "a terrible piece of youthful callousness," he suggested that he remain with the already straining Tate household through the summer. Caroline Gordon had three guests and her own family to cook and clean for and was writing a novel as well. The northern youth did not understand the Tates' demurrer that if he stayed they would have to put him in a tent and so went to Sears, Roebuck, bought a tent and rigged it on their lawn, living there for two months and taking his meals with the family and other guests. That summer Lowell began to fall under the sway of the Vanderbilt poets who, in Lowell's words, were "partly a continuation of Pound and Eliot and partly an attempt to make poetry much more formal than Eliot and Pound did: to write in metres but to make the metres look hard and to make them hard to write."[34]

Ransom returned from Colorado for the fall semester, and Lowell enrolled in his classes at Kenyon. There he majored in classics, was elected to Phi Beta Kappa, and was awarded the Bachelor of Arts degree *summa cum laude* in 1940. In 1940, also, Lowell married Jean Stafford. In a fictionalized account of their meeting, courtship and marriage, Miss Stafford has written that she

> met Theron Mayband [Robert Lowell] in Adams [Boulder] Colorado . . . at a writers' convention at Neville University [the University of Colorado] where as a graduate student, I was serving on the arrangements committee. Theron had left

33. Frederick Seidel, "Robert Lowell," *Paris Review*, XXV (Winter–Spring, 1961), 56–95, reprinted in Thomas Parkinson (ed.), *Robert Lowell: A Collection of Critical Essays* (Englewood Cliffs, 1968), 12–35.
34. Parkinson (ed.), *Robert Lowell*, 28.

his native Boston for his first trip West in order to meet the famous . . . American poet Fitzhugh [Ransom]. . . . I found Theron's brilliant talk and dark good looks somehow reminiscent of young Nathaniel Hawthorne. We were married in Adams a few weeks after the conference ended, and left one week later for Baton Rouge.[35]

As early as January, 1940, Ransom had written to Brooks about a possible fellowship for Lowell. Randall Jarrell had advised Lowell to go to LSU for graduate work, Jarrell told Cleanth Brooks, and "if he does, you'll have an awfully good student." Lowell decided to go to Baton Rouge when he graduated in June—he "thinks he'd rather work with you and Red than anywhere else," Ransom informed Brooks—and his Kenyon mentor began to pull strings to get him a scholarship or fellowship. "He's a strong man," Ransom wrote to Brooks, "the last of the line of Lowells bearing the name, due to give a good account of himself before he is done. He is a bit slow and thorough, but he has enormous critical sense. He . . . wants above all things to work into the sort of critic who compares effects in the different languages." Brooks replied to Ransom's recommendation in early February, informing him that Lowell should write directly to William Read for application and that he would speak to the chairman on Lowell's behalf. Brooks entered the caveat, however, that he was less than certain that Lowell really should come to Baton Rouge. "There are many things wrong with LSU," he warned, "and—this is strictly under the rose—some of our best graduate students from away from here who come because of the *Southern Review*, have had disappointments, but I think that a year might not be bad. There are enough good men and good courses," Brooks continued, "to give him something interesting and perhaps valuable for at least that time, and naturally, and selfishly, Red and I should be highly delighted to have him."[36]

Lowell's plans changed, and he did not enter his application until June, after he had graduated from Kenyon. Ransom wanted Lowell

35. Jean Stafford, "An Influx of Poets," *New Yorker*, November 6, 1978, p. 43.
36. Randall Jarrell to Brooks, February, 1940; John Crowe Ransom to Cleanth Brooks, January 15, 1940; Brooks to Ransom, February 7, 1940.

to stay on in Gambier with a full-time post at the *Kenyon Review*, but the college's president appointed another candidate to the position instead. Thus Lowell was left without options, and Ransom rushed off a long letter to Dean Pipkin in hopes of a last minute appointment at LSU for his favorite student. Referring to Lowell as "a very superlative article," he told Pipkin much the same story he had reported to Brooks and Warren. He added, however, that Lowell's marriage had totally dismayed his family, and they had cut off their financial support. Thus, Ransom urged LSU to find some kind of fellowship or job for the young poet. He also proposed that the *Southern Review* take the Lowells on as a team, mentioning that Stafford was not only an accomplished writer but a good typist as well.

Cleanth Brooks replied by wire to Ransom's frantic letter: PLEASE ADVISE BY WESTERN UNION IF MRS. LOWELL KNOWS SHORTHAND. LETTER FOLLOWS.[37] Jean Stafford's secretarial skills proved to be adequate, and the editors of the *Southern Review* were as happy to have her on their staff as they were to have Lowell among their students.

Tuesday, June 10, the morning after Robert Lowell received his diploma at Kenyon, he and Stafford bundled into their car and were off, "Southbound—/ a couple in passage / . . . young as they want to be." Arriving in Baton Rouge the couple took over the Robert Penn Warren establishment on Chimes Street, the Warrens having recently moved to a country house near Prairieville Plantation. Lowell remembered "the torch-pipes wasting gas all night" in the campus oil field where students parked for necking near the flaring gas burn-off pipes, the university's "measureless student prospects," and the "rats as long as my forearm regrouping toward / the sewage cleansing on the open canals."[38]

More important, he remembered, despite "the moisture mossing in the green seminar room," how often "Robert Penn Warren talked three hours on / Machiavelli . . . the tyrannicide of princes, / Cesare Borgia, Huey Long." To the young Lowell, Warren was "an old mas-

37. Cleanth Brooks to John Crowe Ransom, Western Union, n.d.
38. Robert Lowell, "Our After Life (for Peter Taylor)," *Shenandoah*, XXVIII (Winter, 1977), 2.

ter engaging the dazzled disciple." Besides taking graduate work with Warren, Lowell always made it a point to be at the *Southern Review* office at noon when it closed for lunch. Although, as Jean Stafford has written, he would try to help wrap *Southern Reviews* for mailing, he was "not terribly handy." Instead, he and Warren would usually have a sandwich and a soft drink and then read Dante for two hours. "I had just learned enough Italian to read Dante," Warren recalls, "and he was then in the process of learning it, and we read, argued, and it converted him before the year was over." [39]

More influential than Dante in Lowell's conversion was the Reverend Maurice Schexnayder, a native of St. John the Baptist Parish, Louisiana, and chaplain of the Catholic student group at LSU since 1935. During the fall semester of 1940, Warren was teaching his sixteenth-century literature course to an exceptional group of graduate students which included Robert Lowell and asked Reverend Schexnayder to address the class on the Reformation. The chaplain brushed up on his history, made the presentation, and after class was followed into the hall by Robert Lowell, who asked him for instruction in the Catholic faith. He had already been reading the works of Cardinal Newman, Lowell said, but wanted to learn more. Reverend Schexnayder began what Lowell would remember as "long patient explanations" of the *Number Two Catechism*.[40] He also lent Lowell books on the saints and points of theology which Lowell and Warren would argue at lunch time.

Warren spent the spring semester of 1941 teaching at the State University of Iowa and recalls that Lowell "got hooked about that time." Lowell received the Holy Sacrament of Baptism at Christ the King Chapel on the LSU campus on March 29, 1941, and at the same time Reverend Schexnayder rectified his marriage to Jean Stafford, who had become a Catholic convert long before but had lapsed. Soon thereafter the new convert took a one-week religious retreat to a nearby Jesuit monastery and on returning begged Rev-

39. Robert Lowell, "Louisiana State University, 1940," *Day By Day* (New York, 1977), 2; Robert Penn Warren in interview with David Farrell, Oral History Program, University of Kentucky Libraries.

40. Robert Lowell to Maurice Schexnayder, February 13, 1977, in collection of Bishop Maurice Schexnayder, Lafayette, Louisiana.

erend Schexnayder to allow him to go back for another month. The priest counseled moderation, however, and told the young man to concentrate on his studies, believing that "the biggest aim of religious education as applied in universities should be helping students to reconcile problems that come up in connection with their courses."[41]

Warren agreed with almost everyone else who knew Lowell that he was "eager and good company," and Brooks found him to be a brilliant student of Milton and the seventeenth century. "He was always a naif of one kind or another," Warren recalls. "And a calculated naif, too. But he had a charm and he had great intelligence and he read widely, and he could be wonderfully good company." Unfortunately, there was a fairly general agreement that, in Warren's words: "you talk about a man who was really mad . . . he was on his way."[42]

The last person to disagree with Warren's diagnosis would have been Lowell's wife, Jean Stafford, who according to campus rumor was harried from her bed to sleep on a platform of wooden planks as a sign of her husband's new-found piety. In her fictionalized account of their year in Baton Rouge, Miss Stafford tells of life with Robert Lowell:

> Half a year after we were married, Theron immersed in the rhythms of Gerard Manley Hopkins the poet, was explosively ignited by Gerard Manley Hopkins the Jesuit, and, as my mother would have said, he was off on a tear. We were in Louisiana then—in steaming, verminous fetor; almost as soon as the set of Cardinal Newman's works arrived from Dauber and Pine, the spines relaxed, for the Deep South cockroaches, the size of larks, relished the seasoned glue of the bindings and banqueted by night. . . .
>
> Father Neuscheier wore the miasmas from the bayous like a hair shirt, having chosen Baton Rouge out of many possibilities because it afforded him so excellent a chance to chasten his chaste flesh. Air conditioning was in its infancy—

41. "Reverend Maurice Schexnayder," *Louisiana Leader*, IV (December, 1936), 5.
42. Warren, Farrell interview.

not even the movie houses had it, or the saloons—but in most buildings of public nature there were those large, romantic ceiling fans, whirling and whirling quietly, at a slow speed, resembling animated daisies with petals made of wood. But there was no fan in Our Lady of Pompeii, and Father Neuscheier must have suffered as the wet air thickened and warmed, but not a bead of sweat shone on his perfectly round face or on his perfectly bald head. His austerity was right up Theron's alley, and before I knew what had happened to me, I had been dragged into that alley which was blind.

Theron had promised at the start that he would not impose his old-time religion on me, but within a week after he was confirmed I found myself being remarried in the Catholic Church, and a week after that I was going to daily Mass at seven in the morning . . . and to benediction in the late afternoon; together we told two Rosaries a day, and we replaced our reproduction of "A Little Street in Delft" and "La Grande Jatte" with black and white photographs of Bellini's "St. Francis Receiving the Stigmata" and Holbein's "Thomas More." There would be, so did declare the head of the house, no sacrilegious jokes: we did not even laugh one rainy Sunday when Father Neuscheier announced at Mass that if anyone had sneakily or even accidentally caught some raindrops on his tongue, thereby breaking his fast, he would not be eligible to receive Communion.

What had become of the joking lad I'd married? He'd run hellbent for election into that blind alley—and yanked me along with him, and there we snarled like hungry, scurvy cats.[43]

Lowell took Brooks's advice and stayed only one year at LSU, but in that year he made two of the most important decisions of his life. The first was his conversion to Catholicism and the second was his choice not to be anyone's "very distinguished professor of English." He left Baton Rouge to spend some time with the Tates at Sewanee

43. Jean Stafford, "An Influx of Poets," 49.

and from there went to work briefly in 1941–1942 as an editorial assistant for the Roman Catholic publishing firm of Sheed and Ward in New York, a position he acquired on the recommendation of Reverend Schexnayder. He also contributed to the Kenyon critics' volume of essays on Gerard Manley Hopkins. But most important, as Lowell wrote Bishop Schexnayder on February 13, 1977, only a few weeks before his death, "a year or so after leaving Louisiana, I turned out to be a poet, and so it continues."[44]

While Robert Lowell was busy becoming a Catholic and a poet, Jean Stafford occupied herself writing and working in the *Southern Review* office. "The job isn't bad," she wrote their friend from Kenyon, Peter Taylor. The office looked "like a hogsty with an accumulation of years of manuscript," but Erskine and Brooks, she found, were "nice to work for." Despite the city's "hot and steamy" climate and roaches "as big as a calf," she was soon enjoying the place and urging Taylor to join them. "We want you to come here next year (or this summer or this week if possible) instead of Iowa," she wrote. "It would be much more fun."[45] Apparently Taylor agreed, for he was soon boarding with the couple on Chimes Street.

The only native southerner of the three, Taylor had graduated from a Memphis high school in the spring of 1935 and gone down river to New Orleans with a school friend, the two of them intent on working their way to Europe on a freighter. While looking for a suitable ship to hire on, Taylor and his companion heard that Senator Huey P. Long was delivering a radio address from a French Quarter hotel and thought that it would be fun to see the red-neck messiah who was making Franklin Roosevelt doubt his own job security. The two young adventurers found the hotel, climbed an unguarded fire escape, and perched in an open window to watch the Kingfish making his speech. There they remained unmolested while Long went through his flamboyant performance. Growing bored at last with the free show, they withdrew to sample some of the more exciting aspects of the New Orleans evening. Taylor was impressed with the

44. Lowell to Schexnayder, February 13, 1977, in collection of Bishop Schexnayder.
45. Jean Stafford, "Some Letters to Peter and Eleanor Taylor," *Shenandoah*, XXX (Spring, 1979), 27–55.

lax security precautions, not at all like the heavily armed vigil which surrounded the senator while in Baton Rouge; but three months later Long lay dead in his capital despite the bodyguards assigned to protect him.

By then young Taylor had returned from his foreign adventure and within the year had enrolled in Vanderbilt's English program, where he fell under the sway of John Crowe Ransom. When Ransom left Vanderbilt for Kenyon in 1937, Taylor returned to Memphis to enroll at Southwestern University. There he signed up for Allen Tate's creative writing seminar, but Tate found that he "could not teach him anything," and so asked him to leave the class after two weeks. "The simple truth," says Tate, "is that he had a perfection of style at the age of eighteen that I envied." Seeing that he could do nothing for this exceptionally gifted young man, Tate sent him back to Ransom at Kenyon, but not before forwarding two of his stories to Brooks and Warren at the *Southern Review*. "They were obviously the work of a very gifted young writer who had a flavor and a way of his own," says Warren. "The editors of *The Southern Review* recognized these virtues, but decided to wait for the next showing" of Tate's find. "He was very young, just starting college, and there seemed to be plenty of time." Taylor did, however, place his stories in a little magazine called *River*, making Warren wish that he had them back.[46]

In 1939 Taylor moved on to Kenyon to participate in "the creative writing class, which we all acknowledged as our reason for being at Kenyon." There Taylor roomed with Robert Lowell, the Jim Pruitt of his short story "1939." Both of them, in the terms of the story, had "come to Kenyon because we were bent upon becoming writers of some kind or other and the new president of the college had just appointed a famous and distinguished poet to the staff of the English Department."[47] That poet, of course, was Ransom, who insisted when Taylor graduated in 1940 that he go with Lowell to study with Brooks and Warren at LSU.

46. Allen Tate, "Peter Taylor," *Shenandoah*, XXVIII (Winter, 1977), 9; Robert Penn Warren, Introduction to Peter Taylor's *A Long Fourth and Other Stories* (New York, 1948), iii.
47. Peter Taylor, "Sentimental Journey [1939]," *New Yorker*, March 12, 1955, pp. 33–57.

At LSU Taylor enrolled in a seminar with Warren, and the two became quite friendly. As Warren remembers, Taylor was a real asset to the class, never opening "his mouth without uttering a shrewd perception or wry criticism." Student and professor, however, got to know each other outside the classroom as well, for "talk in that little seminar didn't end with the 6 P.M. bell." Thus, with some difficulty Taylor told Warren shortly after his arrival that he was leaving LSU. "With grave kindness," Warren recalls, "Peter tactfully explained that graduate work was not for him. . . . He had to be a writer . . . and he had to put all his eggs in one basket. I knew damned well he was a writer if I'd ever seen one, and I was in no mood to criticize his decision."[48] In fact, Taylor stayed on at LSU for a while, leaving only to enlist in the army at the beginning of World War II. During his Baton Rouge residence, he was "a gift of God to the *Southern Review*," publishing three stories in the journal within two years. One, "A Spinster's Tale" made the O'Brien Honor Roll in 1941, and another, "The Fancy Woman," was selected in 1942.

Next on Warren's list of stand-outs from his writing seminars was Leonard Unger. Like so many of Brooks's and Warren's best students, Unger came to LSU from Vanderbilt with John Crowe Ransom's and Donald Davidson's recommendations. Feeling "no guidance or pressure to specialize or to qualify for a profession," Unger had majored in English at Vanderbilt, he says, "out of a kind of indecision." Like many other Vanderbilt students of that era, he was influenced, charmed, and profoundly impressed by John Crowe Ransom.[49] At the end of Unger's undergraduate career, just before he graduated Phi Beta Kappa in 1937, Ransom advised him to further pursue his career in letters at LSU.

On December 8, 1936, Ransom wrote to Warren informing him that "an excellent man here, Leonard Unger, is putting in his application with Pipkin for a Graduate Scholarship in English. . . . He would make a star pupil for you and Cleanth, being decidedly a modern, and in fact a pretty good practitioner of verse. He would certainly command a scholarship here but for our iron-clad rule that

48. Robert Penn Warren, "Two Peters: Memory and Opinion," *Shenandoah*, XXVIII (Winter, 1977), 8, 10.
49. Leonard Unger to author, October 29, 1979 (in possession of the author).

no town student can get one." Four days later Davidson seconded Ransom's recommendation in a formal letter to Pipkin to which he attached the handwritten addenda, "Mr. Unger is really good," as if the typewritten form letter were insufficient or insincere.[50]

Unger's father, a dry goods merchant, was none too keen on the idea of his son's postgraduate education, but Unger recalls that one day near graduation, Ransom "bought a pair of suspenders from my father, introduced himself, and recommended my going to grad school."[51] Unger came to LSU the next year as reading assistant to Nathaniel Caffee, but from the start he was a Brooks and Warren follower. During his senior year at Vanderbilt, Unger had developed an enthusiasm for the poetry of William Blake, and when he came to LSU, he proposed to do his Master's thesis on that early Romantic poet. Brooks, who was Unger's thesis director, vetoed the idea on the grounds that the LSU library was inadequate for the necessary research. Instead of Blake, Brooks and Unger decided on Eliot's *Ash Wednesday* as a suitable topic.

Unger remembers his first engagement with Eliot's poetry as a brief report in Ransom's class his sophomore year at Vanderbilt. "At the time it seemed like a bright thing to do," he says. Few, if any, of his classmates had even heard of Eliot, and "in addition to the pleasure of appearing bright to Mr. Ransom and myself, I was by that time genuinely enthralled by Eliot's poetry." Unger expanded his brief report into a short paper for Brooks, who had recently published his famous explication of *The Waste Land*, and with Brooks's assistance that short paper grew into Unger's Master's thesis. "Everything else that I have written on Eliot has followed from the experience of exploring *Ash Wednesday*—for indeed the preparation of the thesis was an experience of exploration. It was an education beyond anything else I had encountered in academic routines," he reports. "I had grabbed hold of something and it moved, and I hung on."[52]

During the two years of his Master's degree program, Unger

---

50. John Crowe Ransom to Robert Penn Warren, December 8, 1936; Donald Davidson to Charles Pipkin, December 12, 1936.
51. Leonard Unger to author, October 29, 1979.
52. Leonard Unger, *T. S. Eliot: Moments and Patterns* (Minneapolis, 1966), 4, 5.

proved not only an able scholar, but also a great help to Brooks in the preparation of *Modern Poetry and the Tradition*. Unger ultimately had more pieces accepted by the *Southern Review* than did any other of Brooks's and Warren's students. In his final year at LSU, he placed his first essay with the journal, "Notes on *Ash Wednesday*," based on his Master's thesis under Brooks. In 1942 he contributed four poems to the *Review*, proving Ransom's estimation of him as a "pretty good practitioner of verse," and also his second essay on Eliot entitled "T. S. Eliot's Rose Garden: A Persistent Theme."

On finishing his Master's work at LSU Unger chose to do his Ph.D. at the University of California. Like Alan Swallow, however, he was disappointed in his hopes despite Warren's best efforts to pry a fellowship out of his old friend Bertrand Bronson. Unger was, however, offered scholarships at the University of Chicago and the State University of Iowa. "The one at Iowa pays him a little better," Warren mentioned in his letter of recommendation to Bronson, "so he is taking that one." While teaching there in the spring semester of 1941 Warren was reunited with Unger and a number of other former LSU students as well. "The LSU boys are setting the pace," he proudly reported to Brooks.[53]

Unger put aside the writing of verse soon after his *Southern Review* debut, but his work on Eliot and the moderns has rivaled that of his LSU mentors. Ransom, in fact, considers his essay on Eliot in the Minnesota Pamphlet Series "though crowded as it had to be in about 50 pp., the best thing we have on that poet." Leonard Unger has, to some degree, reacted against the early training he received from Ransom, Brooks, and Warren. In his long essays "Donne's Poetry and Modern Criticism" and "Fusion and Experience," for example, he takes exception to the prevailing notions of Donne's poetry in particular, and all of metaphysical poetry in general, as fostered by Eliot, Ransom, Brooks, and Tate. He denies that metaphysical poetry contains a fusion of thought and feeling and that metaphysical poets possessed a unified sensibility. But he takes

53. Robert Penn Warren to Bertrand Bronson, April 7, 1939; Warren to Brooks, n.d.

great pains to assert that "in these two essays Ransom, Brooks and Tate—the first two my former teachers and all three my present friends—are treated 'impersonally.'" His attacks are purely rhetorical and written for the joy of exercising his wits. "If I have achieved anything of value here," he declares, "then my book is but partial evidence of my grateful indebtedness to these men."[54]

In addition to this array of poets, novelists, short story writers, editors, publishers, and critics which came out of Brooks's and Warren's LSU classrooms, the two *Southern Review* editors influenced and helped to train a number of very highly regarded English teachers, journalists, and social critics while at Baton Rouge. John Edward Hardy, for example, is a Baton Rouge native who completed his Bachelor's degree with Brooks in 1944, and was encouraged by Brooks to do graduate work at the State University of Iowa, where he completed his Master's degree in 1946. From there he moved on to Yale to an instructor's position. After Brooks joined the Yale faculty in 1946 the two completed an edition of *The Poems of Mr. John Milton*, an effort which had begun in Brooks's undergraduate seminar on Milton at LSU. Hardy left Yale in 1948 to pursue his Ph.D. at Johns Hopkins. Finishing there in 1956, he joined the staff of the Department of English at the University of Illinois at Chicago Circle, where he has become coordinator of graduate English studies and has published several volumes of criticism including, in 1973, an analysis of the work of Katherine Anne Porter.

Robert D. Jacobs, a native of Vicksburg, Mississippi, first attended LSU in 1938, having earned Bachelor's and Master's degrees in English at the University of Mississippi. A junior fellowship at LSU entitled him to teach two sections of freshman composition for $60 a month and pursue a Ph.D. specializing in medieval literature. Jacobs had first encountered the poetry of John Crowe Ransom in a course on southern literature at Ole Miss, and not long after arriving at LSU he became aware of the pervasive influence of Brooks and Warren. Although he chose Bosley Woolf, LSU's finest medievalist, as his director, Jacobs chose the structure of *Beowulf* as

54. John Crowe Ransom to Horst Frenz, October 30, 1961, in Young, *Gentleman in a Dustcoat,* 458; Leonard Unger, *The Man and the Name: Essays on the Experience of Poetry* (Minneapolis, 1956), vii, viii.

his dissertation topic and planned to analyze the Anglo-Saxon poem by the Brooks and Warren method. In addition to his study of medieval verse, Jacobs wrote some modern poetry, and saw one of his compositions published in Alan Swallow's *Signets*.

Near completion of his Ph.D. in January, 1941, Jacobs left the university to serve as an officer in the Marine Corps. When he returned to LSU at the end of World War II he was advised by Robert B. Heilman that the department was in decline and that he should finish his degree elsewhere. Jacobs, therefore, moved to Johns Hopkins, changed his major to American literature, and his dissertation topic to Edgar Allan Poe. At Hopkins he met Louis D. Rubin, Jr., a student in the Department of Writing, Speech, and Drama, in which Jacobs was a faculty member while yet a student in the Department of English. Together they took over the student literary magazine, which they coedited as the *Hopkins Review*, modeled on the *Southern Review* which they both greatly admired. Jacobs and Rubin commissioned for this magazine a series of articles on writers in the modern South, including Brooks and Warren, and these they anthologized as *Southern Renascence: The Literature of the Modern South*. Several years later they again collaborated on *South: Modern Southern Literature in its Cultural Setting*.

Jacobs credits his exposure to Brooks and Warren and their textbooks with even more influence on his teaching career than on his publication. Although a writer of very little fiction or verse, Jacobs was "pressed into service" as teacher of a creative writing course at Johns Hopkins where, armed with *Understanding Fiction* and his recollections of overheard conversations between Robert Penn Warren and Walton Patrick at LSU, he "managed somehow to teach the class." Among his students was the now eminent novelist John Barth. "Obviously," Jacobs observes, "this early orientation in the Brooks-Warren method did no harm to his superb talent."[55]

This orientation has not harmed Jacobs either. After leaving Johns Hopkins in 1953 with a new Ph.D. he spent eighteen years teaching American literature at the University of Kentucky before moving on to the Georgia State University, where he now holds the

55. Robert D. Jacobs to author, July 18, 1982 (in possession of the author).

Callaway Professorship in Language and Literature. Among the most memorable occasions of his academic career Jacobs ranks his attendance, as a representative of the American Studies Association, of the Fugitives Reunion in Nashville in 1956, where he renewed his contact with his early mentors, Cleanth Brooks and Robert Penn Warren.

Walton R. Patrick is another Mississippi native who did graduate work with Brooks and Warren and has gone on to a career in academics. Graduated from Mississippi State College in 1933, Patrick came to Baton Rouge for the Master's which he completed in 1934, and in 1937 was granted LSU's first Ph.D. in English. He remained at LSU with the English faculty until the outbreak of World War II, during which he served as an officer in the field artillery. In 1945 Patrick moved to Auburn University where, in 1947, he became chairman of the English department, a position which he held until his retirement in 1978.

In 1931 Arthur H. Scouten came to LSU from upstate New York on a football scholarship, but proved too light to make the team. He stayed with the athletic department, however, as team manager and tutor. In this capacity he made the acquaintance of Huey Long, who got the young man a job with the state construction department and even engaged him as his personal driver. After a few courses with Robert Penn Warren, however, Scouten's main interest switched from football to literature. With a senior fellowship which paid $125 per month for carrying the murderous load of five sections of freshman composition, he remained at LSU doing graduate work until 1942. Since then he has taught Renaissance and Restoration drama at the University of Texas and the University of Pennsylvania and has amassed a bibliography of eight books, thirty-nine articles, essays, and notes, and scores of reviews in learned journals.

Aubrey L. Williams was born in Jacksonville, Florida, in 1922 and came to LSU as an undergraduate in 1940. Although nominally a journalism major and editor of the *Daily Reveille*, Williams found work in that department "shallow, even meaningless," and so "took all the English courses under Brooks that [he] could." Thus he became a strong editorial champion of the *Southern Review* when the administration threatened to shut down the magazine in 1942. Williams left LSU at the end of his junior year to serve in the army through World War II, but returned to finish his degree in 1947. Brooks, at that time, was about to make his move to Yale and asked Williams to come along to do graduate work in English. Williams was, of course, delighted, and intended to work under Brooks on some contemporary southern writer. At Yale, however, despite his mentor's distaste for the subject, Williams became highly involved in eighteenth century studies and since his 1952 Ph.D. has made a major contribution to the understanding of the age of Pope. When questioned on Brooks's influence on his career, Williams maintains that he "finally wanted to be an English teacher because of Cleanth Brooks and Robert Heilman; in what seemed to be the corrupt world of Louisiana politics and LSU academia, they seemed to be the most morally courageous, and the most intelligent and learned, men on the scene." [56]

Another promising young writer who came to LSU to study his craft under Robert Penn Warren was Thomas H. Thompson of Amarillo, Texas. Thompson completed his Bachelor's degree at the University of Southern California in 1932. He became a protégé of Thomas Wolfe, who introduced the young writer to Warren at the Boulder writers' conference in the summer of 1935. Thompson took Wolfe's suggestion that he sign up for graduate work at LSU in order to take advantage of Warren's creative writing course, and Warren was pleased to secure for him a teaching fellowship. Impressed by the young Texan's work, Warren published his first story, "Goodbye, Old Man," in the *Southern Review* in the summer of 1936. This story was selected by Edward O'Brien for the 1937 Roll of Honor and was followed in the *Review* by "Jolly" the following winter and by "A Shore for the Sinking" in the spring of 1938.

In addition to his creative writing course, Thompson took Warren's sixteenth century and Brooks's seventeenth century courses and did his thesis under Brooks, whom he considers to be "the best teacher of literature I ever had." Under anyone else but Warren, he believes he would have "flunked out," and so decided that "the life of scholarship was not for Thompson." [57] When he completed his Master's degree in 1939 Thompson took the advice that Sherwood

56. Aubrey Williams to author, October 2, 1979 (in possession of the author).
57. Thomas H. Thompson to author, October 2, 1979, and November 21, 1979 (in possession of the author).

Anderson had given him at Boulder. He returned to Amarillo and worked his way into the newspaper business. Anderson had told him that he had a storyteller's aptitude, but that he had led a sheltered life. He "hadn't gone hungry," in Anderson's words, and needed raw material. This Thompson hoped to find in the daily newspaper business. Thompson published no more fiction after returning to his Texas hometown, but his newspaper, the Amarillo *Globe-Times*, exposed a breakdown in local law enforcement in 1960 and led an election campaign that swept the lax officials from their posts. This piece of journalism earned for Thompson the Pulitzer Gold Medal Award in 1960, the Pulitzer Prize for his newspaper in 1961, and a seat on the Pulitzer Prize jury in 1962.

Brooks and Warren's Agrarian stand was also responsible for drawing to LSU a student who was to become one of the most articulate voices of the traditional South in the twentieth century. Richard M. Weaver, born at Weaverville, North Carolina, but raised in Lexington, Kentucky, became a member of the American Socialist party after earning his B.A. degree at the University of Kentucky, and remained a staunch leftist despite his graduate work at Vanderbilt with Donald Davidson and John Crowe Ransom. Weaver had entered Vanderbilt in 1933, and in the spring of 1934 received his M.A. in English. His thesis subject was "The Revolt Against Humanism." He continued graduate studies at Vanderbilt for two more years as a candidate for the Ph.D., and also taught in the English department, but left in 1936 without completing the requirements for his doctor's degree.

After leaving Vanderbilt Weaver taught for three years at Texas A&M University, until he realized "that I did not *have* to go back to this job, which had become distasteful, and that I did not *have* to go on professing the clichés of liberalism, which were becoming meaningless to me. . . . It is a great experience to wake up . . . to the fact that one does have a free will, and that giving up the worship of false idols is quite a practicable procedure." At the end of the year he gave up his Texas job "and went off to start my education over at the age of thirty."[58]

58. Richard M. Weaver, "Up from Liberalism," in *Life Without Prejudice* (Chicago, 1965), 129.

Weaver enrolled at LSU, and under Brooks and Warren's influence, undertook a course in extensive reading in the history of the American Civil War, "preferring," he said, "first-hand accounts by those who had actually borne the brunt of it as soldiers and civilians." Weaver states that in his research he has "attempted to find those things in the struggle of the South which speak for more than a particular people in a special situation. The result," he concedes, "is not pure history, but a picture of values and sentiments coping with the forces of a revolutionary age, and though failing, hardly expiring."[59]

In paying special attention to the history and literature of the Confederacy, Weaver "came to recognize myself in the past," and this recognition, according to Davidson, "was something more definite than the so-called 'search for identity' on which many moderns are said to be engaged. Weaver did not need to ask: 'Who am I?' He knew that." But his research fortified his self-knowledge, and, by relating himself more consciously to his southern forebears he was able to ask the larger philosophical questions: "Who are we?" and "What are we doing?" and "What ought we to do?"[60]

Under Brooks's supervision Weaver wrote the dissertation "The Confederate South, 1865–1910: A Study in the Survival of a Mind and Culture," which was later published under the title *The Southern Tradition at Bay: A History of Postbellum Thought*. The preparation of this dissertation, observes Donald Davidson, "marks the turning point of his career—the moment when he renounced the facile radicalism of the Roosevelt period for something more truly radical—the kind of 'radicalism' that the current term 'conservative' does not always suggest." As is true of the Agrarian essays of Tate, Ransom, Davidson, Brooks, and Warren, Weaver's dissertation addresses a far broader question than that posed exclusively by the American South in the fifty years after Appomattox. "As in indirect fire by artillery," Davidson says, "his 'aiming point' is indeed the South, but the 'target' just over the hump is the modern regime both North and South that has emerged in the mid-twentieth century." Weaver left LSU to go on to a highly distinguished career at

59. Richard M. Weaver, *The Southern Tradition at Bay* (New Rochelle, 1968), 388.
60. Donald Davidson, Foreword to Weaver, *Southern Tradition*, 19.

the University of Chicago, but his "flight" to the North was, as he said of that of the first generation of Agrarians, merely a "strategic withdrawal" to a location "where the contest can better be carried on."[61]

Other Brooks and Warren students from 1935 to 1942 include Pier Pasinetti, who left Italy with the Warrens in 1940 and lived in Baton Rouge until moving on to a Yale Ph.D. and a career as a novelist, Hollywood writer, and professor at UCLA; Melvin Watson, chairman of the English department of Chapman College at Orange, California; Ernest Clifton, chairman at North Texas State; Patrick Quinn, chairman at Wellesley; David Malone, chairman of the comparative literature program at the University of Southern California; William Harvard, head of the political science department at Vanderbilt; and Bernard Webb, chairman of the psychology department at the University of Florida.

61. *Ibid.*, 14; George Core and M. E. Bradford, Preface to Weaver, *Southern Tradition*, 10.

EIGHT

The *Review* or the Tiger

I think it better that in times like these
A poet's mouth be silent, for in truth
We have no gift to set a statesman
    right . . .

WILLIAM BUTLER YEATS
"On Being Asked for a War Poem"

I N April, 1938, R. P. Blackmur reported to Robert Penn
Warren that he had read "horrid rumors that *The Southern Review*
might prematurely die," and begged for reassurance that this was
not the case. Warren replied that "the rumor concerning the possible suspension of the publication is absolutely without foundation,"
but he also reported that he and Brooks had picked up the same
rumor elsewhere and were distressed to learn that its circulation
was so wide. "Certainly," he concluded, "the University is making
all plans to continue publication."[1] In the spring of 1938 Louisiana
State University certainly had no plans for discontinuing its prestigious quarterly. Although Huey Long's successor to the governor's
chair, O. K. Allen, and his successor, Richard Leche, had, if possible, even less interest in the *Review* than had the Kingfish, President James Monroe Smith was still firmly committed to the magazine, noting that "from the first this publication has enjoyed an
enthusiastic reception in the highest quarters. It has received the

1. R. P. Blackmur to Robert Penn Warren, April 22, 1938; Warren to Blackmur,
April 26, 1938.

213

most flattering commendations from eminent critics in this country and from some of similar authority in England. Some of its contents have been cited for literary awards, and in this and other respects it has attained a success which is indeed remarkable."

Smith went on to note that although "such an undertaking as *The Southern Review* [is] not an indispensable factor in the educational responsibilities of the University, it is yet an accomplishment in which we take great pride." He claimed to speak not only for himself and the university community but for students of English literature world-wide when he said that "this magazine is an ornament of the highest worth, deserving the esteem of all persons who value superior work in letters and criticism." While Smith was well aware that the readership of the *Review* was relatively small and that it could not be expected ever to pay its own way, he boasted that "whoever sponsors such a publication is . . . conferring upon civilization and culture within its region a benefit which is all the more to be praised," and that the Louisiana State University, by fathering the *Southern Review*, "has gained for itself the admiration of the intellectual world."[2]

But for all the extravagance of praise that Smith heaped upon the *Review*, which was his university's brightest jewel and in which he had played a minor founding role, there still existed a corruption at the core of Huey Long's university. Like the rotten bricks that launched Warren's Willie Stark on his political career in *All the King's Men*, it would soon lead to the collapse of the splendid reputation which the Louisiana State University had achieved since 1924 and would destroy the *Southern Review*, driving its editors from the South. The university which sheltered the *Review* and the literary colony which gathered around it was set in the midst of "a world of parasites of power," says Warren,

> a world that Long had been contemptuous of, but knew how to use. . . . This was a world of sick yearning for elegance and the sight of one's name on the society page of a New Orleans newspaper; it was the world of the electric moon devised, it

2. James Monroe Smith, "Biennial Report of the President, 1935–1937," Louisiana Collection, Louisiana State University, Baton Rouge.

was alleged, to cast a romantic glow over the garden when the president of the university and his wife entertained their politicos and pseudosocialites; it was a world of pretentiousness, of bloodcurdling struggles for academic preferment, of drool-jawed garb and arrogant criminality. It was a world all too suggestive, in its small bore, provincial way, of the airs and aspirations the newspapers attributed to that ex-champagne salesman Von Ribbentrop and to the inner circle of Edda Ciano's friends.[3]

Recalling his tenure at LSU, Warren says that living in Baton Rouge in the 1930s,

> you felt that you were living in the great world, or at least in a microcosm with all the forces and fatalities faithfully, if somewhat comically, drawn to scale. And the little Baton Rouge world of campus and Governor's Mansion and Capitol and the golden bathroom fixtures reported to be in the house of the university contractor was, once the weight of Long's contempt and political savvy had been removed by the bullet of the young Brutus in the Capitol, to plunge idiotically rampant to an end almost as dramatic as the scenes in the last bunkers in Berlin or at least the filling station on the outskirts of Milan. The headlines advertised the suicides and the population and penitentiaries, both Federal and state, received some distinguished additions.[4]

Long himself had put it as succinctly as anyone could when he said only a short time before his assassination: "If anything happens to me, the people who try to wield the powers that I have created will all land in jail." One such unfortunate was none other than James Monroe Smith, "a genius of a sort," according to Robert Heilman, "a big thinker before thinking big had been thought of, an imaginative man who like other men of imagination felt the letter of the law to be too irksome."[5] Although many members of Smith's fac-

3. Warren, "*All the King's Men:* The Matrix of Experience," 164.
4. *Ibid.*
5. Edwin A. Davis, *Louisiana: A Narrative History* (Baton Rouge, 1965), 342; Heilman, "Cleanth Brooks," 134.

ulty thought him a man who should never have been anything but a professor of education at Southwest Louisiana Institute, President Smith had uncontrolled powers at LSU. This was Long's legacy. When the late governor had given an order to his university president he wanted it executed instantly and with no possibility of interference from supervisors or auditors. From 1930 to 1935 Smith had had Long himself to deal with and that had proved check and balance enough to keep Smith in line. But with Long's death, Smith no longer had anyone to reckon with, and his freedom provided temptations too great for the "big thinker" to restrain.

Baton Rouge was the great center for dramatization of the new riches acquired by the heirs of Senator Long. Louisiana's capital in the late 1930s was a boom town, the "Virginia City on the Comstock Lode of Graft,"[6] and President Smith was as conspicuous as any of the others of the Long machine in flaunting his new-found wealth. LSU alumni, returning to campus for football games, were amazed at the extravagance of the parties thrown by the university's president. Among the old graduates who remembered their alma mater when she was an honest woman was Rufus W. Fontenot, collector of internal revenue in New Orleans, and his suspicions that Smith was living beyond his means were borne out when, after a short investigation, he discovered the president was transacting some highly curious dealings in whiskey and wheat.

Smith had undergone a slight apprenticeship in speculation at Lafayette. On savings from his family cafeteria, he had dabbled in real estate. Years before coming to LSU he had started on a stock market career in a small way. On a trip to New Orleans he visited a broker and made a contract to purchase $300 worth of Morrison Cafeteria stock on the installment plan, ten dollars down and ten dollars a month. The monthly payments "came out of the professor's hide." He had to write frequently, asking for extensions of the time in which to scrape together ten dollars for a payment. After a raise in salary at Lafayette, he bought a little more cafeteria stock. During his first years at LSU he continued "nickeling and diming" the stock market, but it was not until after Long's death that he began

6. Johnson, "Louisiana Revolution," 97.

to flash $1,000 bills around like the rest of the Louisiana big spenders. His first large speculation occurred in 1937, when he bought 1,000 barrels of one-year-old Bourbon whiskey in a Kentucky warehouse. The fact that the market broke and left him with a considerable loss did not deter him from further speculation in the immediate future.

Fontenot's investigation revealed that President Smith had forged $1,000,000 in university bonds to invest in wheat futures in the belief that there would be war in Europe in 1938 and that wheat prices would skyrocket. When British Prime Minister Neville Chamberlain came home from Munich and announced that "there will be peace in our time," however, wheat prices fell through the floor, and Smith was frantically seeking a way to cover his losses.

According to an investigative reporter for the *Saturday Evening Post*, Smith's main trouble seemed to be suggestibility. "From his political associates he got the idea that all office-holders were great thieves; from his academic associates he got the idea that all professors are great economists. These two ideas cross-fertilized each other and produced a scheme for a great coup in wheat." Smith had himself introduced, under an assumed name, at the brokerage house of Fenner and Beane, and explained that he and "a group of associates" were planning a large operation. "It filled me with joy when he said this," revealed the head of the firm later, because Smith "belonged to the political crowd. They had all the wherewithal in Louisiana. The old people, our former customers, were out. I felt that we were going to see the color of real money at last." Smith proceeded in the jargon that he had picked up from LSU's school of business, to explain that commodities were what were wanted. War, he said, was inevitable, and inflation would follow. Wheat was the prudent hedge. "He talked economics so masterfully," said the broker at Fenner and Beane, "that I could hardly restrain myself from asking if he would take me into his group."

Smith started by purchasing 2,000,000 bushels of wheat, posting $300,000 in LSU bonds as collateral. Then came Munich, and the brokers demanded more collateral. This time Smith was forced to give them forged bonds. The first bonds that Smith had put up were good in themselves but had been stolen from the university. As wheat continued to slump he walked into a printing house in Baton Rouge with a sample $1,000 bond and said, "Print me three hundred of these." This order was executed without question, but the firm rejected them as unaccompanied by an acceptable legal opinion as to their validity. Smith then deposited a $300,000 cashier's check on a New Orleans bank to cover his wheat purchases. He obtained the check merely by telling the bank that the board of supervisors of the university had authorized him to borrow it. This $300,000 swindle of the New Orleans bank got him in trouble in Baton Rouge. A Baton Rouge banker called and reproached him for giving preference to a New Orleans bank! "You're right," said President Smith. "It was thoughtless of me. But I'll tell you what I'll do. I'll take $100,000 from you."[7] The Baton Rouge banker happily handed over the money. Both banks lost their loans, for neither had been authorized by the board of supervisors of the university. Smith had forged the minutes authorizing the borrowings.

Dean Fred Frey, who worked every day with President Smith, says that Smith "kept his venture a well-guarded secret; so far as I know, no one on the university campus knew he was dabbling in wheat futures." Fenner and Beane, on the other hand, "knew good and well that he was operating under an assumed name." Once the scandal broke, Frey asked Smith what had induced him to get into the stock market and to gamble with the university's money. Smith explained that "after Huey Long's death, as the legislature was gradually cutting down on student aid, he dreamed up the idea of buying wheat futures, making a killing, and in this way providing a very large student aid fund for the university."[8] Smith's hopes of perpetuating his name by leaving a great endowment to the university were killed as soon as his misdeeds were known, and even Smith Hall, a large dormitory on the Baton Rouge campus, had its name chiseled away as soon as it was reported that he had left the country.

On June 21, 1939, Governor Richard Leche—often quoted as declaring, "I swore to uphold the Constitution of Louisiana and the United States, but I did not take any vows of poverty"—announced

7. *Ibid.*, 16, 17, 97, 98, 100, 102.
8. Frey, "Reminiscences of Fred C. Frey," 86.

that he would resign, effective within the week, for the sake of his health. Huey Long had never considered his brother Earl compe-tent to hold any major public office, and Earl had once referred to his famous older brother as "a big-bellied coward." Now, nearly four years after their reconciliation at Senator Long's deathbed, Lieuten-ant Governor Earl K. Long was on the eve of becoming governor. Never a friend of J. M. Smith, the heir to the Long machine was in a position now to do him irreparable damage. On June 25 Smith re-signed from the university and disappeared. Governor Leche re-signed at seven o'clock the following evening, and when the court-house opened on the morn of the new Long administration, the East Baton Rouge district attorney filed formal charges against Smith for embezzling $100,000 from LSU. On June 30 the East Baton Rouge Parish Grand Jury indicted Smith, and on July 1 for-mer LSU President James Monroe Smith, Commendatore of the Order of the Crown of Italy and Chevalier de la Legion d'Honneur, was arrested in Brockville, Ontario, where he had fled with his wife. On Independence Day, 1939, Mr. and Mrs. Smith were returned to face trial. "I'm not going to be a goat," Smith blustered. "I'm sorry I went away. I was ill advised."[9]

Crowds began arriving early at the New Orleans airport, and be-fore the plane bearing the Smiths arrived, the grounds surrounding the administrative building assumed the aspect of the Mardi Gras. Men and women hung over the fence that separated the building from the field. Hundreds of others sought a good view from the roof. Several groups brought along hot dogs and munched away happily as they awaited the arrival of the plane. Smith's misdeeds seemed less like "appalling vice," recalls Robert Heilman, "than like some kind of Gilbert and Sullivan picturesque and picaresque rascality."[10]

In the crowd waiting for the former LSU president's return was *Times-Picayune* reporter Carl Corbin. Corbin was one of the first newsmen to approach Smith after his plane touched down and he had disembarked, and the young journalist began asking Smith some rather pointed questions about his mishandling of university

9. "Jimmy the Stooge," *Time*, July 10, 1939, p. 14.
10. Heilman, "Baton Rouge and LSU Forty Years After," 129.

funds and his flight to avoid prosecution. "I don't know who you are," snapped Smith, "but you're very impertinent." "I thought you knew me, Doc," replied Corbin. "You kicked me out of LSU five years ago."[11] Carl Corbin had been one of the *Reveille* editors who had been expelled in December, 1934, "for issuing statements derogatory to LSU and subjecting it to unjust and unwarranted criticism."

Before Smith could answer he was whisked away into a big black limousine, the centerpiece of an impressive motorcade, complete with motorcycle policemen and wailing sirens, and escorted back to Baton Rouge and a waiting jail cell. Several loyal faculty members were waiting outside the parish courthouse, and John Earle Uhler of the English department was heard to whisper, "There but for the grace of God . . ." as his former boss was led by. Smith refused the offer of $150,000 in bail money from his faculty and friends and instead settled into his specially equipped cell. Unlike the other units of the East Baton Rouge Parish jail, Smith's new quarters boasted a bathtub, electric fans, a store of reading material, and a view of the city. Willie White, a Baton Rouge Negro waiting to be hanged for the murder of a grocer, occupied the adjacent cell. "What you in fo', white boy?" he asked in quiet wonder.[12]

Further investigation produced charges of juggling $400,000, of operating a confidence game, and of forging former governor O. K. Allen's signature to LSU bonds in addition to the embezzling of $100,000 for which he had been extradited from Canada. After a sensational trial J. M. "Jingle Money" Smith was convicted of using the mails to defraud and was sentenced to thirty years in the state penitentiary at Angola. To his credit, he spent his spare prison hours teaching his fellow inmates to read and write. Two members of the LSU Board of Supervisors followed their governor and president with prompt resignations and so did George Caldwell, the university's construction superintendent. Caldwell was promptly arrested, charged with diverting WPA labor and materials to private use, and sentenced to the federal penitentiary at Atlanta, where he soon was joined by former governor Leche. "Indications are," said *Newsweek*

11. New Orleans *Times-Picayune*, July 5, 1939, p. 1.
12. New Orleans *Item*, July 5, 1939, p. 1; "Louisiana Cell," *News-week*, July 17, 1939, p. 15.

at the end of July, "that the Department of Justice has permission from the White House to go through with a Louisiana showdown, let the chips fall where they may." [13]

When the news broke the entire university was shocked and demoralized. Naturally, the scandal rapidly became a news story of national importance, and Donald Davidson wrote to Brooks that "the newspaper accounts of LSU doings fill me with all sorts of apprehensions. . . . I do hope you can give me the reassuring news that you are not affected at all . . . all I know is the N.Y. *Times*!" [14] Brooks responded with a satirical variation on the currently popular Andrews Sisters song, "Three 'itty Fishes in an 'itty Bitty Poo'," which was making the round of the campus under the title "Ballad on Political Flying Fishes."

> Down in a meadow at LSU
> Stood Monroe Smith and Dicke Leche too.
> "Run," said Dick, "as fast as you can
> While I hold your resignation in my hand."
>
> Now Earl told Dick, "You've gone too far.
> You'll resign tonight or I'll tell the law."
> "OK," said Dick, "I'll quit if I can,
> But you know damned well I'm in a hell of a jam."
>
> The football players they swore and swore
> They said that they would play no more
> Because "If we play we'll get no pay
> Unless Dick can steal it from the WPA."
>
> While over in Canada sat the Monroe Smiths
> Telling how they gave us fits:
> "I took their dough and I ran and I ran
> And I ran right over the poor little lambs."

Another local wit suggested that the 1940 LSU football schedule be amended to include games with Leavenworth, Alcatraz, Sing Sing, and Joliet; but despite the display of humor with which some of the LSU faculty faced the crisis at their university, Cleanth Brooks

13. "Louisiana Storm," *News-week*, July 31, 1939, p. 12.
14. Donald Davidson to Cleanth Brooks, July 3, 1939.

and some of his more conscientious colleagues began immediately to try to put their vandalized house back in order. On the day following the resignation of J. M. Smith the LSU Board of Supervisors appointed E. S. Richardson, president of the Louisiana Polytechnic Institute at Ruston, as acting president of LSU. Richardson accepted the new post pending his resignation from Louisiana Tech, but after consideration decided not to take the position. In his place the LSU board elected Paul M. Hebert, dean of the LSU School of Law. Hebert was a native of Baton Rouge who had taken his B.A. and his LL.B. at LSU in the same year and then went to Yale for his J.S.D. degree. After completing his graduate work Hebert became dean of the law school at Loyola University in New Orleans, an action making him one of the youngest law deans in the United States. From Loyola he returned to LSU, and became acting president of the institution at age thirty-two.

His acting vice-president was Colonel Troy H. Middleton, a retired army officer who had been serving as dean of administration and who had served from 1930 to 1936 as commandant of cadets. In addition to his duties as vice-president of the university, Middleton was named comptroller, vowing that "every penny of money that is paid over to, or expended by the Louisiana State University will be expended strictly in accordance with sound educational policies and sound educational practices." A universally admired and respected individual, Middleton was remembered by his former cadets as a man who "always walked seven feet tall, made larger than life by that quiet dignity and command presence that were so integral a part of him, in or out of uniform." After World War II he returned to serve LSU once more from 1951 to 1962 as president of the university.[15]

Within fifteen days of Smith's flight to Canada, acting vice-president Middleton had William B. Franke of the New York CPA firm of Franke, Hannon, and Withey and former technical advisor to the National Committee of Standard Reports for Institutions of Higher Learning on campus to straighten out LSU's tangled fi-

15. Frank James Price, *Troy H. Middleton: A Biography* (Baton Rouge, 1974), 129; "Troy H. Middleton, 1889–1976," *LSU Alumni News*, LII (December, 1976), 2, 3.

nances. On July 11 Franke presented his plan embodying recommendations for the revision of the methods of control of financial and business activities. The board of supervisors authorized Franke's firm to proceed with the preparation of a budget for the next fiscal year and the installation of a modern institutional accounting system. Franke's report was long delayed, however, because of what he called the "unbelievably bad conditions of the accounts and the accounting records." Franke found LSU's previous budget to be inadequate and of little value for purposes of administrative control and its accounting systems entirely unsuited to its operations. Franke's investigation revealed a deficit in general funds of almost $600,000, a condition reported immediately to Governor Long. Within three weeks, funds were provided by the state to make good the sinking fund requirement of the coming year, and Franke's report concluded that "by exercising rigid economies, by careful administration and by efficient operation we think there can be no question but that financial solvency of the University can be quickly restored." [16]

In early August, 1939, J. Harvey Cain, director of the American Council of Education, issued his group's report on the academic situation at LSU. "Because an accomplished and likable university president chose to use his talents for alleged criminal purposes, rather than for the common good of the institution," said the ACE report, "Louisiana State University has held a conspicuous spot on the pages of nearly every newspaper in America during the past month." Despite the unpleasant notoriety, however, the council concluded that "the academic standing of Louisiana State University has long been unquestioned. The present institutional illness has been due to temporary financial difficulties. This institution, once the lengthened shadow of Huey Long, is now far bigger than any one man, and the present situation should prove a blessing in disguise." [17]

Despite Cain's rosy observation that the unfavorable publicity regarding its financial difficulties had only served to "focus attention upon the university's splendid educational facilities," and despite the fact that on campus students were apparently carrying on busi-

16. "Report on Investigation as of June 30, 1939," Franke, Hannon, and Withy, CPA's, 1–6, Louisiana Collection.
17. Cain, "Situation at Louisiana State University," 215–16.

ness as usual and most professors reported that "if it were not for the newspaper reports they would be unaware of anything unusual going on," unrest and confusion were spreading through the student body, the faculty, and the administration. Dean Frey recalls that the "administrative officers of the university were getting all kinds of conflicting suggestions as to what should be done to reorganize" the system. The primary point of contention was the succession to the LSU presidency, a deeply divisive issue for the Baton Rouge campus, and, says Dean Frey, "some of the more liberal faculty members wanted to turn the major part of the university's administration over to faculty committees. This further agitated the situation."[18] Among the foremost of those "liberal faculty members" was Cleanth Brooks.

Leonard Unger has testified that although "an unhealthy atmosphere was pervasive" at LSU during his years there as graduate student, Brooks and Warren and Robert Heilman "were for me and others healthy and valuable presences in that atmosphere." Robert Penn Warren gave his name and prestige to the reform movement at LSU, identifying himself with the liberal cause although, as one former student recalls, he "had about all he could say grace over with teaching, editing the *Southern Review*, and beating out his novels and poetry." When the James Monroe Smith scandals struck, Warren was in Italy at work on *All the King's Men*. Cleanth Brooks, present on the scene, "had a high degree of institutional concern and . . . loyalty; unlike many members of the profession, he did not use the pressure of other concerns (teaching, editing, and an extensive program of criticism and scholarship) to justify indifference to the university." Brooks recalls the "hours and hours" spent in trying to eradicate the poor courses, insisting on higher academic standards, and attempting to inject faculty opinion into the university policy-making apparatus. As early as 1935 he had been active in a movement to refute the "charges and insinuations reflecting upon the high standing of Louisiana State University and the integrity of members of its faculty," and in 1939 he became one of the nineteen faculty members most vigorous in the search for a suitable perma-

18. Frey, "Reminiscences of Fred C. Frey," 98–100.

nent president for LSU and for a restoration of the university's good name. Brooks, Heilman, Warren, Charles Hineman, and scattered allies from classics, romance languages, music, political science and "a scientist here and there" talked Hebert into instituting a faculty senate, and Brooks soon became a major leader on the side of reform. "His deftness in words and tenacity in issues," says Robert Heilman, "naturally made him a leader in academic matters in which he took part. He led best in smaller group meetings, in sessions to identify ends and plan means; he had a mildness, courteousness, and inclination to subtlety that were not the best equipment for open combat."[19]

The day that former president Smith was returned from Canada, LSU Alumni President Tom W. Dutton demanded in a statewide radio broadcast that Governor Long "depoliticalize" the university so that its president would not have to "bootlick the legislature" for funds, "depoliticalize" the board of supervisors of the university by asking for the resignation of every office holder or active politician and replace them with LSU graduates, and "depoliticalize" the faculty and the presidency. To Dutton's address, Brooks and the other members of "the Nineteen," as he and his "liberal" coalition came to be called by friend and foe alike, replied with enthusiasm: "Your courageous radio speech of Monday night," they wrote to him in an open letter, "offers a challenge to the faculty of the Louisiana State University. The press, clergy, and others have declared, as you have, that the university can regain the confidence of the people of the state only if it is cleaned from top to bottom."[20]

Brooks and his colleagues proposed a list of seven measures which they felt would most quickly return LSU to its accustomed place in the ranks of America's institutions of higher learning. They recommended that the university be placed under a board which was free from political control, that the faculty be established as an organized group actively participating in the formation and expres-

19. Leonard Unger to author, October 29, 1979 (in possession of the author); Thomas Thompson to author, October 2, 1979 (in possession of the author); Heilman, "Cleanth Brooks," 132–34, 142; Brooks, *et al.*, "Facts Concerning Academic Freedom at Louisiana State University," 1–3, Louisiana Collection, LSU.

20. Cleanth Brooks, *et al.*, open letter to Tom W. Dutton, July 8, 1939, quoted in *School and Society*, July 22, 1939, pp. 111–12.

sion of university policy, and that political influence must play no part in determining whether or not persons on the university staff— in administrative or teaching positions—were to be retained. Further, "the Nineteen" insisted that new appointments to faculty and administrative posts must be determined solely by evidence of merit, that promotions in rank and salary be determined by considerations absolutely divorced from politics, and that academic standards no longer be jeopardized by political favoritism toward students whether through political fellowships and scholarships or unwarranted grades. Finally, the group demanded, "there must be an end to the situation whereby a university publication edited by faculty members can be forced by political pressure to alter its content."[21] The *Southern Review* had at no time during its tenure been subjected to any political pressure whatsoever, but in 1938 Professor Daniel Borth had resigned as editor of the *Louisiana Business Review*, a College of Commerce publication, after Governor Leche objected to President Smith that statistics on business conditions of the state differed with figures printed in the *Progress*, the house organ of the Leche administration. That such tampering with university publications had not interfered with the editing of the *Southern Review* was no doubt a result of the fact that neither Governor Leche nor any of his henchmen were even aware of the literary quarterly.

By the morning of July 10 the LSU campus was buzzing with discussion of the unprecedented faculty action taken by "the Nineteen." Although only one dean signed the seven-point "Magna Carta," the New Orleans *States* reported that "many faculty members who have hesitated in the past to raise their voices at conditions on the campus that, to say the least, involved a threat to academic freedom, appeared heartened" by the action of alumni officials and "the Nineteen." "The general attitude of the teaching staff," the *States* concluded, "is that, with an aroused faculty *en masse* demanding a change in conditions, LSU will quickly regain its place in the educational world."[22]

21. New Orleans *States*, July 10, 1939, p. 1.
22. *Ibid.*

On a second front the Nineteen were battling to prevent the appointment of an unqualified candidate to the presidency of the university. Since the days of Sherman, LSU had for most of its years been run by more or less distinguished military men, and so there was some enthusiasm for the candidate proposed by the New Orleans *Item*, General Malin Craig, the retiring chief of staff of the United States Army. Speaking for himself and for the other members of the Nineteen, Brooks's close friend Charles S. Hineman of the government department protested his nomination. He agreed with the stand taken by the editor of the *Item* calling for an end to political control of the university, but confessed to being "not at all attracted . . . by your suggestion that a military figure can supply the kind of leadership which this institution needs." To the contrary, Hineman pointed out, LSU "has had already too much of military methods in its administration." Had deans and department heads not felt so strongly that it was their duty to obey without question the dictates of former president Smith, his questionable practices might have been terminated before they became criminal and destructive. Hineman was willing to concede that the appointment of a highly respected soldier might restore much of the moral confidence that the people of Louisiana once had in their university, but "it would not . . . restore the university to a place of esteem in the educational world."[23]

Exactly how much influence Hineman's open letter had on the board of supervisors' decision is hard now to determine, but General Craig, much to the relief of the Nineteen and other advocates of academic excellence at LSU, was not elevated to the presidency of the university. Encouraged by their successes in their initial attempt to save LSU from the politicians and for the scholars, the Nineteen issued a second statement on the state of affairs on the Baton Rouge campus and what might best be done to rectify the situation there. "The significance of the present state of affairs" at LSU, they maintained, "depends wholly upon one's interpretation of the intellectual good health of the university when the recent scandals began." For those who were confident that the university was a "good and per-

23. *Ibid.*

haps great institution at that time, that its reputation among its sister institutions was high, that its standards of achievement were known and honored in this state and throughout the United States" it was perfectly logical to believe that "the removal of one or two subordinate rascals, and the institution of a fool-proof and crook-proof book-keeping system" was sufficient to clear the university's name and to ensure its thorough recovery. Contrary to the findings of J. Harvey Cain's American Council of Education, however, the Nineteen had no cause to believe that LSU was even a very good academic institution at the time of the Smith scandals, or to believe that Smith was an educational leader of wisdom and discernment. Since, they maintained, the university was far from intellectually healthy, "the mere removal of a local wart can hardly have, in itself, effected a cure," and the retention of the deans and department chairmen who led it to the present fiasco "is hardly a good omen now." With regard to the selection of a permanent president for the university, the group insisted that, "however good and honest," to appoint a man who "lacks all information about what has to do with intellectual health and disease, is an injustice to the institution, and indeed, an injustice to the man himself."[24]

"To our astonishment," recalls Heilman, the appearance of this statement "filled the air with the noise of denial and denunciation." "The Nineteen" became the strongest term of abuse heard in the faculty club, and 160 members of the faculty signed a counter-statement to the effect that LSU was "a treasury of academic excellences." There was even some vague talk of "haircutting," that is, the non-reappointment or non-promotion of the offending members.

Acting president Hebert, however, while not publicly siding with the Nineteen, took to heart many of their proposals and went ahead with a full-scale cleansing of the academic temple. In his commencement address at the end of the summer term, Hebert told the graduating class that "in any university there are two distinct phases of the institution's affairs. On the one hand, there are administrative, financial, and business aspects; on the other, there are purely educational and academic activities. Although the latter activities

24. Cleanth Brooks, *et al.*, n.d.

constitute the fundamental and exclusive reasons for a university's existence, the former are nevertheless indispensable to the function of any organization." Hebert took issue with the judgment of Brooks and the Nineteen by claiming that "the recent distressing events at LSU have been entirely concerned with the administrative and financial aspects of the University's affairs" and that "these have not in any way disrupted the continued and beneficial functioning of the purely educational and academic activities." Hebert promised to completely reorganize the financial affairs and business management of the university, but stated his opinion that, "in general, academic conditions at the University are sound. We have a talented faculty," he maintained, "devoting their earnest efforts to the rendition of a high type of educational service." Perhaps with the recent prodding of the Nineteen in mind, he further promised, "at the proper time," to augment the faculty to meet the needs of the university, and to lend every encouragement and assistance to all kinds of scholarly work.

An even deeper bow in Brooks's direction was his highly favorable comment on the *Southern Review*. In pointing to the bright spots and encouraging accomplishments in the university's recent history, the acting president cited as one "special field of accomplishment by faculty and students" their various kinds of publications. There were published on the campus "several journals and periodicals—literary, scientific, and professional. One of these has received such wide acclaim that it has been described by national and international critics as one of the most outstanding in its field."[25]

In a long and thoughtful letter to Donald Davidson on the ninth of August, Brooks recapped the events of the past several weeks at LSU and tallied up the score. "I take it," he began, "that the newspapers, even distant ones, have carried a full account of what has occurred" but went on to give an insider's account of LSU's time of troubles. He and his friends had feared that the federal investigation of the Smith scandal would be a whitewash in exchange for support of New Deal programs in Louisiana by the newest inheritors of the Long machine, but they were pleased to learn that on

25. Paul Hebert, "Address delivered to the commencement exercises of the summer session, 1939," Louisiana Collection, LSU.

August 8 Richard Leche had received a federal indictment and that the federal government was going to make a complete and thorough investigation. Several other big figures in the state machine were indicted, and "Smith himself has been indicted forty-one times and the end is not yet." Brooks told Davidson of his relief that E. S. Richardson, "a completely unsatisfactory person," had turned down the offer of the presidency at LSU and of his good feeling toward Hebert.

Referring to his own embroilment in campus politics, Brooks reported that

> some two or three weeks ago, nineteen of us wrote a letter to the alumni secretary (who had made a strong speech demanding a clean-up), a letter in which we listed certain things which that clean-up should secure. It was not the strongest letter in the world, but it was sufficiently sharp. The newspapers displayed it prominently and we were immediately attacked by the reactionary members of the faculty. First, they tried to get Hebert to denounce us; next they got out a statement which they tried to drum up signatures for, which stated that the university was sound academically and in every regard it was intended to suggest that we were a bunch of mudslingers and radicals.

But, Brooks reported, Hebert had refused to denounce the Nineteen or to publish the opposition's counter-statement and in fact "has indicated a steady progress toward our position." The local chapter of the American Association of University Professors, for example, had appointed a committee to suggest to Hebert that he allow an impartial investigation of the academic quality of the university. This Hebert had already done. "The summer campaign against the reactionaries on the campus," therefore, "has ended in a thoroughgoing triumph for ourselves."

Brooks ended his missive on a note of guarded optimism for the future. He believed, he told Davidson:

> If Hebert pursues the course which I think he will pursue, I think that LSU may actually profit by the disaster, not only in fact but in public esteem. There is still a difficulty, however, that people here do not realize how much the University has

been discredited over the country, whether rightly or wrongly, by what has happened to it. We believe that the only way salvation lies is in realizing that fact and in taking drastic, convincing, and even dramatic steps to indicate to the country at large that the University is really sound and really a University.[26]

For his and Warren's magazine, Brooks had no fears. To Davidson he said that "Hebert has taken occasion to emphasize the good work of *The Southern Review* in several speeches, and I believe that he wishes us well and will give us thorough support. As a matter of fact, I think that under the new administration *The Southern Review* should prosper." Four days later he wrote to John Berryman that "the trouble at the University has not contributed to peace and calm" but that "bad as it is," the scandal and restructuring of the LSU system "is going to rebound finally to the University's good and to the good of the *Review*." Through the autumn and into the winter events bore out Brooks's prediction. George Fort Milton, writing in the *Yale Review*, cited the *Southern Review* as "a Baton Rouge offset to James Monroe Smith," and Brooks was able to write to Caroline Gordon at the end of October that although "the faculty is still boiling hard with the events of the past summer, and there is much politicking and skirmishing on one front and another," he was sure that "our bogy man will not inherit the headship" and jeopardize the continued existence of the *Review*. The situation had not changed by mid-November when Brooks wrote to Frank L. Owsley that "matters are going pretty well here with the usual amount of skirmishing and backstairs brawling. I think that our side is winning, however, and I hope that by the end of this year our situation in the department and in the University will be clarified and strengthened."[27]

The first month of the new year saw not only Brooks's university but his department as well seeking a new leader. When English department chairman William A. Read announced his retirement on January 17, Brooks was appointed to chair a special committee of the Department of English, charged with the duty of making a

26. Cleanth Brooks to Donald Davidson, August 9, 1939.
27. *Ibid.*; Brooks to John Berryman, August 14, 1939; George Fort Milton, "The South Do Move," *Yale Review*, XXIX (September, 1939), 150; Brooks to Caroline Gordon, October 29, 1939; Brooks to Frank Owsley, November 11, 1939.

study and report, on or before February 15, to the dean of the College of Arts and Sciences and to acting president Hebert regarding the appointment of a new head for the English department for the following June. In charging Brooks with this responsibility Hebert also instructed Brooks to cooperate with the commission of the Educational Survey, appointed by the American Council on Education. In this connection Brooks was made responsible for outlining the basic educational needs and policies of the English department with particular reference to the direction that the program had followed and suggesting routes for sound development in the future. Robert Heilman was Brooks's ally on the selection committee and W. John Olive constituted the swing vote. Unfortunately for the smooth functioning of the committee's business, President Hebert also appointed Professors Uhler and Bradshear to the committee. Uhler and Bradshear were, of course, of the faculty's reactionary right.

"His institutional concern led Cleanth to invest a great deal of time in seeking desirable appointments when the department chairman and the university presidency became vacant," Heilman recalls, and Brooks took out time from his other concerns for caucusing, politicking, and searching. "Since most people want to put allies into chairmanships, it is worth reporting that Cleanth's candidate shared with him, I am sure, not one literary or social or political idea; Cleanth was simply supporting an honorable man."[28] Brooks's choice in the matter was Adolphus Bryan, a Harvard Ph.D. who had joined the LSU faculty in 1926 and had proven himself a capable administrator if not a convert to the New Critical approach to the teaching of literature. Uhler, embittered by the fact that he had lost his promised chairmanship when Smith resigned from the presidency, nominated Thomas Kirby as an obstructionist move. Kirby, who had come to LSU in 1935 with a Johns Hopkins Ph.D., was chosen by President Hebert, and although he made the English department an excellent chairman and subsequently became a good friend of Brooks and the department's New Critical wing, Brooks and his allies saw the imminent doom of the reform movement at

28. Heilman, "Cleanth Brooks," 133–34.

LSU. At the end of 1939 William Empson wrote to Brooks in hopes that his fellow New Critic might help him to secure a teaching position at LSU. Brooks was quick to reply that although he was most interested in Empson's career and avid to have him as a colleague in Baton Rouge, "I have very little influence, not only in my own University but generally."[29] He had tried to stir up interest in Empson's behalf, but did not think the chances at LSU were very promising.

By April, 1940, Brooks's suspicions were borne out. "I had hoped," he wrote to his English friend, "as I told you earlier, that I could arouse . . . the University to make you an offer and induce you to stay with us for at least a time." "Unfortunately," he reported, "the scandals broke about our heads some eight or nine months ago and since then the University has been agitatedly (and properly) reforming and reorganizing itself. That is all to the good, but it has made it very difficult to get anything done, for everyone is in a stir."[30] The rejection of such a renowned critic as William Empson meant a great loss to the prestige of the Louisiana State University, but the worst was yet to come.

The campaign for the Louisiana governor's chair, conducted through the last months of 1939 and brought to a vote in February, 1940, matched Earl K. Long's caretaker administration and the battered Long machine against Sam Houston Jones, the main plank of whose platform was to get Louisiana schools out of Louisiana politics. A faculty wit remarked that since Huey's death Louisianans had "a choice of stupid do-gooders or bright crooks." One of the few men to prove wrong one of his brother's predictions, Earl Long held together the efficient Long machine that Huey had created, and with a genius for organization possibly improved upon it. In his campaign for the statehouse, the younger Long appealed to the voters to develop a sense of selectivity, and not to condemn the barrel because of a few rotten apples. "Smith was one man," he exhorted his constituents. "Don't blame anybody. Look at Jesus Christ. He picked twelve. And one of them was a son-of-a-gun." The motto of his administration had been "Better a little with righteousness than great revenues without right," and however sanctimonious this

29. Brooks to Empson, December 23, 1939.
30. Brooks to Empson, April 10, 1940.

credo might have sounded to the anti-Long faction of the electorate, the Earl of Louisiana had received very high marks for his handling of the crisis of money and morale at LSU. Sam Jones beat Earl Long by 20,000 votes—by 50,000 in reality if one accepts the *Saturday Evening Post*'s estimate of the number of ballots stolen by the Long machine. The reform government took office, but according to young Hubert H. Humphrey, then a graduate student in the government department at LSU, "the signs of reformation were barely discernible to the trained eye."[31] The new broom had vowed to sweep clean, but in cleaning up the mess left by the heirs of the Kingfish much of the good that he had wrought was swept away as well. Among the treasures thrown out with the trash was the *Southern Review*.

The remainder of 1940 was relatively calm for the editors of the embattled quarterly. The only major change in the magazine was the departure of Albert Erskine, who went east to pursue a career in publishing. Erskine left for a position with New Directions in November, and John E. Palmer replaced him as managing editor in December. At the same time Brooks and Warren were promoted to full editorial status in name as well as in fact. January of 1941 came, however, and LSU still had no president. Confusion was still the keynote of campus activities, and Cleanth Brooks wrote to R. P. Blackmur, "We are hoping for the best but we are very far from confident." At the end of the month, in a letter to Davidson, Brooks seemed even more concerned for his university's future. "Things are still a mess here as you may have heard. The Board has still to elect a permanent president, and until he is elected, there is going to be little more than rumor and counter rumor around here, alarms and excursions. We are doing what we can but without too much confidence. It's all pretty exciting but pretty hard on the nerves, for I fear that we will get something very bad unless we get something very good."[32]

One of the immediate causes for Brooks's concern was the pres-

31. Hubert H. Humphrey, *The Education of a Public Man: My Life in Politics* (New York, 1976), 64.
32. Cleanth Brooks to R. P. Blackmur, January 30, 1941; Brooks to Donald Davidson, January 30, 1941.

sure that the *Southern Review* was beginning to feel. With the coming of World War II to the United States, both state and university administrations began to look for ways to cut back ever further the budget allocated to the university. On January 15 acting president Hebert appointed a committee to consider certain matters relating to the policy of the *Southern Review,* and on February 8 that committee brought in its report. It had found but two minor points with which to quibble with the policy of the *Review.* The first of these dealt with the distribution of complimentary and sample copies. The members of Hebert's commission recommended that the members of the editorial staff be assigned only five copies of the magazine, that sample copies "be carefully and conservatively" assigned, and that the mailing of copies be done by the *Review*'s secretary only and that accounts of sample copies be strictly kept. The committee's second point concerned payment of the editors for their own contributions to the *Southern Review.* At first chary of allowing the editors to accept compensation for work which they contributed to the journal, the committee validated Brooks's and Warren's right to publish and be paid for their own fiction, poems, and criticism only after the editors explained their position in a strongly worded letter to the chairman. "The editors of *The Southern Review,*" they wrote, "certainly do not wish to embarrass the University or themselves" by publishing their own material, and they are "perfectly willing to abstain in practice from making further contributions" to the *Southern Review.* "They do not, however, admit the principle that payment for such contributions is bad practice with the implication that the magazine has erred in this regard in the past. Their informal decision to abstain from making contributions in the future, if taken, will be based solely on grounds of expediency, and a desire to cooperate with the University in the most whole-hearted manner."

Brooks and Warren defended past selections of their work— Brooks's "Three Revolutions in Poetry" and his analysis of *The Waste Land* and Warren's "Goodwood Comes Back," "How Willie Proudfit Came Home," "When the Light Gets Green," and "Letter from a Coward to a Hero" among them—as the subjective value judgments of the editors themselves.

With so heavy a reliance on the integrity and judgment of the editors, it is probably not "good business" for the University to support the *Review* at all. If so heavy a realiance on the editors *is* justified, the editors feel that they have a right to consider the work of their colleagues on the staff as well as that of writers not on the staff. In any case the editors are perfectly willing to stand on the record and to stake their reputations for integrity and good judgment on the reputation of the magazine—including the past contributions of the editors.[33]

During the summer semester of 1941 Warren served as visiting professor of English at the State University of Iowa, where he continued the search for a suitable candidate for the presidency of Louisiana State. His search was in vain, and toward the end of the semester he wrote to Brooks: "I ache for LSU news, if there is any. And God knows, there must be, or times have changed."[34] News from Baton Rouge there was, and none of it good. Brooks's quest for an acceptable presidential candidate had borne no better fruit than had Warren's, and his fight with the present administration was even more frustrating than his colleague's want of news of the fight. "We were immensely busy about the succession," recalls Robert Heilman, and "saved from hopelessness by ignorance of our own impotence." As an example of the obstacles facing Brooks and his more progressive-minded colleagues, Heilman tells the story of one Sunday when he and Brooks and several other young men of the faculty drove several hundred miles to call upon the president of the board of supervisors "hoping to urge our candidate upon him and to register our dismay over the rumored front-runner." Brooks's tactics were ingenious but unavailing. He adopted what Heilman calls a "very ingratiating approach: a sort of naïvely earnest throwing of us appellants on the mercy of a court admittedly dedicated to all worthy ends. Cleanth did not have to be a serpent to be a little less the dove he was content to appear, trusting to the goodness in men who have crumbs to toss to hungry mouths."

33. Brooks and Warren, "Note on Section 2," n.d., in *Southern Review* Collection, Yale.

34. Robert Penn Warren to Cleanth Brooks, n.d.

The sixtyish-or-so president . . . was courteous and friendly,
professed gratitude for our concern, and said he had the best
interests of the University at heart. Then with Cleanth and
me he took a tack that was devastating in effect, though I am
unsure whether he just fell into it, made honest use of a good
thing, or took a deadpan demonic revenge for our bothering
him. Having found that we professed literature, he took on
the air of a kindly benefactor: "Gentlemen, I know that you
will be interested, etc." Then he revealed to us a manuscript
or privately printed pamphlet, the poetry of his wife, and introduced us to the maker herself. He was like a plantation
owner letting an oil prospector in on a hidden gusher on the
back forty. I am not sure whether we were to assay the crude
on the spot or send in a laboratory report by mail. On the
scene I limped in clichés while Cleanth managed benign
words, in which the chilly critical spirit was somewhat muffled
in the folds of courtesy and in which he gave only the mildest
of gentlemanly turns of the screw that might have capped
that well of English a little defiled by gentle reading and un-
fettered memory.[35]

Brooks and Heilman might have saved their effort and embarrassment and put their Sunday afternoon to a more pleasant use, for
on the twelfth of March Brooks received a letter from John Crowe
Ransom concerning the LSU presidency. "I was terribly depressed
the other day to see in the Columbus paper that you are going to
have a MILITARY head at LSU," he wrote. "The gentleman made
the headlines because he commanded a post near here recently;
which doesn't make him smell any sweeter." No more prophetic
words were ever written than Ransom's sad prediction that "I suppose the upshot practically will mean that you are all now at the
mercy of your Deans; a military man won't know anything at all
about literature. Bad. Bad."[36]

Several weeks before, Fred Frey, LSU's new dean of the university, had received a telephone call from James Smitherman, chair-

35. Heilman, "Cleanth Brooks," 134–35.
36. John Crowe Ransom to Cleanth Brooks, March 12, 1941.

man of the board of supervisors, and was requested to meet with him at the Heidelberg Hotel. Dean Frey arrived at Smitherman's room, indulged in a bit of conversation about the weather, and was informed that he had been appointed the next president of Louisiana State University. Before the board made its action public and official, however, Frey was informed that he must first talk a few things over with Governor Jones "so that the Governor could tell me what changes he wanted made at the University and whom he wanted fired." At this point Dean Frey interrupted the chairman, declaring that "if you folks elect me president, I'm going to run the university, Sam Jones isn't."[37] A brief and strained conversation followed, and several weeks later the board of supervisors announced the election of General Campbell Blackshear Hodges as president of the university.

General Hodges had two nicknames—"Black" and "Scraggy"— both originating from the condition of his hair. "He's short, handsome, and extraordinarily gifted in making and keeping friends," *Newsweek* reported, and like most military officers he was exceptionally well traveled. His most recent state-side assignments had been as commandant of cadets at West Point and as military aides to Presidents Hoover and Roosevelt before being given command of the V Army Corps. Only after receiving LSU's offer did the native Louisianian resign his commission. His tenure as president, with its $12,000 a year stipend, became effective July 1, 1941, and right away he began organizing his personal staff. Once again Dean Frey was called to the Heidelberg, this time to be informed that the new president "was going to make me his chief of staff. He said he didn't know too much about a university and he planned to lean heavily on me." One observer of the LSU scene has commented that it was extremely fortunate that General Hodges was appointed to head the university or else he would have been given a combat command in Europe and set the war effort back at least two years for the Allies.[38]

One of the last official acts of the Hebert administration was an attempt to make restitution to the seven members of the *Reveille*

37. Frey, "Reminiscences of Fred C. Frey, 101.
38. "New Deal at LSU," *News-week*, March 24, 1941, pp. 52, 54; Frey, "Reminiscences of Fred C. Frey," 101.

staff fired and expelled by Huey Long and James Smith seven years earlier. In attempting to offer formal amends, acting president Hebert remembered the wisdom of Benjamin Disraeli's aphorism that "apologies only account for what they do not alter." As young men "who have suffered a grave injustice in your experience at LSU, it would be only natural for you to have a feeling of bitterness against this institution which no apology can alter," he said. "Yet, somehow, I feel that as we write 'finis' to this sorry episode you will accept the apologies of the University with a spirit of generosity and good will." [39]

With the ascendancy of General Hodges to the presidency of LSU, however, the administration of the Louisiana State University made yet another mistake as tragic in its implications and even more wasteful in terms of potential good than had been the expulsion of the *Reveille* staff. One of Hodges' first acts in office was to expunge the faculty senate for which Brooks had worked so hard, and with the dissolving of the senate the reform movement at LSU collapsed. Under pressure from the state government to remove all vestiges of Longism and to reduce all expenses to an absolute minimum in face of the American war effort, and due to the weakness and jealousy of many of the faculty, early in the fall semester General Hodges personally informed the staff of the *Southern Review* that the indefinite suspension of the publication of their magazine was under serious consideration.

The June 10, 1940, issue of *Time* had run a commendatory notice of the *Southern Review*'s special Thomas Hardy number in which the news magazine had noted that "while the people of Europe turn to mass murder, training in the sciences of murder, or defense against it, intelligent U.S. citizens are becoming solemnly aware that the arts, scholarship and precious thought of Western culture are in their keeping. For in Europe's desperate atmosphere the free life of the intelligence is suspended where it has not been crushed." The *Time* reviewer placed the center of America's struggle to maintain those precious traditions squarely on the banks of the Mississippi at Baton Rouge, Louisiana. The *Southern Review*, which he found superior to any other journal in the English lan-

39. Paul Hebert to Jesse H. Cutrer, March 14, 1941, in J. H. Cutrer's personal files.

gauge, "has applied no standards save excellence," and "has been subject to no political pressure whatever." The editors of the magazine, their students, and their contributors, "prove, if any proof was necessary, that there exists in the U.S. a community of scholars and artists, alive to their own time and country, and capable of preserving the traditions of the West."[40]

Yet President Hodges and his deans felt that money spent on the *Review* could be put to better use elsewhere under the current exigencies of a nation gearing up for war. Ironically, LSU was actually making millions of dollars from the U.S. government during World War II for teaching military personnel in the ATS Program. Apparently none of the administration were struck by the irony of the fact that the cost of maintaining the Royal Bengal Tiger, which was the LSU football team's mascot, was nearly as great as that of maintaining the *Southern Review*; and the new administration further revealed its callousness toward the history and traditions of the university and to the nation when it authorized the melting down as scrap the two priceless ten-pounder Parrott rifles that William T. Sherman had captured at Charleston in 1865 and had presented to the school in 1868.

The editors, of course, did not acquiesce to the termination of their magazine without first putting up a considerable fight. In asking the administration to reconsider its decision, Brooks and Warren made three general points. First, as the magazine was supported entirely by the university with the small exception of advertising revenue amounting to little more than $300 yearly, with a net cost to LSU of about $7,000 annually, the editors offered to reduce their budget request by $750. This, they felt, could be accomplished by the elimination of one signature (16 pages), a reduction which they felt would not seriously impair the program of the magazine. Brooks, Warren, and Palmer felt that for the magazine to continue to operate in its accustomed form and under its standard policy no further budget cuts could be supported. There was, in fact, a real need for additional space, student help, and funding for advertising, "without which it is difficult to see how the magazine can appreciably

40. "Wessex and Louisiana," *Time*, June 10, 1940, p. 92.

widen its audience and maintain its record of a slowly rising income," they reported to the budget committee.[41]

Reducing pay to contributors to one and a half cents per word for prose and thirty-five cents per line for verse was considered, but the suggestion that the prestige of the *Review* was such that many writers might be willing to contribute for a very low rate or for nothing was rejected out of hand. Although it might be true, the editors maintained, that certain writers who had sources of income from activities other than writing and very young writers who had no established reputations might still contribute to the *Review*, "for the truly professional writers, who depend to a considerable extent upon their writing for income, this would not apply." The editors candidly believed also that raising the price of the magazine, as suggested by the budget committee, from 75¢ to $1.00 per copy "would not increase net income, and would definitely reduce the number of subscribers."

Other proposed economy measures were vetoed as well. A further reduction in the number of pages would result in the disruption of either the long fiction or the review/essay policy, and the editors said they would rather go down with their banner nailed to the masthead than to compromise the quality of the magazine. Second, they reopened the question of the value of the quarterly to the university, a contribution which they felt to be two-fold. The *Review* had helped to offset the extremely unfavorable publicity that the university had received from the Smith affair, and, the editors pointed out, the *Review* had gained recognition for LSU as a center of intellectual activity. Finally, Brooks and Warren rebutted the budget committee's assessment that the university should not "continue to support so heavily an activity which relatively reaches so small a number of people regardless of the fact that the Committee is fully cognizant of the high standing of the magazine in literary circles."[42] The editors called attention to the fact that the influence of the magazine was not to be determined by the number of subscriptions.

41. Brooks, Warren, and Palmer to LSU Budget Committee, n.d., in *Southern Review* Collection.
42. Cleanth Brooks and Robert Penn Warren, "Proposed economy measures," n.d., in *Southern Review* Collection.

A substantial percentage of the circulation was with libraries, and a good deal of evidence indicated that each library copy was heavily used. For instance, one library had a triple subscription, and it had been reported by one correspondent from Harvard that the copy of the magazine received by the Widener Library was worn out before he had the opportunity of reading it. A second point made in this connection was that the *Review* reached an audience which was both vocal and influential. In reaching such an audience, Brooks and Warren maintained, the magazine did not merely render a service to the university but also to society at large.

With the budget committee's recommendation that the *Southern Review* be suspended came the simultaneous decision to let go the *Journal of Southern History*, the official organ of the Southern Historical Association, then in its eighth year at LSU and running on a subsidy of $5,000 per annum, and the *National Mathematics Magazine*, begun sixteen years earlier by Professor S. T. Sanders of the LSU Department of Mathematics. Although the latter magazine had no formal connection with any mathematics association, it had been endorsed "without reservation" by all of America's mathematics societies. It had a wide United States and foreign circulation and subscriptions for about two hundred libraries at a cost to the university of slightly less than $1,500 per year for eight issues.

With the impending demise of the *Southern Review* bruited about the campus, the state, the nation, and, indeed, the entire republic of letters, it was announced that senior editor Charles W. Pipkin had died of a heart attack at the Hotel Dieu hospital in New Orleans on August 4, 1941. Dean Pipkin had been in failing health for more than two years and had been quite ill for the previous three months. "To those who cherish liberty, racial tolerance, a love of mankind, and above all, the right to think," the *Reveille* eulogized, "the sad news of his departure from their midst is a terrific blow."[43]

The Louisiana press rallied a few of its editorial pages to the defense of the beleaguered *Review*. The editor of the New Orleans *States*, for example, told his readers that "it is well that LSU should study how it can stretch its dollars as far as possible. . . . The gov-

43. "Veritas," *Reveille*, August 4, 1941, p. 4.

ernment needs money, it needs material, it needs services in the present all-out world-fight for democratic principles." But, he argued, it would be a mistake to drop the *Southern Review* "just as it would be a mistake to close the art galleries and the libraries; just as it would be a mistake not to seek individual enlightenment and inspiration and courage in such appeals to the higher self as the Symphony Orchestra."[44]

Readers and admirers of the *Review* also wrote to its editors and to the administration from all corners of the English speaking world. From Yaddo Katherine Anne Porter sent her hope that the *Southern Review* "is going on, that it does well. I have always loved it, from the first."[45] But on December 20, 1941, Brooks wrote to Allen Tate, "This spring number will be our last: we are announcing in the Winter number our probable suspension with Volume VII, No. 4." Brooks sent his apologies for not having informed his old friend earlier of the troubles he and Warren were having, but explained that the end came quite suddenly. "There have been rumors for several weeks, but we have faced such rumors on and off for years. The final decision came only today." Brooks also said that he had not written of the *Review*'s impending doom because the magazine's enemies had always attributed any favorable comment which the *Review* received directly to the machinations of its editors. Thus, Brooks explained, "we have wanted to lean over backwards in keeping completely quiet about our shaky situation." Particularly in view of the university's recent scandals, Brooks and Warren were especially sensitive to adverse comment that the school might receive. "LSU is apparently considered licensed game for the ironic commentator," Brooks observed, and "what they *could* make of the suspension of the *Review* could be pretty nasty." The war might have diverted comment, or there may have been no notice of the end of the magazine anyway, Brooks conceded, but "at any rate, Red and I want to be in the position of having done nothing to solicit protests or comment of any kind."

Always the consummate gentleman, Brooks went even further to

44. New Orleans *States*, October 1, 1941, p. 6.
45. Katherine Anne Porter to John E. Palmer, October 6, 1941.

avoid bringing embarrassment to his antagonists with a few kind words for the university's new president. Despite the fact that on the very morning of his letter to Tate Hodges had personally reported his decision to shut down the magazine, Brooks wrote that "it is only fair to say that the General has been fair and very sympathetic. I think that he honestly regrets the loss of *The Southern Review*." Taking Hodges' point of view, Brooks explained that "he has been with the University only six months and you can scarcely blame him if he feels that he has to take the advice of his committee. He has dealt very fairly and straightforwardly with Red and me, and this has constituted another reason for our saying nothing about the suspension until we had talked over the matter of the announcement with him." On the brighter side, Brooks saw the end of the quarterly as a release from a heavy obligation. "Red and I ought to get some books finished now."[46]

The end of the *Review* was announced in the Winter 1942 issue of the magazine, a special William Butler Yeats number, and one of the quarterly's most successful. In a brief editorial the editors informed their readers:

> The magazine faces suspension of publication with the spring issue of 1942 unless arrangements not now foreseen can be made before that date. The editors wish to express their appreciation to the Louisiana State University and the officers of its administration for the generous support accorded *The Southern Review* during the past seven years, not only in financial matters but in an understanding of the ends to which the *Review* has attempted to dedicate itself. The editors are confident that the magazine's contributors and readers will share with them this feeling of gratitude, but they are also confident that the contributors and readers will agree with the administration and with the editors that the pursuit of these ends, in times such as these, be curtailed.[47]

That the editors were being more kind than candid is evidenced

46. Cleanth Brooks to Allen Tate, December 20, 1941.
47. Cleanth Brooks and Robert Penn Warren, "Editorial," *Southern Review*, VII (Winter, 1941–1942), n.p.

by their statement to *Time* magazine's New Orleans correspondent. "It is always difficult to put a commercial value on intangibles," they said, "and the pressure of economy probably always prejudices the case against intangibles. The editors of *The Southern Review*, as interested parties, are scarcely in a position to appraise the value of the services rendered by the magazine to Louisiana State University." But the budget committee had made such an appraisal, and the editors could not help but feel that "the ends to which the magazine was dedicated are valid and important at any time, and may be especially valid and important at the present time."[48]

W. T. Couch, not always a friend of the editors, at least in their Agrarian aspect, was outraged when he heard of the end of the *Review*. "How your university can permit this I do not understand," he said in a telegram to Brooks. "You have been creating more values for LSU and this part of the country than could possibly be created in any other way with anywhere near comparable expenditures. I would appreciate your writing and telling me what has happened." As always, Brooks's reply was mild and non-inflammatory; he made every effort to express the administration's point of view as well as his own. "The subsidy which has been given us through the last seven years has been generous, and because generous, onerous," he said. "Therefore when the pressure for economy began to impinge on the University, it was not surprising that the magazine should come under heavy attack." With characteristic modesty, Brooks told Couch that "it is hardly profitable to go further into the matter of whether or not we were a suitable economy as compared to other activities and projects: first because we lack the facts; and second, because we are interested parties." Quite naturally, he confessed, he and Warren believed personally in the purpose of their quarterly, but maintained that they were "hardly the people to assess those ends and what is the value to Louisiana State University and to the South of what we have accomplished."[49]

Far from agreeing with the university's administration, the contributors and readers of the *Southern Review* fell solidly behind

48. Brooks and Warren to *Time*, n.d., in *Southern Review* Collection.
49. W. T. Couch to Cleanth Brooks, January 28, 1942; Brooks to Couch, February 3, 1942.

Couch's estimation. In a bitterly ironic letter to the editor of the *Reveille*, one undergraduate spoke for many when he asked why, after "the dropping of that obnoxious publication, the *Southern Review*, from the university's budget," the administration should be content with half-measures and not go ahead and do away with the English department entirely? The money saved could buy the "things the school really needs," for example an innerspring mattress for Mike the Tiger, "who has been sleeping in disgustingly uncomfortable quarters for all these years while LSU spent money on, of all things, a literary magazine!" *Reveille* editor John E. Hardy echoed this disgust at "the action of the Babbitts of the budget committee." According to his January ninth editorial, the curtailing of the *Review* was "a deliberate sabotage of our intellectual tradition from our own faculty and administration." Joining the student protest, the faculty of LSU's College of Arts and Sciences voiced unanimous protest against the suppression of the magazine in a resolution stating that the publication had brought "enviable distinction" to the university. Submitted to General Hodges on January 10, 1942, the resolution urged the administration "to explore most earnestly every possibility by which the university could retain this needed source of acclaim in the intellectual world."[50]

Not confining itself to the LSU campus, the protest against the suspension of the *Review* spread across the nation. During the last week of 1940 more than 230 members of the Modern Language Association signed a petition to General Hodges expressing their "feeling of dismay at the possibility of the discontinuance of *The Southern Review*. We feel that its loss would be irreparable, particularly in view of the national crisis when efforts to preserve cultural continuity should be redoubled." John Crowe Ransom editorialized in the *Review*'s behalf in the pages of the *Kenyon*, and R. P. Blackmur wrote that "the general sorrow and dismay over the death of *The Southern Review*" was so great that he and some of his Princeton colleagues were attempting to start a journal to be operated along similar lines. And Randall Jarrell wrote to Brooks that "You

50. Coy Wynn to Editor, *Reveille*, January 9, 1942, p. 2; John E. Hardy, "Editorial," *Reveille*, January 9, 1942; Baton Rouge *Morning Advocate*, January 11, 1942, p. 14.

and Red made it the best literary magazine in the world. It's a great loss." Even the *New Republic*, ideologically no friend of the *Southern Review*, lent its voice to the hue and cry. Noting that with the coming of the war weekly magazines and daily newspapers would inevitably be cutting back on the space formerly given to literary discussion, the *New Republic*'s editors saw that now more than ever the country had great need of a literary quarterly. Therefore they were happy to join with the members of the Modern Language Association in urging the authorities at LSU to revise their decision.[51]

Even after the university cut its support to the *Southern Review* and the editors announced its suspension, Brooks and Warren continued an energetic fight to keep their magazine alive. The John Guggenheim Memorial Foundation, the Rockefeller Foundation, the Carnegie Corporation, and the Rosenwald Fund all were consulted in hopes of finding a new source of funding, and everywhere the response was the same. The *Southern Review*, they were told, was a worthy project, but no money was available. Through the month of March, Philip Davidson held out a faint glimmer of hope that the magazine might move to Agnes Scott College in Decatur, Georgia, but funding there too failed, and one more mirage disappeared.

The *Southern Review*'s last, best hope was offered by the editors' old mentor and friend, John Crowe Ransom. Warren had visited in Kentucky and Ohio during the Christmas vacation, and in Gambier he had personally warned Ransom, who was having his own problems keeping the *Kenyon Review* afloat, of the imminent demise of the *Southern Review*. On January 21, Ransom wrote to Warren that he was anxious to know the fate of the Baton Rouge quarterly just as soon as the LSU board of supervisors made its final decision. At Kenyon, too, belts were tightening, and a faculty committee was examining the budget for possible economies. Ransom was certain that "they'll remark the matter of the *Review* expense," but he was equally sure that "the President is very much behind us, and we

51. "Petition," Modern Language Association to General Campbell B. Hodges, December 30, 1941, in *Southern Review* Collection; R. P. Blackmur to Cleanth Brooks and Robert Penn Warren, February 9, 1942; Blackmur to Warren, March 14, 1942; Randall Jarrell to Brooks, n.d.

have other warm supporters" and expected to save his magazine. Brooks and Warren had been advisory editors on the *Kenyon Review* since its founding in 1938 and now Ransom wrote, "I do *powerfully* hope that, if you discontinue there, you may go in with us in some fashion."[52] Not only would the proposed merger keep alive the *Southern Review* in spirit if not in name, but there would be many practical advantages to the *Kenyon* as well. Greatest of these, Ransom admitted, was an increase in circulation. The *Kenyon Review* at that time was selling 1,200 copies an issue. Ransom offered to fulfill unexpired subscriptions to the Baton Rouge quarterly in expectation that the profit of such an exposure would soon accrue to Gambier.

The rationale behind the proposed merger was far from mercenary, however. Like the *Southern Review*, the *Kenyon Review* was a strong voice for the New Critics, and Morton D. Zabel had noted in 1939 that Ransom's editorial emphasis on "the aesthetic discipline promises to make it an important medium of literary education in the coming decade." The affinity between the two magazines was obvious, and went so far as to include a jointly sponsored symposium in the autumn of 1940 in which the contributors to both defended the teaching of criticism rather than history in college English courses. Ransom declared, in fact, that "there is no other publication with which we have felt so much community of literary purpose; but in some respects its performance has excelled ours, and notably in the display of the modern short story."[53]

The LSU Board of Supervisors met on March 10, and late in the day's proceedings Thomas W. Leigh moved that "the university continue its sponsorship and publication as in the past for another year of the *National Mathematics Magazine*, and that an amount of $2,000 be provided in the budget for this purpose." The motion was seconded by John Y. Fauntleroy but failed to pass. Leigh then moved "that the University continue its sponsorship and publication of *The Southern Review* and that the necessary budgetary adjustments in the proposed budget be made so as to provide a sum of not more

52. John Crowe Ransom to Warren, January 21, 1942.
53. Zabel, "Condition of American Criticism: 1939," 426; John Crowe Ransom, "War and Publication," *Kenyon Review*, IV (Spring, 1942), 218.

than $12,000 for that purpose."[54] The motion failed for lack of a second. Leigh at last proposed that the board set aside $2,000 for the support of the *Journal of Southern History*. This motion, too, died for want of a second.

Following the meeting of the LSU board Brooks and Warren wired Ransom: "Can proceed with merger negotiations if desired. Our full cooperation. Editorship from this end not important. Reply immediately by Western Union." Unfortunately the telegram was "much garbled," but toward the end of March Brooks was once again in touch with Ransom on the subject of the two magazines combining. "I feel chances for a merger good," he wired, and promised to send by airmail a copy of the memorandum on the subject which he had turned in to President Hodges. Ransom's return letter was optimistic, and raised only a few minor problems. The name, for example, was subject to negotiation. Ransom favored "The Review," but wondered if that were "too cocky?" He thought as well that it would be best to keep a provisional editor "down in Baton Rouge, for the sake of the happiness of the present *Southern Review* fans," and to ensure that "the merger magazine really makes some adaptation to the style and tradition of *The Southern Review* and not come out merely as an enlarged *Kenyon Review*." As for form, Ransom thought it would be simplest to keep the *Kenyon*'s present printer and type and page style but to change only the cover to reflect the new status of the old magazines. At any event, he hoped that Brooks would edit the first number of the merger, which he was confident would be effected by summer.[55]

The terms of the merger that Brooks submitted to General Hodges were very advantageous to LSU and to the *Southern Review*. LSU's part of the bargain would be to supply the part-time services of the editors of the *Southern Review*. The university would turn over to the *Kenyon* the money representing the defunct *Southern Review*'s

54. Minutes of the Meeting of the Board of Supervisors, Louisiana State University, March 9–10, 1942, Louisiana State University.

55. Robert Penn Warren and Cleanth Brooks to John Crowe Ransom, Western Union, n.d.; Brooks to Ransom, Western Union, n.d.; Ransom to Brooks, March 30, 1942.

unexpired subscriptions. This sum would amount to only $653.40, and since the sum representing unexpired subscriptions would have to be repaid to the subscribers even if the merger were not entered, the merger would require no special outlay of funds. The merger would demand some additional expense on the part of the university in that the time that Brooks devoted to teaching in the English department would have to be cut from twelve hours to nine hours—the same arrangement as existed with the *Southern Review*—and some secretarial assistance would have to be provided for his work as editor of the joint magazine. Ransom's plan was proposed before Robert Penn Warren had accepted a teaching post at the University of Minnesota. Since Ransom's plan envisaged two editors from Louisiana State, Brooks conceded that the time allotted for his editorial work might have to be increased to six hours. By allowing Brooks three to six hours per week editorial time and by providing him with secretarial assistance, the university would be allowed equal representation with Kenyon College in the new review. "It would seem," Brooks argued, "that the terms are weighted rather heavily in favor of this university, if any premium is to be placed upon equal representation in such an enterprise." [56]

With the memorandum outlining the *Southern Review/Kenyon Review* merger, Brooks enclosed a note to President Hodges expressing his own feelings on the matter. Brooks stressed the absolute objectivity of the memorandum, and added that although he believed that the terms of the proposal were extremely favorable to LSU, with regard to his own personal position, he "would almost prefer that it not be entered into." The work that his editorial position had demanded for the last seven years had taken a heavy toll on his time and energies, and Brooks was not at all sure that they were "altogether rewarding in terms of one's personal career." If General Hodges were to decide that the merger was in the best interest of the university, Brooks pledged himself to continue the work that he and Warren had begun with the *Southern Review*. But he did wish to emphasize the fact that, so far as his personal feelings were

56. Cleanth Brooks to Campbell Hodges, April 30, 1942.

concerned, his "attitude toward the proposed merger is wholly disinterested."[57]

Meanwhile, at Gambier, Kenyon President Gordon K. Chalmers was composing his own letter to General Hodges in regard to the two institutions' literary magazines. John Crowe Ransom, Chalmers informed Hodges, had explained to him fully the matter of the merger, and, to his mind, "not only the friendship of the editors of the two *Reviews* and the fact that many of them have studied under Professor Ransom, but also the opinion frequently expressed by literary critics who admire the two *Reviews* to the effect that their purposes and functions are similar, make it natural . . . that the merger be brought about." After receiving Brooks's memorandum and personal addendum and the letter from President Chalmers on May 7, President Hodges sent a memo to Dean Frey on May 8 asking for his advice on the matter, but stating that he personally doubted the wisdom of entering the merger. Eight days later Brooks met with Dean Frey; Dean Wendell Holmes Stevenson of the College of Arts and Sciences, whose own *Journal of Southern History* had just been suspended; Thomas Kirby, the new chairman of the English department; and President Hodges on the matter of the merger. While Brooks, Kirby, Stevenson, and Frey recommended that the merger be made, Hodges demurred, wishing to delay final action until the board of supervisors met on May 30. At that meeting Mr. Daniel Debaillon proposed and Major Tom W. Dutton seconded a motion, unanimously carried, that the recommendation of President Hodges regarding the proposed merger of the *Southern Review* and the *Kenyon Review* "be accepted and approved and that no steps be taken at this time toward effecting such a measure."[58]

Although almost immediately the painters and floor sanders began to take possession of the *Southern Review* offices, stacking files and furniture in the corridors, Brooks had one last issue of the journal to edit and get to the press. "We have on hand a great deal of material," he wrote to R. P. Blackmur after the suspension was an-

57. Cleanth Brooks to Campbell Hodges, May 5, 1942.
58. Gordon K. Chalmers to Campbell Hodges, May 7, 1942; Minutes of the Meeting of the Board of Supervisors, May 30–31, 1942, Louisiana State University.

nounced, "and feel that we must stand by all commitments which were made before bad weather set in for the magazine. This means that we shall have to publish an enormous issue and divide up what is left in our budget. As it is, our rates for this last issue will be very drastically reduced."[59] Equally depressing was the return of scores of usable manuscripts to which the editors had not yet committed themselves. In addition to poems returned to LSU students Thomas McGrath, Frederick Brantley, and Alan Swallow, Brooks had the un-pleasant duty to send back poems, stories, and essays to Marshall McLuhan, Maxwell Geismar, Wallace Stegner, Marianne Moore, Delmore Schwartz, and a host of other first-rate writers.

It is impossible to judge to what degree General Hodges' decision was swayed by the personal note that Cleanth Brooks attached to the memorandum explaining the terms of the merger as proposed by the *Kenyon Review*. It is certain, however, that Brooks was near exhaustion from his long fight for an acceptable president for the university and chairman for the English department and from his battle to keep the *Southern Review* alive at LSU. The final and most demoralizing blow was no doubt his friend and colleague's decision to accept the offer of a $200 raise and a full professor's chair as direc-tor of the creative writing program at the University of Minnesota.

Warren announced his resignation from LSU simultaneously with the announcement of the demise of the *Review*. "I don't like to see you go to Minnesota," wrote Allen Tate, "but you will have to be somewhere, and I hear it's a good place." Minnesota was a fine uni-versity with a splendid English department, but Warren did not leave LSU quite of his own accord. "I loved it there," he says, "and never wanted to leave," but LSU would not match the salary offered by Minnesota. "That's an invitation to leave," says Warren, "and I did." If Warren was bitter over the losing battles in Baton Rouge, however, he never said so publicly. More than twenty years later, when he returned to Baton Rouge to gather material for his docu-mentary *Who Speaks for the Negro?*, he would only say that the tur-moil in Louisiana's politics was not the reason he left the university. "I think there was a deep attachment of many of the LSU faculty

59. Cleanth Brooks to R. P. Blackmur, February 13, 1942.

members toward the University at that time," he added. "It was the only place that was expanding—it was an exciting place." [60]

If Warren was not outraged at the shabby treatment that he and Brooks had received at the hands of the university administration, much of the student body certainly was. The *Reveille* ran nearly a full page of editorial condemnation of the administration's negligence in allowing Warren to leave. Observing that when recognized ability goes unrewarded, it is only logical that it seek recompense elsewhere, one correspondent noted that "well known Southerners who have traveled North in recent years include John Crowe Ransom . . . who left Vanderbilt University for Kenyon College in Ohio . . . W. Y. Elliott, political theorist who left the same university for Harvard, Allen Tate who left North Carolina State College for Women to teach at Princeton" and a list of others. "Mr. Warren's leaving means that another distinguished man of letters has taken wing in the flight of talent from the South." [61]

Warren spent his last few days on the LSU campus working with Brooks toward the completion of their third textbook, *Understanding Fiction*. This book was an attempt to do for short fiction what *Understanding Poetry* had done for verse, to revolutionize the teaching of the short story and the novel by concentrating the reader's attention on the text rather than on the biography of its author. Their publisher, F. S. Crofts, wrote to Brooks on May 16 advising him that publication would have to be delayed from late summer to some future date for fear that it would not be completed in time. This was due largely to the fact that the company had not yet received permission to use all of the copyrighted material that Brooks and Warren wished, but more importantly, because its authors, in their embroilment in saving the *Review*, had fallen behind schedule for the book's completion.

Brooks responded to Croft's letter with a progress report on May 23. "You will see that we are nearly through with the basic work," he informed his publisher; "as for the time of the publication, we leave that entirely up to your best judgment. Red and I feel that we can

60. Allen Tate to Robert Penn Warren, March 2, 1942; "America's Dean of Letters," *Newsweek*, 66; Baton Rouge *State-Times*, February 4, 1964.
61. Jewel Claitor, "Robert Penn Warren," *Reveille*, May 9, 1942, pp. 1, 6.

have everything in to you by the middle of July." Brooks confided that he and Warren were both "very confident about the first part of the book," which was then nearly in order. "We feel that it has turned out better than we had a right to hope for," and offered to send the complete text of Section One and the Introduction in a few days. The separation of the two authors further delayed the book's completion, however, and *Understanding Fiction* did not appear until 1943. On June 30, 1942, the last number of the *Southern Review* rolled off the press. *Reveille* editor Aubrey Williams noted that the last issue "is a bit different and larger; the poetry section is differently organized and the editors have used all the manuscripts at their disposal to make up the contents." In a special poetry section the works of eleven poets were presented.[62]

Perhaps the most eloquent farewells to the *Southern Review* came from a long-established and well-respected critic and from a young lady whose fiction was almost unknown until she was published in the Baton Rouge magazine. F. O. Matthiessen wrote to Brooks that the end of the *Review* "could hardly have come at a worse time," for the coming of the war had accelerated the tendency, which Auden among others had observed, that the great majority of the people "prefer opinion to knowledge." Matthiessen saw the greatest danger in the vigorously pragmatic American spirit to be the probability of mistaking essentials for inessentials and "cutting down on the arts as though they were excess sugar." Even in peace time, he noted, the national bias had been heavily toward the immediately instrumental, and to carry that tendency one step farther, he maintained, would so weaken the nation's cultural tradition that soon our society would be "producing narrowly trained technicians whose state of mind was almost indistinguishable from the hard efficiency of the fascists." "At such a time all modes of free communication should be encouraged, so that the artist will know that he continues to have an audience, and the critic that his responsibilities remain. The loss of *The Southern Review* is that of an indispensable resource."[63]

62. Brooks to Fred S. Crofts, May 23, 1942; Aubrey Williams, "The *Southern Review* Is No More," *Reveille*, June 30, 1942, p. 2.
63. F. O. Matthiessen to Cleanth Brooks, n.d.

And Eudora Welty wrote from Jackson, Mississippi, of her distress over the magazine's suspension.

> It would have been better if something else, less high and good in intent, had been sacrified when a time for sacrificing came—people will all know that someday, if they don't know now. My heart is sad when I see a thing to which good minds and good wills had been devoted tossed away, and so quickly, just when good minds and good wills need to keep their even ways known. A spirit devoted to honesty should be allowed to keep its voice and not be hushed because the times are evil— the spirit was never irrelevant.

Miss Welty acknowledged her debt to the *Southern Review* and its editors for their "vital encouragement" of her early work, and lamented the loss of such aid for future writers. The *Review* would be missed, she predicted, "nobody will know how much. If our pride is in that, our hope must lie in the expectation that one day *The Southern Review* will be again, taking up where it leaves off."[64]

64. Eudora Welty to Cleanth Brooks and Robert Penn Warren, n.d.

Epilogue

O N May 16, 1942, Brooks's and Warren's textbook publisher, F. S. Crofts, wrote to Cleanth Brooks: "I am sorry that you are going to lose Red. On the other hand, I think he has made a wise decision, and only hope that a similarly good offer will come your way." Offers did come, but Brooks chose to stay on in Baton Rouge. Attention from *Modern Poetry and the Tradition*, *Understanding Poetry*, and the *Southern Review* brought him a visiting professor's appointment at the University of Michigan for the summer of 1942, and in December, 1944, he delivered the annual Francis Bergen Memorial lecture at Yale, choosing as his topic "Shakespeare as a Symbolist Poet." For the fall and winter quarters of 1945 and 1946, Brooks served as visiting professor at the University of Chicago, giving his colleagues at LSU "a taste of department life without the intellectual vitality and the general zest which he contributed," so that on his return to Baton Rouge in the spring, he was named as the first occupant of the William A. Read chair of English. No sooner was he settled into his new sinecure than he was off again, this time to Vassar to conduct a seminar on critical theory and the poetry of William Butler Yeats.[1]

1. F. S. Crofts to Cleanth Brooks, May 16, 1942; Heilman, "Cleanth Brooks," 145.

Epilogue

In 1943, F. S. Crofts brought out Brooks's and Warren's *Understanding Fiction*. Dedicated to their old Vanderbilt teacher and Agrarian comrade Donald Davidson, the new text contained fiction by Warren and many former *Southern Review* contributors such as Eudora Welty and Katherine Anne Porter, and sought by means of critical notes and questions to redirect the course of study of the short story in American college classrooms as *Understanding Poetry* had altered the study of verse. *Understanding Fiction* was followed in July, 1945, by *Understanding Drama*, a joint venture of Cleanth Brooks and Robert Heilman, and in 1947 Reynal and Hitchcock brought out Brooks's second volume of essays, *The Well Wrought Urn*. A collection of his best work since the publication of *Modern Poetry and the Tradition*, *The Well Wrought Urn* is a touchstone for new criticism. The idea behind the organization of the volume was Brooks's belief that "authentic poems from various centuries possessed certain common elements."[2] Conscious of the fact that by stressing commonalities he was going against the tide of English scholarship as then practiced—the historical and evolutionary approach to literature—Brooks wished to demonstrate that once the work of art was stripped of all references to the artist and culture from which it came, the "residuum" would be the elements which made the poem a work of art.

With the publication of *The Well Wrought Urn*, Brooks began to experience "the sense of a period's having been fulfilled." The criticism characteristic of the seven years of the *Southern Review*, he felt, had "come to fruition," or had, at least, reached a turning point. Thanks to their labors with the *Review*, their textbooks, and their individual works of criticism, Brooks and Warren had brought academic respectability to the New Criticism. From then the movement could only "consolidate its gains." Ceasing to be "new," the New Criticism lost its attractiveness as a romantic innovation and with its novelty, some of its less dedicated proponents. At the same time, Brooks observed, it was gaining the allegiance of another set of followers "who hope to exploit it mechanically."[3]

LSU had little time to bask in the reflected glory of Brooks's great

2. Brooks, "The State of Letters: The New Criticism," 594.
3. Cleanth Brooks, Foreword to Robert W. Stallman (ed.), *Critiques and Essays in Criticism, 1920–1948* (New York, 1949), xv, xvi.

achievement. On November 1, 1946, the *Reveille* announced that Brooks was joining the hegira of southern scholars to northern universities. With Warren at Minnesota, Ransom at Kenyon, and Tate back in New York after two years at Princeton, Brooks joined the faculty of Yale University in the fall of 1947. Although the move north was a permanent one, with Brooks retiring from Yale as Grey Professor of Rhetoric in 1974, he never thought of it as a desertion of his homeland. Rather, New Haven became a new position from which to carry on the old fight, and there he would be joined by many members of the old Baton Rouge literary community.

Robert Penn Warren, in the meantime, volunteered for service during World War II but "the Navy didn't want me, and the Army would have to come and get me," and so he accepted the post of consultant of poetry in the Library of Congress.[4] There his office adjoined that of Katherine Anne Porter, who had taken the place of the ailing John Peale Bishop as resident fellow in comparative literature. It was there that Porter showed Warren a copy of *The Confession of J. O. Beauchamp*, the principal document of "the Kentucky Tragedy," an 1826 cause célèbre which became the basis for Warren's 1950 novel *World Enough and Time*. In 1944, also, Warren issued his *Selected Poems, 1923–1943*, a collection of the best of his work from the Tennessee and Louisiana years. In 1946 Harcourt, Brace and Company published the novel version of Warren's verse play, under the title *All the King's Men*. The novel brought a storm of protest from the left and right over the author's supposed sympathy with tyrants or tyrannicides, depending on the political bias of the reviewer. It also brought Warren his first Pulitzer Prize.

In 1950 Warren rejoined Brooks at Yale, where the former *Southern Review* editors issued *Modern Rhetoric*, an anthology of *Stories from the Southern Review*, and *American Literature: The Makers and the Making*. Warren's 1955 novel *Band of Angels* is set in Civil War and Reconstruction era Louisiana and was filmed by Warner Brothers in and around Baton Rouge in 1956. Warren himself did not visit the set, however, and did not see Baton Rouge again until

4. Robert Penn Warren, quoted in Edwin Newman, "Speaking Freely," in Floyd C. Watkins and John T. Hiers, *Robert Penn Warren Talking: Interviews, 1950–1978* (New York, 1980), 158–72.

February, 1964, when he returned to do research for *Who Speaks for the Negro?* and to give a lecture at his old university. He did, however, maintain contacts with many of his former LSU colleagues and students. Besides the ongoing alliance with Brooks, with whom he continued to collaborate on critical anthologies and textbooks, Warren brought Leonard Unger to Minnesota after World War II and worked very closely with Albert Erskine.

After leaving LSU for New Directions in 1940, Erskine moved on in 1941 for a one-year stay with the *Saturday Review of Literature*, then to Doubleday Doran and to Reynal and Hitchcock before settling in 1947 with Random House, where William Faulkner identified him as "the best book editor I know." Bennett Cerf, Erskine's supervisor, noted that it was Erskine who brought Robert Penn Warren to Random House. "They were practically like brothers," he remarked.[5] Albert Erskine served as best man in 1952 when Warren married Eleanor Clark, and the Warrens returned the honor as best man and matron of honor when Erskine married Countess Marisa Bisi. Together Warren and Erskine edited *Short Story Masterpieces* (1953), *Six Centuries of Great Poetry* (1955), and *A New Southern Harvest* (1957), and it was to Albert and Marisa Erskine that Warren dedicated his eighth novel, *Flood*, in 1964.

John E. Palmer, after four year's service as an officer in the U.S. Navy during World War II, returned to the editing business, taking over the *Sewanee Review* when Allen Tate resigned as its editor in the spring of 1946. Under Palmer's editorship that review became stronger than it ever had been. From the University of the South, Palmer went to New Haven, there to take over as editor of the *Yale Review* and president of Silliman College. On December 3, 1946, the *Reveille* announced that Robert B. Heilman had accepted a position at the University of Washington as chairman of the English department, where he was to achieve eminence as the author of a number of books of Shakespeare criticism.

When Warren returned to Baton Rouge in 1964, he saw south of town "the great campus of LSU, where grandeur has long since

5. William Faulkner to Bennett Cerf, quoted in Bennett Cerf, *At Random* (New York, 1977), 133, 235, 236.

flowered beyond Huey P. Long's wildest dreams." As one faculty member has noted who stayed on at LSU beyond the demise of the *Southern Review* and through World War II, "The war took various good people away from LSU, some into other lifetime careers. Continuing productivity brought others into professional visibility, and offers from other universities kept coming in. Some people moved. Many good ones stayed—more than enough to contradict the supposition, heard occasionally, that at LSU some sort of bubble had burst."[6]

The vacuum left at LSU by the departure of Brooks and Warren was partially filled by the arrival in 1941 of historian T. Harry Williams. And Thomas Kirby, who served the LSU English department admirably for nearly forty years despite the controversy by which he came to its chair, attempted to bolster the southern New Critical and creative wing of his department by bringing in perhaps the most promising of the second-generation Agrarians and New Critics, George Marion O'Donnell. As a graduate student at Vanderbilt, O'Donnell had published a selection of poems in the *Southern Review*, had contributed to *Who Owns America?*, and had published elsewhere a small but distinguished body of fiction and criticism. When O'Donnell was called to LSU in 1947, he seemed likely to become a major figure in southern letters. O'Donnell was the first of the southern New Critics to grasp William Faulkner's central role in the southern literary renaissance, and according to his best biographer, "tended to be more of the renaissance than his mentors," Ransom, Tate, and Davidson.[7] O'Donnell lasted at LSU for only two years, however, before succumbing to a drinking problem, and William Van O'Connor, another early Faulkner critic, and Bosley Woolf, editor-in-chief of *Webster's New Collegiate Dictionary*, remained at LSU only marginally longer.

Another loss which the university struggled to overcome was that of the *Southern Review*. With the end of the Baton Rouge quarterly in the autumn of 1942, Brooks and Warren became associated with John Crowe Ransom's *Kenyon Review*, which became one of

6. Warren, *Who Speaks for the Negro?*, 14; Heilman, "LSU," 143.

7. Lewis P. Simpson, "O'Donnell's Wall," *The Man of Letters in New England and the South* (Baton Rouge, 1973), 192–94.

the most significant journals of literary criticism in America. Fortunately for LSU, two of its English faculty's keenest and most productive members, Lewis P. Simpson and Donald Stanford, joined forces in the winter of 1964 to bring out the first issue of the new series of the *Southern Review*. With the aid and encouragement of Thomas Kirby and LSU President John Hunter, Simpson and Stanford began editing a magazine of a quality comparable to its 1930s namesake. "I hope," declared President Hunter, "that if my administration is remembered for one thing it will be for the revival of *The Southern Review*."

According to Simpson, "the historical connection between the *Southern Review* of the 1960's and 1970's and the *Southern Review* of the 1930's and 1940's is absolutely fundamental to our place in the present-day spectrum of American literary quarterlies." Except for an alteration in the cover design, even the format of the new series is identical to that of its predecessor. The continuity between the old series and the new runs deeper than mere similarities of type and printing style, but, Simpson maintains, the continuity was not sought as a deliberate editorial policy. The new editors asked Cleanth Brooks what direction he believed a reinstated *Southern Review* should take and were told that "it should take one as different from that of the magazine of 1935–1942 as the literary situation demanded." Simpson and Stanford found, however, that that direction was not at all different from the one that Brooks and Warren pioneered in 1935. "A divergent road might have been taken in the new series if its editors had been younger," Simpson says. "But their literary education was primarily shaped by the age which nurtured the original series—that of the southern renaissance, or, more broadly speaking, of the second American renaissance." Stanford agrees that "the major problem the editors faced in the publication's revival was to insure the high standards established and maintained in the first 28 issues." The new editors "adopted a policy to avoid extremely experimental works," he continues, "and to emphasize conservative literature." The response of Simpson and Stanford to contemporary literature, therefore, is dominated by the work of Brooks and Warren in the 1930s, an age which "seemed to be revolutionary," Simpson notes, but which, in perspective, is one which found its motivation in the struggle "to recover the use of letters as a functional arena of civilization . . . in which the drama of existence is portrayed and the proper relation and separation of the elements of order is discussed."[8]

If Simpson and Stanford have not been as fortunate in discovering new literary talent as were their predecessors, it may be as Warren has suggested that the times rather than the men are to blame. In a statement to a *Daily Reveille* reporter in 1964, Warren observed that "there is not the floating talent now that was available when we first published the magazine at LSU. The morning mail brought in unsolicited short stories from Eudora Welty, and two of Katherine Anne Porter's best short novels were first published by us." Militating against the revival of the *Review*, in Warren's opinion is the fact that "there are more markets today, but fewer writers. When we were editing *The Southern Review*, there was less competition."[9]

To some contributors to the old series, though, the new is equally good. Eudora Welty, for example, is well pleased that "Lewis P. Simpson is doing a fine job" with the revival of the magazine that gave her her start. The new *Review* is "still exceedingly good," she says, "and they still are printing Brooks and Warren, among other people who began it. It has been a continuing influence all along."[10]

8. Lewis P. Simpson, "*The Southern Review* and Post-Southern American Letters," 81–82.

9. Warren, quoted in the *Daily Reveille*, February 5, 1964.

10. Interview with Eudora Welty, June 17, 1978.

Bibliography

PRIMARY SOURCES

I. Manuscripts

Louisiana Collection. Troy H. Middleton Library, Louisiana State University, Baton Rouge, Louisiana.
Southern Review Collection. Beinecke Rare Book and Manuscript Library, Yale University, New Haven, Connecticut.
Southwest Review Papers. Repository, Southern Methodist University, Dallas, Texas.

II. Books

Boyd, David French. *General History of the Louisiana State University and Agricultural and Mechanical College*. Baton Rouge: Bauer Printing Company, 1899.
Brooks, Cleanth. *Modern Poetry and the Tradition*. Chapel Hill: University of North Carolina Press, 1939.
———. *Relation of the Alabama-Georgia Dialect to the Provincial Dialect of Great Britain*. Baton Rouge: Louisiana State University Press, 1935.
———. *The Well Wrought Urn: Studies in the Structure of Poetry*. New York: Reynal and Hitchcock, 1947.
———, et al. *Facets*. Nashville: Calumet Club of Vanderbilt, 1928.
Brooks, Cleanth, and Robert Penn Warren. *Understanding Fiction*. New York: F. S. Crofts, 1943.

*Unless otherwise indicated, all letters cited come from this collection.

———. *Understanding Poetry: An Anthology for College Students.* New York: Henry Holt, 1943.

———, eds. *Stories from the Southern Review.* Baton Rouge: Louisiana State University Press, 1953.

Brooks, Cleanth, Robert Penn Warren, and John Thibaut Purser. *An Approach to Literature: A Collection of Prose and Verse with Analyses and Discussions.* Baton Rouge: Louisiana State University Press, 1936.

Corley, Sheila, and Fredrick Brantley, eds. *Signets: An Anthology of Beginnings.* Baton Rouge: Alan Swallow, 1940.

Fain, John Tyree, and Thomas D. Young. *The Literary Correspondence of Donald Davidson and Allen Tate.* Athens: University of Georgia Press, 1974.

Foley, Martha. *The Story of Story Magazine.* New York: W. W. Norton, 1980.

Ford, Ford Madox. *The Great Trade Route.* New York: Oxford University Press, 1937.

Hansen, Harry, ed. *O. Henry Memorial Award: Prize Stories of 1939.* New York: Doubleday, Doran, 1939.

Humphrey, Hubert H. *The Education of a Public Man: My Life in Politics.* New York: Doubleday, 1976.

———. *The Political Philosophy of the New Deal.* Baton Rouge: Louisiana State University Press, 1970.

Long, Huey P. *Every Man a King: The Autobiography of Huey P. Long.* New Orleans: National Book Company, 1933.

O'Brien, Edward J., ed. *Best Short Stories of 1937.* Boston: Houghton Mifflin, 1937.

———. *Best Short Stories of 1938.* Boston: Houghton Mifflin, 1938.

———. *Best Short Stories of 1939.* Boston: Houghton Mifflin, 1939.

———. *Best Short Stories of 1940.* Boston: Houghton Mifflin, 1940.

Pilkington, John, ed. *Stark Young: A Life in the Arts: Letters, 1900–1962.* 2 vols. Baton Rouge: Louisiana State University Press, 1975.

Porter, Katherine Anne. *Flowering Judas and Other Stories.* New York: Modern Library, 1940.

———. *Pale Horse, Pale Rider: Three Short Novels.* New York: Harcourt, Brace, 1939.

———, et al. *Recent Southern Fiction: A Panel Discussion.* Macon, Ga.: Wesleyan College, 1960.

Purdy, Rob Roy, ed. *Fugitives' Reunion: Conversations at Vanderbilt, May 3–5, 1956.* Nashville: Vanderbilt University Press, 1959.

Ransom, John Crowe. *The New Criticism.* Norfolk, Conn.: New Directions, 1941.

Sherman, William T. *Memoirs of General William T. Sherman.* 2 vols. New York: D. Appleton, 1889.

Bibliography

Smith, James Monroe. *A Few Facts About LSU*. Baton Rouge: Louisiana State University Press, 1934.

Swallow, Alan. *An Editor's Essays of Two Decades*. Denver: Experiment Press, 1962.

Tate, Allen. *Memoirs and Opinions: 1926–1974*. Chicago: Swallow Press, 1975.

Tate, Allen, and Herbert Agar, eds. *Who Owns America? A New Declaration of Independence*. Boston: Houghton Mifflin, 1936.

Taylor, Richard. *Destruction and Reconstruction*. New York: D. Appleton, 1879.

Thorndike, Rachel Sherman, ed. *The Sherman Letters: Correspondence Between General and Senator Sherman from 1837 to 1891*. New York: Scribner's, 1894.

Uhler, John Earle. *Cane Juice: A Story of South Louisiana*. New York: Century, 1931.

Warren, Robert Penn. *All the King's Men*. New York: Harcourt, Brace, 1946.

———. *All the King's Men: A Play*. New York: Random House, 1960.

———. *At Heaven's Gate*. New York: Harcourt, Brace, 1943.

———. *Eleven Poems on the Same Theme*. Norfolk, Conn.: New Directions Press, 1942.

———. *Night Rider*. Boston: Houghton Mifflin, 1939.

———. *Selected Essays*. New York: Random House, 1958.

———. *Selected Poems, 1923–1943*. New York: Harcourt, Brace, 1944.

———. *Thirty-six Poems*. New York: Alcestis Press, 1935.

———. *Who Speaks for the Negro?* New York: Random House, 1965.

———, ed. *A Southern Harvest*. Boston: Houghton Mifflin, 1937.

Watkins, Floyd C., and John T. Hiers, eds. *Robert Penn Warren Talking: Interviews, 1950–1978*. New York: Random House, 1980.

Welty, Eudora. *The Collected Stories of Eudora Welty*. New York: Harcourt, Brace, Jovanovich, 1980.

Wilkerson, Marcus M. *The Louisiana State University Press and the Advancement of Learning*. Baton Rouge: Louisiana State University Press, 1937.

Young, Stark. *So Red the Rose*. New York: Scribner's, 1934.

———, ed. *Southern Treasury of Life and Literature*. New York: Scribner's, 1937.

III. Articles, Essays, Short Stories, and Poems

Botkin, B. A. "*Folk-Say* and *Space*: Their Genesis and Exodus." *Southwest Review*, XX (July, 1935), 321–36.

Boyle, Hal. "A Correspondent's Notebook." Baton Rouge *Morning Advocate*, November 9, 1949, p. 6A.

Brooks, Cleanth. "Brooks on Warren." *Four Quarters*, XXI (May, 1972), 19–22.

———. "The Christianity of Modernism." *American Review*, VI (February, 1936), 435–46.

———. "Edna Millay's Maturity." *Southwest Review*, XX (January, 1935), 1–5.

———. "The English Language in the South." In Stark Young (ed.), *A Southern Treasury of Life and Literature*. New York: Scribner's, 1937.

———. Foreword to Robert W. Stallman (ed.), *Critiques and Essays in Criticism, 1920–1948*. New York: Ronald Press, 1940.

———. "Forty Years of Understanding Poetry." *College English Association Forum* (April, 1980), 5–12.

———. "Literature and Human Beings." *Louisiana State University Bulletin*, XXVIII (October, 1936), 18–30.

———. "Literature and the Professors: Literary History vs. Criticism." *Kenyon Review*, II (Autumn, 1940), 403–12.

———. "Metaphor and the Tradition." *Southern Review*, I (Summer, 1935), 151–63.

———. "Metaphysical Poetry and the Ivory Tower." *Southern Review*, I (Winter, 1936), 568–83.

———. "The Modern Southern Poet and Tradition." *Virginia Quarterly Review*, XI (April, 1935), 305–20.

———. "On the Reading of *All the King's Men*." *Sewanee Review*, LV (Spring, 1947), n.p.

———. "The Poem as Organism: Modern Critical Procedure." In *The Proceeding of the Second English Institute*. New York: Columbia University Press, 1941.

———. "Poets and Laureates." *Southern Review*, II (Autumn, 1936), 391–98.

———. "The Present State of Literary Scholarship." *South Atlantic Bulletin*, XLIV (September, 1979), 49.

———. "The State of Letters: The New Criticism." *Sewanee Review*, LXXXVII (Fall, 1979), 592–607.

———. "What Deep South Literature Needs." *Saturday Review of Literature*, September 19, 1942, pp. 8–9, 29–30.

———. "The Vision of William Butler Yeats." *Southern Review*, IV (Summer, 1938), 116–42.

———. "*The Waste Land*: An Analysis." *Southern Review*, III (Summer, 1937), 106–36.

———. "Wit and High Seriousness." *Southern Review*, I (Fall, 1935), 328–38.

Brooks, Cleanth, and Robert Penn Warren. "Dixie Looks at Mrs. Gerould," *American Review*, VI (March, 1936), 585–95.

―――. "Editorial." *Southern Review*, VII (Winter, 1941–42), n.p.

―――. "The Reading of Modern Poetry." *American Review*, VIII (February, 1937), 435–49.

Chamberlain, John. "Books of the Times: Huey Long's Quarterly." New York *Times*, August 6, 1935, p. 15.

Davidson, Donald. "I'll Take My Stand: A History." *American Review*, V (Summer, 1935), 301–21.

―――. "The 'Mystery' of the Agrarians." *Saturday Review of Literature*, XXVI (January, 1943), 6–7.

Davis, Robert Gorham. "Dr. Adam Stanton's Dilemma." *New York Times Book Review*, August 18, 1946, pp. 3, 24.

DeMott, Benjamin. "Talk with Robert Penn Warren." *New York Times Book Review*, January 9, 1977, p. 1.

Dobie, J. Frank. "Son-of-a-Gun Stew." *Southwest Review* XIX (Fall, 1933), 13–19.

Erskine, Albert. "The Sempiternal Rose." *Southwest Review*, XX (April, 1935), 21–27.

"Father Gassler Attacks *Cane Juice* and Dr. Uhler Replies," Baton Rouge *State Times*, October 6, 1931.

Faulkner, William. "Knight's Gambit." *Knight's Gambit and Other Stories*. New York: Random House, 1949.

Girault, Norton R. "Recollections of Robert Penn Warren as a Teacher in the 1930's." *Texas Writers Newsletter*, XXXI (April, 1982), 3–6.

Heilman, Robert B. "Baton Rouge and LSU Forty Years After." *Sewanee Review*, LXXXVIII (Winter, 1979–1980), 126.

―――. "Cleanth Brooks: Some Snapshots, Mostly from an Old Album." In Lewis P. Simpson (ed.), *The Possibilities of Order*. Baton Rouge: Louisiana State University Press, 1976.

―――. "On the Reading of *All the King's Men*." *Sewanee Review*, LV (Spring, 1947), n.p.

Jarrell, Randall. "Ten Books." *Southern Review*, I (Fall, 1975), 397–410.

Lowell, Robert. "Louisiana State University, 1940." *Day By Day*. New York: Farrar, Straus, Giroux, 1977.

―――. "Our After Life (for Peter Taylor)." *Shenandoah*, XXVIII (Winter, 1977), 5–7.

Meyers, S. D., Jr. "Agrarianism as Economics." *Southwest Review*, XX, 6–12.

Pipkin, Charles W. "Social Legislation in *Culture in the South*." *Tribune Book Review*, October 12, 1952, p. 8.

Porter, Katherine Anne. "Happy Land." In Frank Crowninshield (ed.), *Vogue's First Reader*. New York: J. Messner, 1942.

―――. "Introduction" to Eudora Welty, *A Curtain of Green and Other Short Stories*. New York: Harcourt, Brace, 1941.

————. "Now at Last, a House of My Own." In Frank Crowninshield (ed.), *Vogue's First Reader*, New York: J. Messner, 1942.

Simpson, Lewis P. *"The Southern Review* and Post-Southern American Letters." *Triquarterly 43: The Little Magazine in America: A Modern Documentary History*, XLIII (1978), 78–99.

Stafford, Jean. "An Influx of Poets." *New Yorker*, November 6, 1978, pp. 43–60.

————. "Some Letters to Peter and Eleanor Taylor." *Shenandoah*, XXX (Spring, 1979), 27–55.

Swallow, Alan. "Road South: Wyoming to Louisiana." *Poetry*, LI (January, 1938), 194–95.

————. "Story of a Publisher." *Wyoming Library Roundup*, XXI (September, 1966), 32.

Tate, Allen. *"The Fugitive, 1922–1925*: A Personal Recollection Twenty Years After." *Princeton University Library Chronicle*, III (April, 1942), 75–84.

Taylor, Peter. "Sentimental Journey [1939]." *New Yorker*, March 12, 1955, pp. 33–57.

Thompson, Barbara. Interview with Katherine Anne Porter. *Writers at Work: The Paris Review Interviews*. 2nd series. New York: Viking Press, 137–63.

Warren, Robert Penn. *"All the King's Men*: The Matrix of Experience." *Yale Review*, LIII (Winter, 1964), 161–67.

————. "Christmas Gift." *Virginia Quarterly Review*, XII (Winter, 1937), 73–85.

————. "Her Own People." *Virginia Quarterly Review*, XI (April, 1935), 289–304.

————. "How a Pulitzer Prize Novel Was Created." *Chicago Sunday Tribune Magazine of Books*, May 11, 1947, p. 14.

————. "How Willie Proudfit Came Home." *Southern Review*, IV (Fall, 1938), 299–321.

————. "Industrialization: The Old South Fades." In Robert Heilman (ed.), *Aspects of a World at War: Radio Forum of the Louisiana State University*. Baton Rouge: General Extension Division, Louisiana State University, 1942.

————. Introduction to *Katherine Anne Porter: A Collection of Critical Essays*. Englewood Cliffs: Prentice-Hall, 1979.

————. Introduction to Peter Taylor, *A Long Fourth and Other Stories*. New York: Harcourt, Brace, 1948.

————. "John Crowe Ransom: A Study in Irony." *Virginia Quarterly Review*, X (Winter, 1935), 93–112.

————. "Katherine Anne Porter: Irony with a Center." *Kenyon Review*, IV (Winter, 1942), 29–42.

———. "Love and Separateness in Eudora Welty." *Kenyon Review*, VI (Spring, 1944), 246–59.

———. "Not Local Color." *Virginia Quarterly Review*, VIII (January, 1932), 153–60.

———. "A Note on the Hamlet of Thomas Wolfe." *American Review*, V (May, 1935), 191–208.

———. "A Note on Three Southern Poets." *Poetry*, XL (May, 1932), 103–13.

———. "A Note to *All the King's Men*," *Sewanee Review*, XLI (May, 1952), 476.

———. "Notes." In Kimon Friar and John M. Brinnin (eds.), *Modern Poetry, American and British*. New York: Appleton-Century-Crofts, 1951.

———. "The Present State of Poetry in the United States." *Kenyon Review*, I (Fall, 1939), 384–98.

———. "Prime Leaf." In Alfred Kreymborg, Lewis Mumford, and Paul Rosenfeld (eds.), *American Caravan IV*. New York: Macaulay Co., 1931.

———. "Pure and Impure Poetry." *Kenyon Review*, V (Spring, 1943), 228–54.

———. "Set in a Silver Sea." *Poetry*, XLVI (September, 1935), 346–49.

———. "The Situation in American Writing, Part II." *Partisan Review*, VI (Fall, 1939), 112–13.

———. "Some Don'ts for Literary Regionalists." *American Review*, VIII (December, 1936), 142–50.

———. "Some Important Fall Authors Speak for Themselves." *New York Herald Book Review*, XXX (October 11, 1953), 10.

———. "Some Recent Novels." *Southern Review*, I (Winter, 1936), 645–47.

———. "A Special Message to Subscribers from Robert Penn Warren." In *All the King's Men*. Franklin Center, Pa.: Franklin Library, 1977.

———. "T. S. Stribling: A Paragraph in the History of Critical Realism." *American Review*, II (February, 1934), 463–86.

———. "Testament of Flood," *The Magazine*, II (March–April, 1935), 230–34.

———. "Two Peters: Memory and Opinion." *Shenandoah*, XXVIII (Winter, 1977), 8.

———. Untitled statement in *Louisiana State University Alumni News*, XV (March, 1939), 3.

———. Untitled statement in *Wilson Library Bulletin*, XIII (June, 1939), 652.

———. "When the Light Gets Green." *Southern Review*, I (Spring, 1936), 799–806.

Young, Stark. "On Reeking of the Soil." *Texas Review*, I (June, 1915), 80–81.

Bibliography

IV. Newspapers and Periodicals

Amite *Progress*. June 25, 1936.
Baton Rouge *Morning Advocate*. January, 1934–December, 1942.
Baton Rouge *State Times*. January, 1934–December, 1942.
Louisiana Leader. I–IX (December, 1933–June, 1942).
Louisiana Progress. III (1931).
Reveille [Louisiana State University]. January, 1934–December, 1942.
Southern Review. I–VII (Summer, 1935–Spring, 1942).

V. Other Sources

Brooks, Cleanth, *et al. Facts Concerning Academic Freedom at Louisiana State University*. Baton Rouge: Louisiana State University Press, 1935.
Brooks, Cleanth, and Robert Penn Warren. "Note on Section 2" to LSU Budget Committee, n.d. Typescript in *Southern Review* Collection, Beinecke Rare Book and Manuscript Collection, Yale University.
Commission of the American Council on Education. *Louisiana State University and Agricultural and Mechanical College: A Survey Report by a Commission of the American Council on Education*. Washington: American Council on Education, 1940.
Dalrymple, William Haddock. *A Brief Sketch—Illustrated—of the Louisiana State University and Agricultural and Mechanical College*. Baton Rouge: Louisiana State University, 1922.
Farrell, David. Interview with Robert Penn Warren. Oral History Program. University of Kentucky Libraries. Lexington, Kentucky.
Franke, William B., Raymond J. Hannon, and Howard P. Withey. *Louisiana State University: Report on Investigation as of June 30, 1939*. New York: Franke, Hannon and Withey, 1940.
Frey, Fred C. "Reminiscences of Fred C. Frey." n.p.: n.p., 1975.
Gossett, Thomas F. "A History of the *Southwest Review*: 1915–1942." M.A. thesis, Southern Methodist University, 1948.
Hebert, Paul M. "Louisiana State University: Retrospect and Prospect." Commencement Address, Louisiana State University, summer, 1939. Louisiana Collection, Middleton Library, LSU.
Holtman, Robert E. *Aspects of a World at War: Radio Forum of the Louisiana State University*. Broadcast over WJBO radio, Baton Rouge, Louisiana. November, 1941–May, 1942. Baton Rouge: General Extension Division, Louisiana State University, 1942.
Louisiana State University, *Report of the Board of Supervisors*, 1920–1937; 1938–1942.
Lowell, Robert. Letter to Bishop Maurice Schexnayder, February 13, 1977. Papers of Bishop Maurice Schexnayder, Lafayette, Louisiana.
Minutes of the Meeting of the Board of Supervisors Louisiana State University. March 9–10 and May 30–31, 1942. Louisiana State University.

Montesi, Albert J. "The *Southern Review* (1936–1942): A History and Evaluation." Ph.D. dissertation, Pennsylvania State University, 1955.

Personal Correspondence with Cleanth Brooks, Albert Erskine, Walton Patrick, Arthur H. Scouten, Thomas Thompson, Leonard Unger, and Aubrey Williams.

Personal Interviews with Cleanth Brooks, W. T. Couch, Jesse H. Cutrer, Alex Daspit, Fred C. Frey, Robert D. Jacobs, Thomas A. Kirby, Andrew Lytle, John E. Palmer, John T. Purser, Bishop Maurice Schexnayder, Lewis P. Simpson, Donald Stanford, Allen Tate, Peter Taylor, Arlin Turner, Robert Penn Warren, Eudora Welty, and T. Harry Williams.

Rock, Virginia. "The Making and Meaning of *I'll Take My Stand*." Ph.D. dissertation, University of Minnesota, 1961.

Sullivan, James P. "A Study of the Critical and Pedagogical Works of Cleanth Brooks and Robert Penn Warren." Ph.D. dissertation, New York University, 1970.

Tassin, Anthony G. "The Phoenix and the Urn: The Literary Theory and Criticism of Cleanth Brooks." Ph.D. dissertation, Louisiana State University, 1966.

"Transcript of the Meetings of the Conference on Literature and Reading in the South and Southwest." Baton Rouge, Louisiana, April 10 and 11, 1935.

Trippet, Mary Maude. "A History of the *Southwest Review*: Toward an Understanding of Regionalism." Ph.D. dissertation, University of Illinois, 1966.

SECONDARY SOURCES

I. Books

Anderson, Elliott, and Mary Kinzie. *The Little Magazine and Contemporary Literature.* New York: Modern Language Association of America, 1966.

Bain, Robert, Joseph M. Flora, and Louis D. Rubin, Jr., eds. *Southern Writers: A Biographical Dictionary.* Baton Rouge: Louisiana State University Press, 1979.

Barrett, William. *The Truants: Adventures Among the Intellectuals.* New York: Anchor/Doubleday, 1982.

Blotner, Joseph. *Faulkner: A Biography.* New York: Random House, 1974.
———, ed. *Selected Letters of William Faulkner.* New York: Random House, 1977.

Bradbury, John M. *The Fugitives: A Critical Account.* Chapel Hill: University of North Carolina Press, 1958.

Cerf, Bennett. *At Random.* New York: Random House, 1977.

Claire, William F., ed. *Publishing in the West: Alan Swallow; Some Letters and Commentaries.* Santa Fe: Lightning Tree, 1974.

Bibliography

Couch, William Terry, ed. *Culture in the South: A Symposium of Thirty-One Authors*. Chapel Hill: University of North Carolina Press, 1934.

Cowan, Louise. *The Fugitive Group*. Baton Rouge: Louisiana State University Press, 1959.

Cowley, Malcolm, ed. *Writers at Work: The Paris Review Interviews*. 1st series. New York: Viking Press, 1959.

Davis, Edwin Adams. *Louisiana: A Narrative History*. Baton Rouge: Claitor's, 1965.

Davis, Forrest. *Huey Long: A Candid Biography*. New York: Dodge, 1935.

Fineran, John Kingston. *The Career of a Tinpot Napoleon: A Political Biography of Huey P. Long*. New Orleans: John Kingston Fineran, 1932.

Fleming, Walter L. *Louisiana State University: 1860–1896*. Baton Rouge: Louisiana State University Press, 1936.

―――. *General W. T. Sherman as College President*. Cleveland: Arthur H. Clark, 1912.

Givner, Joan. *Katherine Anne Porter: A Life*. New York: Simon and Schuster, 1982.

Hamilton, Ian. *Robert Lowell*. New York: Random House, 1982.

Hendrick, George. *Katherine Anne Porter*. New York: McGraw Hill, 1957.

Hoffman, Frederick J. *The 20's*. New York: Free Press, 1965.

Kane, Harnett T. *Louisiana Hayride: The American Rehearsal for Dictatorship, 1928–1940*. Gretna, La.: Pelican, 1971.

Krieger, Murray. *The New Apologists for Poetry*. Minneapolis: University of Minnesota Press, 1956.

Lee, David D. *Tennessee in Turmoil: Politics in the Volunteer State, 1920–1932*. Memphis: Memphis State University Press, 1979.

Lewis, Lloyd. *Sherman: The Fighting Prophet*. New York: Harcourt, Brace and Co., 1932.

Liddell-Hart, B. H. *Sherman: The Genius of the Civil War*. London: Ernst Benn, 1930.

Liebling, A. J. *The Earl of Louisiana*. Baton Rouge: Louisiana State University Press, 1970.

Lopez, Enrique Hank. *Fugitive from Indian Creek: Conversations with Katherine Anne Porter*. New York: Little, Brown, 1981.

McCallum, James Dow, ed. *The College Omnibus*. New York: Harcourt, Brace, 1934.

O'Brien, Michael. *The Idea of the American South: 1920–1941*. Baltimore: Johns Hopkins University Press, 1979.

O'Connor, William. *An Age of Criticism: 1900–1950*. Chicago: Henry Regnery, 1951.

Price, Frank James. *Troy H. Middleton: A Biography*. Baton Rouge: Louisiana State University, 1974.

272

Reed, Germaine M. *David French Boyd*. Baton Rouge: Louisiana State University Press, 1977.

Rubin, Louis D., Jr. *The Wary Fugitives: Four Poets and the South*. Baton Rouge: Louisiana State University Press, 1978.

Schlesinger, Arthur M., Jr. *The Politics of Upheaval*, Vol. III of *The Age of Roosevelt*. Boston: Houghton Mifflin, 1960.

Simpson, Lewis P. *The Man of Letters in New England and the South*. Baton Rouge: Louisiana State University Press, 1973.

————, ed. *The Possibilities of Order: Cleanth Brooks and His Work.*, Baton Rouge: Louisiana State University Press, 1976.

Sindler, Allan P. *Huey Long's Louisiana: State Politics, 1920–1952*. Baltimore: Johns Hopkins University Press, 1956.

Smith, James Monroe. "The Old War Skule." *New Louisiana*. New Orleans: Franklin Press, 1936.

Stephens, Edna. *John Gould Fletcher*. New York: Twayne, 1967.

Swing, Raymond G. *Forerunners of American Fascism*. New York: Julian Messner, 1935.

Tate, Allen, ed. *Recent American Poetry and Poetic Criticism: A Selected Use of References*. Washington, D.C.: Library of Congress, 1943.

Taylor, Joe Gray. *Louisiana: A History*. New York: W. W. Norton, 1976.

"Unofficial Observer." [John F. Carter.] *American Messiahs*. New York: Kennikat Press, 1935.

Vandekieft, Ruth M. *Eudora Welty*. New York: Twayne, 1962.

Watkins, Floyd C., and John T. Hiers. *Robert Penn Warren Talking: Interviews, 1950–1978*. New York: Random House, 1980.

Weaver, Richard M. *The Southern Tradition at Bay*. New Rochelle: Arlington House, 1968.

Williams, T. Harry. *Huey Long: A Biograhy*. New York: Knopf, 1969.

Woodward, C. Vann. *The Burden of Southern History*. Rev. ed. Baton Rouge: Louisiana State University Press, 1968.

Young, Thomas Daniel. *Gentleman in a Dustcoat: A Biography of John Crowe Ransom*. Baton Rouge: Louisiana State University Press, 1976.

II. Articles, Essays, and Reviews

"A Commemoration 1980, *The Southern Review, Original Series*, 1935–1942." Baton Rouge: Louisiana State University Press, 1980.

"America's Dean of Letters." *Newsweek*, August 25, 1980, pp. 66–69.

"Announcement of Awards." *Poetry*, XLIX (November, 1936), 104–106.

Armfield, Eugene. "Moonshine and Honeysuckle." *Saturday Review of Literature*. December 18, 1937, pp. 10–11.

Baker, Howard. "In Praise of the Novel." *Southern Review*, V (Spring, 1940), 778–93.

Baker, Nina Brown. "Jean Stafford." *Wilson Library Bulletin*, XXV (April, 1951), 578.

Basso, Hamilton. "Books in Brief." *New Republic*, September 25, 1935, p. 195.

———. "The Huey Long Legend." *Life*, December 9, 1946, pp. 106–108ff.

Beatty, Richmond Croom. "Personal Memoir of the Agrarians." *Shenandoah*, III (Summer, 1952), 11.

Bentley, Eric. Review of *All the King's Men*. *Theatre Arts*, XXXL (November, 1947), 72–73.

Blackmur, R P. "Modern Poetry and the Tradition." *Modern Language Notes*, LVI (May, 1941), 388–90.

Blaisdell, Gus. "Alan Swallow, 1915–1966." *New Mexico Quarterly*, XXXVI (Winter, 1966–1967), 325.

Block, Maxine, ed. "Katherine Anne Porter." *Current Biography*. New York: Wilson, 1940.

Boyle, Kay. "Full Length Portrait." *New Republic*, November 24, 1941, pp. 707–708.

Breit, Harvey. "Talk with Mr. Warren." *New York Times Book Review*, June 25, 1950, p. 20.

Bridson, D. G. "American Periodicals." *Criterion*, XV (January, 1936), 368–69, and XV (July, 1936), 777–78.

Brinton, Crane. Review of *Who Owns America? Southern Review*, II (Summer, 1936), 15–21.

Brown, Stuart G. "Poetry and Tradition." *Sewanee Review*, XLVIII (October, 1940), 547–52.

"Building Program of LSU." *School and Society*, June 6, 1936, p. 763.

Cain, J. Harvey. "Situation at Louisiana State University." *School and Society*, L (August 12, 1939), 215–17.

Carter, Hodding. "Huey Long: American Dictator." *American Mercury*, April, 1939, pp. 435–37.

Claitor, Jewel. "Robert Penn Warren." *Reveille*, May 9, 1942, pp. 1, 6.

Clark, Eleanor. "No More Swans." Review of *A Southern Harvest. Partisan Review*, IV (March, 1938), 56–58.

Corbin, John. "A Share for All in America." *New York Times Book Review*, May 10, 1936, pp. 1, 13.

Cowley, Malcolm. "Partisan Review." *New Republic*, October 19, 1938, p. 311.

Crume, Paul. "Pale Horse, Pale Rider." *Southwest Review*, XXV (January, 1940), 214.

Curtiss, Nina. "Tragedy of a Liberal." *Nation*, April 29, 1939, pp. 507–508.

Daniel, Robert. "*Modern Poetry and the Tradition.*" *Sewanee Review*, XLVIII (July, 1940), 419–24.

Daspit, Alex. *LSU Graduate Report*, XXI (Spring, 1976), 5.

Davenport, Basil. "The Tobacco War." *Saturday Review of Literature*, March 18, 1939, p. 6.

Davidson, Donald. Introduction to *So Red the Rose*, by Stark Young. New York: Scribner's, 1953.

Davis, Robert Gorham. "On the Reading of *All the King's Men*." *Sewanee Review*, LV (Spring, 1947), n.p.

Deutsch, Babette. "Poets—Timely and Timeless." *New Republic*, March 19, 1943, pp. 420–21.

Ellman, Richard. "Publisher for Poets." *Saturday Review of Literature*, July 22, 1961, pp. 33–34.

Empson, William. "A Masterly Synthesis." *Poetry*, LV (December, 1939), 154–56.

Fadiman, Clifton. "Mr. Marquand, Mr. Thackery and Others." *New Yorker*, March 18, 1939, pp. 68–69.

Fletcher, John Gould. "The Modern Southern Poets." *Westminster Review*, XXIII (Winter, 1935), 229–51.

Flint, F. Cudworth. "Five Poets." *Southern Review*, I (Winter, 1936), 650–74.

Forgotson, E. Shirley. "The Poetic Method of Robert Penn Warren." *American Prefaces*, VI (Winter, 1941), 130.

Frank, William. "Warren's Achievement." *College English*, XIX (May, 1958), 365–66.

Gallagher, Wes. "Wes Gallagher." *Broadcasting*, July 9, 1973, p. 57.

Gannett, Lewis. "Books and Things: Landmarks in the History of the Short Story." New York *Herald Tribune*, May 25, 1937, p. 27.

G[elatt], R[oland]. "The Author of *World Enough and Time*." *Saturday Review of Literature*, June 24, 1950, p. 11.

Gelder, Robert van, ed. "Katherine Anne Porter at Work." In *Writers and Writing*. New York: Scribner's, 1946.

Gerould, Katherine Fullerton. "A Yankee Looks at Dixie." *American Mercury*, XXXVII (February, 1936), 217–29.

"Give Him Honor or Give Him Death!" *Time*, April 1, 1935, pp. 15–17.

Gross, Seymour. "The Achievement of Robert Penn Warren." *College English*, XIX (May, 1958), 361–65.

Guerard, Albert, Jr. "Four Ways of Criticism." *Virginia Quarterly Review*, XVI (Winter, 1940), 150–56.

———. "Criticism and Commodity." *New Republic*, December 8, 1941, pp. 796, 800.

Haber, Thomas Burns. "Understanding Poetry." *English Journal* (College Edition), XXVII (December, 1938), 870.

Hardin, J. Fair. "The Early History of Louisiana State University." *Louisiana Historical Quarterly*, XI (January, 1928), 1–31.

Hardy, John Edward. "The Achievement of Cleanth Brooks." In Louis D.

Bibliography

Rubin, Jr., and Robert D. Jacobs (eds.), *Southern Renascence: The Literature of the Modern South.* Baltimore: Johns Hopkins University Press, 1953.

Harris, Mark. "Speaking of Books: Alan Swallow, 1915–1966." *New York Times Book Review*, December 18, 1966, p. 2.

Hartley, Lodwick. "Katherine Anne Porter." *Sewanee Review*, XLVIII (Spring, 1940), 206–16.

Hawkins, A. Desmond. "Periodicals: American." Criterion, XVII (July, 1938), 796, and XVIII (January, 1939), 405–406.

"Headlong Week." *Time*, November 19, 1934, p. 17.

Heilman, Robert. "The Southern Temper." *Hopkins Review*, VI (Fall, 1952), 5–15.

———. "Williams on Long: The Story Itself." *Southern Review*, n.s., VI (Autumn, 1970), 935–53.

Holmes, John. "Five American Poets." *Virginia Quarterly Review*, XII (April, 1936), 288–95.

Hubbell, Jay B. "Southern Magazines." In W. T. Couch (ed.), *Culture in the South.* Chapel Hill: University of North Carolina Press, 1935.

"Huey Long's University." *Time*, December 10, 1934, pp. 42–45.

Hutchens, J. K. "On an Author." *New York Herald Tribune Book Review*, July 2, 1950, p. 2.

Isherwood, Christopher. "Tragic Liberal." *New Republic*, May 31, 1939, p. 108.

Jack, Peter Monro. "The New Books of Poetry." *New York Times Book Review*, April 26, 1942, p. 4.

Jarrell, Randall. "Critical Scholars." *New Republic*, October 6, 1940, p. 439.

———. "Contemporary Poetry Criticism." *New Republic*, July 21, 1941, p. 88.

"Jimmy the Stooge." *Time*, July 10, 1939, 14–16.

Johnson, Alva. "Louisiana Revolution." *Saturday Evening Post*, May 11, 1940, pp. 16–17; 97–98; 100; 102.

Jones, Frank. "A Poet." *Nation*, September 26, 1942, p. 277.

Kalb, Bernard. "The Author [Robert Penn Warren]." *Saturday Review of Literature*, August 20, 1955, p. 9.

"Katherine Anne Porter." *New York Times Book Review*, April 14, 1940, p. 20.

"Katherine Anne Porter Receives New York University Medal." New York *Herald Tribune*, April 4, 1940, p. 19.

"Katherine Anne Porter at Yaddo." New York *Times*, December 21, 1940, p. 15.

Kelvin, Norman. "The Failure of Robert Penn Warren." *College English*, XVIII (April, 1957), 355–64.

Bibliography

Kenner, Hugh. "Omnibus Review of Poetry Textbooks." *Poetry*, LXXXIV (April, 1954), 45–53.

Kreymborg, Alfred. "Poets and Poetry: Peasants and Intellectuals." *Living Age*, March 1940, pp. 95–96.

Lann, Robert. Review of *Thirty-six Poems*, by Robert Penn Warren. *New Republic*, July 15, 1936, p. 304.

Leach, Henry Goddard. Review of *Thirty-six Poems*, by Robert Penn Warren. *Forum*, XCVI (August, 1936), 96.

Lechlitner, Ruth. Review of *Thirty-six Poems*, by Robert Penn Warren. New York *Herald Tribune Book Review*, February 16, 1936, p. 10.

———. "Selected New Poetry." *New York Herald Tribune Book Review*, July 19, 1942, p. 13.

Legaré, Hugh Swinton. "Prospectus." *Southern Review* (Charleston), I (February, 1828), n.p.

Long, Louise. Review of *Night Rider*, by Robert Penn Warren. *Southwest Review*, XXIV (July, 1939), 498–500.

"Louisiana Cell." *News-week*, July 17, 1939, p. 15.

McDowell, Fredrick. "Robert Penn Warren's Criticism." *Accent*, XV (Summer, 1955), 173–96.

Mack, Maynard. "Critical Synthesis." *Yale Review*, XIX (Winter, 1939), 398–402.

Marshall, Margaret. "Notes by the Way." *Nation*, January 4, 1941, p. 22.

Milton, George Fort. "The South Do Move." *Yale Review*, XXIX (Fall, 1939), 138–52.

Mizener, Arthur. "Recent Criticism." *Southern Review*, V (Fall, 1939), 376–400.

———. "Equality of Poetry: Review of *The Well Wrought Urn* by Cleanth Brooks." *Poetry*, LXXI (March, 1948), 318–24.

Morris, R. L. "Can Poetry Be Taught?" *Sewanee Review*, XLVII (January, 1939), 89–94.

Muller, Herbert J. "Violence upon the Roads." *Kenyon Review*, I (Summer, 1939), 323–24.

———. "The New Criticism in Poetry." *Southern Review*, VI (Spring, 1941), 811–39.

"My University." *Time*, December 10, 1934, pp. 42–45.

"New Deal at LSU." *News-week*, March 24, 1941, p. 52.

"New Home of Louisiana State University." *School and Society*, XXXI (October 31, 1925), 551–52.

Nichols, Lewis. "In and Out of Books." *New York Times Book Review*, July 16, 1966, p. 8.

Nims, John Fredrick. "Two Intellectual Poets." *Poetry*, LXI (December, 1942), 505–508.

O'Connor, William Van. "A Short View of the New Criticism." *The English Journal*, XXXVIII (November, 1949), 489–97.

Olive, W. J. "John Earle Uhler." *Studies in English Renaissance Literature*, edited by Waldo F. McNair. Baton Rouge: Louisiana State University Press, 1962.

"One Was a Son-of-a-Gun." *Time*, July 17, 1939, p. 15.

"Opportunity Unlimited." *LSU Alumni News*. January–February, 1957, p. 21.

Payne, Ladell. "Willie Stark and Huey Long: Atmosphere, Myth or Suggestion?" *American Quarterly*, XX (Fall, 1968), 580–95.

Prescott, Orville. "Outstanding Novels." *Yale Review*, XXXVI (Autumn, 1946), 192.

"Presidency of Louisiana State University." *School and Society*, July 8, 1939, p. 45.

"Profiles in Editorship." *LSU Outlook*, January, 1981, n.p.

"Promise Kept." *Time*, April 10, 1939, p. 75.

Pruette, Lorine. "A Tobacco War in Kentucky." *New York Herald Tribune Books*, March 19, 1939, p. 2.

Pulos, C. E. "Warren as Critic." *Prairie Schooner*, XXXIII (Spring, 1959), 1–2.

Rahv, Philip. "A Variety of Fiction." *Partisan Review*, VI (Spring, 1939), 112–13.

Ransom, John Crowe. "Apologia for Modernism." *Kenyon Review*, II (Spring, 1940), 247–51.

―――. "The Aesthetics of Regionalism." *American Review*, II (January, 1934), 290–310.

―――. "The Inklings of 'Original Sin.'" *Saturday Review of Literature*, May 20, 1944, pp. 10–11.

―――. "The Teaching of Poetry." *Kenyon Review*, I (Winter, 1939), 81–83.

―――. "War and Publication." *Kenyon Review*, IV (Spring, 1942), 217–18.

―――. "Why Critics Don't Go Mad." *Kenyon Review*, XIV (Spring, 1952), 331–39.

Recommendation of the Faculty." *School and Society*, L (July 22, 1939), 111–12.

"Reverend Maurice Schexnayder." *Louisiana Leader*, IV (December, 1936), 5.

Review of *Eleven Poems on the Same Theme*, by Robert Penn Warren. *New Yorker*, May 9, 1942, p. 64.

Review of *Night Rider*, by Robert Penn Warren. *Booklist*, April 15, 1939, p. 271.

Review of *Night Rider*, by Robert Penn Warren. *Vanderbilt Alumnus*, XXIV (April, 1939), 10–11.

Rosenfeld, Paul. "An Artist in Fiction." *Saturday Review of Literature*, April 1, 1939, p. 7.

Rushton, Peter. "The Unrational Muse." *Virginia Quarterly Review*, XVIII (Summer, 1942), 479–80.

Schutte, W. M. "The Dramatic Version of the Willie Stark Story." *Symposium: All the King's Men*. Carnegie Studies in English, #3. Pittsburgh: Carnegie Press, 1957.

Scouten, Arthur H. Review of *Huey Long's Louisiana*, by Allen P. Sindler. *American Quarterly*, IX (1957), 189.

————. "Warren, Huey Long, and *All the King's Men*." *Four Quarters*, XXI (May, 1972), 23–26.

"Second Southern Novel." *LSU Alumni News*, XV (March, 1939), 3–4.

Seidel, Frederick. "Robert Lowell." *Paris Review*, XXV (Winter–Spring, 1961), 56–95.

Shapiro, Edward S. "American Conservative Intellectuals, the 1930's, and the Crisis of Ideology." *Modern Age*, XXIII (Fall, 1979), 370–89.

Smith, Harrison. "Standards of Criticism." *Saturday Review of Literature*, November 4, 1950, p. 20.

Smith, Henry Nash. "The Dilemma of Agrarianism." *Southwest Review*, XIX (April 1934), 215–32.

————. "McGinnis and the *Southwest Review*: A Reminiscence." *Southwest Review*, XL (Fall, 1955), 299–310.

————. "A Note on the Southwest." *Southwest Review*, XIV (Spring, 1929), 267–78.

Sochatoff, A. Fred. "Some Treatments of the Huey Long Theme." *Symposium: All the King's Men*. Carnegie Studies in English, #3. Pittsburgh: Carnegie Press, 1957.

"*The Southern Review*." *Harvard Alumni Bulletin*, XXXVIII (November, 1935), 174–75.

"*The Southern Review*." *New Republic*, January 19, 1942, p. 68.

"*The Southern Review*." *Vanderbilt Alumnus*, XXVI (November, 1940), 8–9.

"South's Shortage." *Time*, January 7, 1935, p. 34.

Stauffer, Donald. "Cooperative Criticism: A Letter from the Critical Front." *Kenyon Review*, IV (Winter, 1942), 133–44.

Stegner, Wallace. "Conductivity in Fiction." *Virginia Quarterly Review*, XV (Summer, 1939), 443–44.

Stewart, John L. "The Achievement of Robert Penn Warren." *South Atlantic Quarterly*, XXVII (October, 1948), 562–79.

Swallow, Alan. "The Careful Young Men: Tomorrow's Leaders Analyzed by Today's Teachers." *Nation*, March 9, 1957, pp. 209–10.

————. *U.S. Quarterly Booklist*, II (December, 1946), 283–84.

Swing, Raymond G. "The Menace of Huey Long." *Nation*, January 9, 1935, pp. 36–39; January 16, 1939, pp. 69–71; January 23, 1935, pp. 98–100.

Tate, Allen. "Criticism and Creation." In Joseph Twadell Shipley (ed.), *Dictionary of World Literature*. New York: Philosophical Library, 1943.

―――. "My Debt to Alan Swallow." *University of Denver Quarterly*, II (Spring, 1967), 43.

―――. "Peter Taylor." *Shenandoah*, XXVIII (Winter, 1977), 10.

―――. "The Present Function of the Critical Quarterly." *Southern Review*, I (Winter, 1936), 551–59.

―――. "Tradition." In Joseph Twadell Shipley (ed.), *Dictionary of World Literature*. New York: Philosophical Library, 1943.

―――. "Understanding Modern Poetry." *English Journal*, XXIX (April, 1940), 263–74.

Tentarelli, Ronda Cabot. "The Life and Times of the *Southern Review*." *Southern Studies*, XVI (Summer, 1977), 129.

"Then and Now . . . A Review in Review." *LSU Outlook*, January, 1981, n.p.

Thompson, Ralph. "Outstanding Novels." *Yale Review*, XXVIII (June, 1939), vi.

―――. Review of *The Best Short Stories of 1937*, edited by Edward J. O'Brien. New York *Times*, May 26, 1937, p. 23.

"Tobacco War." *Time*, March 27, 1939, p. 73.

Trilling, Diana. Review of *All the King's Men*. *Nation*, August 24, 1946, p. 220.

Trilling, Lionel. "The Sense of the Past." *Partisan Review*, IX (May, 1942), 229–41.

Troy H. Middleton, 1889–1976." *LSU Alumni News*, LII (December, 1976), 2–3.

"Two Heavy Brickbats Hit Huey Long's University." *News-week*, January 5, 1935, p. 34.

Unger, Leonard. *The Man and the Name: Essays on the Experience of Poetry*. Minneapolis: University of Minnesota Press, 1956.

―――. *T. S. Eliot: Moments and Patterns*. Minneapolis: University of Minnesota Press, 1966.

Untermeyer, Louis. "Complex but Clear." *Saturday Review of Literature*, January 13, 1940, p. 17.

―――. "Cream of the Verse." *Yale Review*, XXXII (Winter, 1943), 370.

"Veritas." *Reveille*, August 6, 1941, p. 4.

W[allace], M[argaret]. "Southern Writers." *New York Times Book Review*, November 21, 1937, p. 28.

Wanning, Andrews. "A Primer for Modern Poetry." *Furioso*, I (January, 1940), 23–26.

Warren, Austin. "Achievement of Some Recent Critics." *Poetry*, LVII (January, 1951), 239–43.

Weaver, Richard. "Agrarianism in Exile." *Sewanee Review*, LVIII (Fall, 1950), 586–606.

―――. "Aspects of the Southern Philosophy." In Louis D. Rubin, Jr., and Robert D. Jacobs (eds.), *Southern Renascence: The Literature of the*

Modern South. Baltimore: Johns Hopkins University Press, 1953, pp. 14–30.

———. "The Tennessee Agrarians." *Shenandoah*, III (Summer, 1952), 3–23.

———. "Up from Liberalism." In *Life Without Prejudice*. Chicago: Henry Regnery, 1965.

Webb, Max. "Ford Madox Ford and the Baton Rouge Writers' Conference." *Southern Review*, n.s., XX (Fall, 1974), 892–903.

Wescott, Glenway. "Katherine Anne Porter Personally." In Lodwick Hartley and George Core (eds.), *Katherine Anne Porter: A Critical Symposium*. Athens: University of Georgia Press, 1969.

———. "Praise." *Southern Review*, V (Summer, 1939), 161–37.

"Wessex and Louisiana." *Time*, June 10, 1940, p. 92.

West, Ray B., Jr. "Truth, Beauty and American Criticism." *University of Kansas City Review*, XIV (Winter, 1947), 137–48.

Wharton, Don. "Louisiana State University." *Scribner's*, September, 1937, pp. 33–34, 38.

"When the Dam Breaks." *Time*, January 23, 1939, p. 45.

Williams, Aubrey. "The *Southern Review* Is No More." *Reveille*, June 30, 1942, p. 2.

Williams, Oscar. "More Poets of the Month." *New Republic*, July 6, 1942, p. 28.

Winsten, Archer. "Presenting the Portrait of an Artist." New York *Post*, May 6, 1937, p. 17.

Winters, Yvor. "Alan Swallow: 1915–1966." *Southern Review*, n.s., III (Summer, 1967), 796.

Yueh, Norma N. "Alan Swallow, Publisher, 1915–1966." *Library Quarterly*, XXXIX (July, 1969), 223.

Zabel, Morton D. "Announcement of Award." *Poetry*, XLIX (November, 1936), 104–106.

———. "Condition of American Criticism: 1939." *English Journal* (College Edition), XXVIII (June, 1939), 417.

———. "Problems of Knowledge: *Thirty-six Poems*." *Poetry*, XLVIII (April, 1936), 37–41.

———. "Recent Magazines." *Poetry*, XLVIII (April, 1936), 51.

Index

283

Index

Index

Index